W9-BYX-116

Clockwork Garden

ROGER J. FABER

# Clockwork Garden

## ON THE MECHANISTIC REDUCTION OF LIVING THINGS

THE UNIVERSITY OF MASSACHUSETTS PRESS

AMHERST, 1986

Printed in the United States of America
Set in Linotron Sabon by G&S Typesetters
Printed by Cushing-Malloy and bound by John Dekker & Sons

Library of Congress Cataloging-in-Publication Data

Faber, Roger J., 1931–
Clockwork garden.
Bibliography: p.
Includes index.
1. Mechanism (Philosophy) 2. Mind and body.
3. Quantum theory. 4. Teleology. I. Title.
BD553.F25 1986 113'.8 85-28408
ISBN 0-87023-521-4 (alk. paper)

To my father

CONTENTS

# PREFACE

IN THIS BOOK I TRY TO DISCERN THE HUMAN SIGNIFICANCE of our current scientific world picture, evaluating competing interpretations and arguing finally for one of them. Now arguments do not spring spontaneously out of the air; we develop them in order to organize our intuitions, the informal distillation of our experiences of the world. Nor do arguments complete the effort to understand; they serve only insofar as they help to make sense of further experiences, clarifying and perhaps correcting our intuitions. Experiences are both the source and the end of reasoning; we cannot rest until we have brought intuition and argumentation into harmony. It seems appropriate, therefore, to introduce this volume on the mechanist philosophy of nature by recounting one of the sources of my own intuitions.

Looking for a colleague, a herpetologist, I once wandered into an unoccupied research laboratory, where what seemed to be the postmortem dissection of a turtle stood in a state of temporary suspension. The body, minus the lower shell, was pinned on its back to a wooden slab, its internal organs exposed. I soon saw, however, that this was no corpse; the creature's legs were slowly tracing a crawling motion in the air. The image of that disturbing sight stayed with me. To cool my indignation, I told myself that the body I had seen was only a mechanism made of cells; that nothing was occurring on the dissecting board that differed significantly from what goes on in an automobile repair shop. The turtle with beating heart and waving limbs was in all respects—except for the stuff from which it was made—like a Volkswagen on a repair rack with its engine idling and wheels spinning. Was it trying to escape? No, not in the full sense of "trying." Not more so than a heat-seeking missile, say, could try to hit a target. Was it feeling pain? No; like any mechanism it could not feel, it could only function. The firing of its pain-sensing neurons was like the glowing of a lamp that warns about oil pressure or overheating in an automobile. I learned later that the dissection had begun with the routine precaution of severing the animal's spinal cord just below the head, so the possibility of pain did not arise. The warning lamp had been disconnected. Still, a wider question remained: It is the common thread running through this volume. Does a living organism differ from a functioning machine only in being made of carbohydrates rather than high-carbon steel and in having been formed by the spontaneous self-assembly of molecules rather than by design in a factory? Having some personal experience of what it is like to be a living organism, I felt inclined to answer no.

To give that answer is to make an antireductive conjecture about the organic world. Finding support for the conjecture is a daunting task, not least because the mechanistic view of living things is firmly rooted in modern evolutionary biology. Nevertheless, the attempt to counter, or at least to temper, mechanistic reductionism appeals to humanists of all ideological stripes. Some Christians have objected to evolutionism because it conflicts with a literal interpretation of the Book of Genesis; some Marxists have objected to the elevation of parts over wholes because it degrades the collective in favor of the individual. But I submit that threats to these special orthodoxies pale to insignificance compared with the insult that reductionism offers to ordinary, nondenominational humanism. That threat, the demeaning of the human person, touches religious and nonreligious alike.

Having exposed a little of the origin of this study, let me also alert the reader to the character of its destination. This book is offered in support of the antimechanist conjecture. Chapters 1 through 7 explore what can be done without raising the ancient riddle of mind and body. In them I look for antireductive arguments that will stand up to the severest criticism a reductionistic materialist could level at them without challenging the materialist's ontology. I conclude that arguments of that type do not deliver what antireductionists seek. Turning, then, to the mind–body question, I argue in chapters 8 through 11 along two independent lines for a deservedly unpopular metaphysical position, a dualism of mind and matter.

Does a dualist conjecture hang together logically? Does it accurately reflect the nature of things? How we answer those questions depends finally on whether or not we can bring our best arguments and our trusted intuitions into harmony. Pending the ultimate judgment on the truth of dualism, however, it is proper at this stage to note some of its attractive features as well as its repulsive ones. Both kinds provide reasons for taking an interest in the conjecture.

On the sinister side, one may fear that adding minds to the furniture of the universe would crack the dike of Reason, flooding the intellectual landscape with mind reading, spoon bending, and fortune telling. On the other hand, one might welcome a dualistic framework in which we could honor more wholeheartedly some reasonable and humanistic issues, such as traditional concerns with aesthetics, ethics, and the disciplined mysticisms of West and East. Besides, dualism, for all its internal problems, offers a more interesting program; it is a more entertaining source of puzzles and speculations than its monist alternatives. Can we accommodate dualism without succumbing to blind unreason? I think we can. I want to urge that we need not dwell in desert landscapes in order to preserve a rational sobriety.

Many people have helped to move this work along with inspiration, criticism, and advice. Foremost among them is Abner Shimony, who guided me in my first venture into a new area, who suggested doing a book, and whose thoughtful criticism kept it more or less on track. Many others have also read and commented encouragingly on various stages of portions of the manuscript: especially William C. Wimsatt, Donald T. Campbell, Claire Michaels, Forest Hansen, Laurie Shrage, Robert Glassman, Patricia McGoldrick, and Robert Mannweiler. The exposition of quantum mechanics is considerably less muddled than it might have been, because of the challenging criticism of David Kavesh. I thank Juliana H. Feder and Charles A. Louch for showing me some of the oddness and excitement of modern biology. Formative stages of several chapters were read at the Center for the Interdisciplinary Study of Science and Technology of Northwestern University, to the faculty sack-lunch seminar, whose ability to survive the emigration of its nucleus, Donald T. Campbell, testifies to how well he founded it. A paper read to the Boston Colloquium for the Philosophy of Science grew in two directions: more technically, into an article in *Boston Studies in the Philosophy of Science*, vol. 84, and less technically, into chapters 4, 5, and 6 of this work. I wish to thank M. Patricia Faber for moral and practical support that carried the writing over major hurdles. Thanks are due also to Lake Forest College for its financial support, and to Boston University, especially the Department of Physics and the Department of Philosophy, for its stimulating hospitality while I was taking sabbatical leave from Lake Forest. Finally, I am grateful to Virginia Crist, whose skillful typing made progress possible during the early and late phases of this project.

# Clockwork Garden

ONE

# Wholes and Parts: Introductory Survey

COMMON WISDOM ABOUT THE WORLD GUIDES US WELL in daily living, but getting along practically is not enough; we also want to weave a natural philosophy with yarns pulled from the workbasket of common sense. The task is challenging, because our beliefs and speculations about ourselves and our place in nature make a knotty snarl, whose strands pull in contrary directions. In this book I try to disentangle two strong threads of opinion about human nature without cutting either one. I want to preserve the traditional, humanistic idea that human beings act as causal and moral units; and I want to do equal justice to the modern, scientific story that we operate as cellular or biochemical mechanisms. The humanistic view grows out of ordinary human experience and has been enshrined in law and in the world's religions. The mechanistic has been assembled piece by piece as scientists and others have sought to work out the assumptions of realism, materialism, and atomism; it finds an institutional home in Western medicine.

Atomism, the source of the latter view, is a program for research, a prescription for how to set about the task of making sense of the world. This program has persisted as an element of Western science and of Western common sense from the days of Democritus and Epicurus to the age of Watson and Crick. Though some have pronounced it terminally ill, atomism will not lie down. Nor should it. The revelations produced almost daily by researchers in molecular biology attest to the present vigor of the mechanist philosophy. Rumblings of dissatisfaction with the atomist program may echo down the corridors of the physics building, but in the genetics laboratory mechanistic reductionism lives secure and breathes with new vitality.

## A DILEMMA

Despite the triumphs already achieved by the atomist program, however, and its promise of still deeper insights into the mechanism of life, there are reasons to feel distressed about mechanism as a philosophy. If scientific knowledge is continuous with common sense, extending and correcting the knowledge of the marketplace, then our most trustworthy information about the nature of things comes from our best scientific theories. And they are atomistic. Atomism as a philosophy of nature casts a chilling shadow upon our image of human nature. In this gloom ordinary things, human beings among them, acquire a shadowy ontological status because, according to the atomist program, parts are specifiably more real than the wholes they compose. The fundamental reality is Democritus's "atoms and void." The patterns of arrangement and interaction that characterize the objects of everyday experience are merely the automatic outcome of the activities of the atoms. The patterns have no causal efficacy; they are not imposed upon brute matter but are spun off from the mindless dance of the atoms. According to Lucretius,

> Slavery, riches, freedom, poverty,
> War, peace, and so on, transitory things
> Whose comings and goings do not alter substance—
> These, and quite properly, we call *by-products*.
> [LUCRETIUS, trans. HUMPHRIES, 1968, p. 33]

In our ordinary talk about the world, we habitually ascribe causal agency to macroscopic things which, according to atomist reductionism, are either conglomerates of atoms or whirling patterns whose atomic memberships continually change. We name these things as causal agents for convenience, to simplify the stories we tell, or out of ignorance; but true causal agency resides in the particles alone. According to atomism, we *are* what our atoms *do*.

Here is a dilemma. On the one hand we hold that one can say what something really is—what it is in itself and apart from the relations it sustains with ourselves or other things—by listing its parts, telling how they are arranged and move, and mentioning the general laws that govern their interactions. In this we echo a recurrent theme of Lucretius, whose three-point program of reduction lacks only a reference to general laws:

> . . . many things have elements in common,
> But differently combined . . .
> . . . It is most important
> Both with what other elements they are joined,
> In what positions they are held together,
> And their reciprocal movement.
> [P. 43]

On the other hand, we take a human being to be the very model both of causal agency and of individuality. Our notions of what it is to be a unified whole and of what it is to act are both derived from our experience as human beings.

Sometimes atomism is criticized on the grounds that it entails a deterministic negation of human will. But the objection to mechanism raised by Brand Blanshard, himself an avowed determinist, clearly shows that the offense is caused not by determinism per se but by the peculiar nature of mechanistic determinism:

> What most affronts [the plain man], I think, is the suggestion that he is only a machine, a big foolish clock that seems to itself to be acting freely but whose movements are controlled completely by the wheels and weights inside.
> [BLANSHARD 1958, p. 10]

Blanshard goes on to assert that neither he nor the plain man feels affronted by a determinism that treats the thinking, willing human being as an individual causal agent, constrained by the logical and aesthetic necessities inhering in the objects of his thought and will. If I have correctly pointed to the reason for mechanism's repellent visage, then it is easy to see both why Blanshard could accept a form of determinism while rejecting mechanism and why introducing indeterminism into an atomist philosophy would not soften its features. We object not to determinism as such but to the transferral of causal agency from human beings to their parts. Whether those parts move and collide in strict conformity to the laws of a Laplacean universe or swerve freely as Epicurus and Lucretius were forced to assume or, indeed, whether those parts exhibit quantum indeterminacy, the atoms retain their claim to be the real actors on the stage of the universe; whatever there may be of freedom or necessity in the world remains the freedom or necessity of the atoms.

The dilemma implicit in common sense (augmented by science) is sharpened by the fact that the general program of reduction need not always produce a dehumanized picture of things. The world seems to be so constructed that the reduction of wholes to parts can be carried out in stages—there are parts within parts. At certain stages, declaring the inner reality of a composite entity to be comprised in the arrangement and interactions of its parts may lead to a more, not less, humane understanding of the system. Consider for example the tension between our upper-level discourse about state and society and our lower-level talk about individual persons. Jean Jacques Rousseau, who favors holism here, criticizes those who consider "the moral person which constitutes the State as a creature of the imagination, because it is not a man" (Rousseau 1791, 1947, p. 18). Rousseau's description of democracy further illustrates his holism:

> But when the whole people determines for the whole people, it considers only itself; and if a relation is then formed it is only a relation of the whole object from one point of view to the whole object from another point of view, and the whole itself is not divided.
> [P. 33]

In contrast to Rousseau's favoring of the upper level, John Stuart Mill (1859, 1975) takes his stand against the control of individuals by the state simply by refusing to treat the composite entity as a unit:

> It is now perceived that such phrases as "self-government" and "the power of the people over themselves," do not express the true state of the case. The "people" who exercise the power are not always the same people with those over whom it is exercised; and the "self-government" spoken of is not the government of each by himself, but of each by all the rest.
> [P. 5]

The humane effect of Mill's resolute reductionism is not lost in this age of genetic engineering: We need to be reminded that lofty talk about Man controlling his own evolutionary destiny translates into the plain and ancient fact of some men controlling others. But a principle, once adopted, must be applied consistently. And it seems that the consistent application of atomism must carry us down through the world's levels of organization until we acknowledge that the full truth about anything whatever resides in stories about the particles of physics.

## POPULAR REMEDIES

Can the conflict between the reductionist and holist strands of common sense be as sharp and intractable as I have suggested? Only a close scrutiny of carefully constructed arguments and counterarguments will lead to a satisfactory answer to that question. But before undertaking such a study, and to make the labor seem worthwhile, let me briefly consider and briefly dispose of five simple, yet popular attempts to escape the reductionist horn of the dilemma.

1. *A whole, any whole, is more than a mere collection of parts.* This reply is certainly true, but it misrepresents the atomist program; hence, it is not a reply to reductionism. As noted above, Lucretius recommends a three-part program: The atomist sets forth the true nature of any composite entity, not only by listing its parts but also by specifying their relative positions and their motions. To this prescription a modern atomist would add a reference to the law-governed interactions among the parts. So the first reply fails by underestimating the resources of the atomist program. The nature of a composite thing may not be conveyed by a simple enumeration of its parts, but we can capture the whole dynamical activity in a complete description of what the parts are doing.

2. *No one will ever be able to turn the science of human behavior into a branch of applied physics.* This reply is also correct in what it states but misrepresents the question. Not even the most enthusiastic reductionist thinks that upper-level sciences such as biology and psychology will in fact be replaced by applied physics. Any attempt to explain any part of the natural world must strike a balance between the competing claims of utility and literal truth. For all sorts of reasons, the need for brevity perhaps the least of them, sciences that treat composite entities as units will always be necessary in practice. The question is whether they are necessary in principle. So the second reply fails by answering an irrelevant question.

3. *The properties of water cannot be explained by the properties of hydrogen and oxygen.* This reply is a sample of a class of replies asserting that upper levels of organization display irreducible, emergent properties. I do not know how to make a general criticism of the whole class, and I intend to consider some more challenging examples of supposed emergent properties in subsequent chapters. But this particular reply is easily met. Of course the properties of water in bulk cannot be understood in terms of the bulk properties of hydrogen and oxygen. The macroscopic substance water is not made up of the two substances hydrogen and oxygen; it is composed of water molecules. And, although chemists still write the formula for a molecule of water as $H_2O$, no chemist actually thinks of the molecule as thus composed. Rather, a single molecule is pictured as made up of two protons, an oxygen nucleus, and eighteen electrons, interacting dynamically by means of the electromagnetic force and according to the laws of quantum mechanics. The atomist must be sure to identify correctly the constituents of the composite entities he studies; the recent successes of ab initio quantum-mechanical calculations of the properties of fairly complex molecules show that modern chemistry has made the right identification. The properties of water can be explained by reference to the properties (including the interactive propensities) of neutrons, protons, and electrons. So this attempt to establish an irreducible property fails by incorrectly identifying the constituents of the upper-level entity.

4. *The components of a system cannot be understood apart from their membership in the whole.* This reply points out, quite

rightly, that to understand what one cell of a living organism is doing we must study not just the properties of the isolated cell but also how the cell interacts with others. And to understand a human being we must note how the person is affected by, and in turn affects, other members of society. An ecological attitude toward nature emphasizes the interrelatedness of things—the balance of opposing forces in the equilibrium between predator and prey, and the cooperation among other living things for mutual benefit. But interaction does not erase distinctions. Things that influence one another causally still retain their individuality. Atomic particle *A* would be doing something else today had it not collided with *B* yesterday, but even without that encounter *A* would still exist and would still have the same mass and charge—would have them, indeed, even if B had never existed. Causal interdependence does not entail ontological dependence, still less the undifferentiated wholeness advocated by some Western interpreters of Eastern thought. The atomists' world contains distinct, individual particles, but the atoms do interact. Pointing out that the pieces are not isolated merely brushes aside a straw opponent. This reply shows that any adequate account of a composite entity must encompass a sufficiently large set of parts; a picture of an isolated part is not a picture of a system of interacting parts, and a history of an isolated part is not a history of the part as it is acted upon by others. But, as I shall argue in more detail in chapter 2, it is essential to distinguish an appeal for adequate scope at the lower level from an argument for the irreplaceability in principle of upper-level language. The fourth reply establishes the need for scope but fails to block the move from upper to lower level.

5. *Reality has no structure of its own.* According to this reply, such structure as the world seems to display is imposed upon it by the arbitrary linguistic and conceptual categories we employ in our descriptions. Thus the partition of the world into atoms recommends itself with no greater force than do alternative partitions that present other things—human beings, for instance—as the causal agents. To satisfy our descriptive purposes, we are free to choose any of these apparently rival ways of dividing up reality. This criticism of atomism was raised by Ludwig Wittgenstein (1958), given a measure of scientific standing by Benjamin Whorf (1956), and popularized by Carlos Casteneda (1974).

But the criticism ignores the fact that we cannot freely adopt just any set of descriptive categories. Most of our attempts to formulate the organizational patterns of the world raise expectations that subsequent experience dashes to pieces. In this way the world itself disposes of all but a tiny fraction of the theories we propose in our attempts to understand it (Campbell 1960; 1974*a*). The scientific enterprise succeeds only because it meekly approaches the world on its own terms, without insisting on preconceived conceptual schemes.

Sweeping aside these weak or misdirected attacks on reductionism merely clears the way for the main effort. Many more carefully constructed arguments remain, arguments that promise to refute, or at least to mitigate, the mechanistic picture I have sketched. Of one major class of replies, however, I shall have nothing to say until the closing chapters, namely, those based on a dualist ontology, such as the mind–brain interactionism of Popper and Eccles (1977). I shall consider at first only replies that are, if not explicitly materialist, at least compatible with a materialist ontology. Such replies appeal because of their economy: If they work, their success is the more impressive for their having drawn upon a minimal theoretical arsenal. If, even within a materialist philosophy, mechanism could be softened or refuted, then the refutation would be secure indeed.

## SUMMARY

Let me summarize this introduction by stating my central question in a form that shows how I intend to approach this assessment of the mechanist world picture.

I wish to ask what Willard Quine (1960) identifies as the central question of ontology: What is there? And, although I shall be satisfied with a less formal criterion than his, I shall follow Quine in looking to our current scientific world picture for at least part of the answer. What we acknowledge as real, our "ontological commitment," is revealed, he says, in our logically formalized scientific theories: the terms over which the quantifiers of the theories range represent the items that populate the universe. A less formal test of ontic commitment will suffice for my purposes. The picture of the world that we get from science and from common sense highlights a multitude of activities: the gravitational tugging that diverts Jupiter into its elliptical orbit; the pressing of a quantity of helium gas against the walls of a neoprene blimp; the surviving into later generations, through natural selection, of certain alleles instead of others less favored; the responding of persons' mental states to the phases of the moon, and so on. What, in fact, is being done out there? Is natural selection truly an activity performed by some agent? Does a person's mental state really depend on where the moon is in relation to the sun?

Having settled such questions as well as we can, we next inquire, for each activity: What is doing it? Here we strive for parsimony: Our task must be to winnow the list of actors. This paring down, the principal task of reductionism, produces an increase in understanding. The gas presses on the inner walls of its container; but the molecules of which the gas is composed collide with the molecules that compose the walls. Should we retain both activities on our list? No, answers reductionistic science, the pressing done by the gas is nothing over and above the colliding done by the molecules. The activity of the whole is built up out of the aggregated activities of its parts. What they do includes, by aggregation, what the gas does; and they do much more besides. Therefore, the great drama of the universe is not played out by both gases *and* molecules; only the molecules need to be featured on the marquee. Throughout this investigation, then, I shall focus upon activities, assuming throughout that every real activity is done by some real, individual doer or set of doers. These agents are the inhabitants of the universe. Atomistic science has taken up the challenge of trying to understand every activity as built up by the bustling of material particles. I want to ask whether we can find any activities that cannot be so understood.

TWO

# The Case for Mechanism

ATOMISM IS, OF COURSE, MERELY A STRATEGY OR PRE-scriptive program for research, but its successes have made it virtually synonymous with the content of modern science. Although philosophers of science have undertaken quite properly to produce general analyses of causal explanation, in the practice of science we are not satisfied with an explanation that fails to establish the connection between cause and effect; and "connection" here means "mechanism." The associations and correlations reported by medical researchers and sociologists (e.g., the statistical association of smoking with various diseases) are regarded as mere indications of underlying mechanisms. When we claim that a correlation discovered in a system is more than a coincidence, we imply that some pattern of interactions among the parts of the system lies out there, waiting to be discovered.

Three features characterize atomic theory: separability, context-independence, and locality. The parts must be separable from the wholes they compose, not just conceptually but physically as well. They must be capable of independent existence.[1] Second, the parts must carry their properties unchanged from one complex situation to another. The intrinsic properties and modes of interaction that distinguish the various types of particle belong to them absolutely—they do not depend upon the degree of complexity or the organizational patterns of the larger system. In practice this means that the parts can be characterized by the properties they reveal in simple experimental contexts and that these properties account for all that goes on in more complicated contexts. Consequently, the direction of theoretical explanation must run exclusively from the parts to the whole. Now this explanatory asymmetry between theories about parts and theories about wholes reflects its ontological counterpart: The wholes do not exist in their own right but depend upon the existence of their parts. When we list the parts and tell how they are arranged and interact, we make it clear what the whole really is.

Third, with the single and perplexing exception of quantum mechanics (Bell 1965; Clauser et al. 1969), all atomistic theories exhibit what has been called locality; that is, they present each particle as being affected by and as acting upon only the objects (including the particles that mediate force fields) in its immediate spatiotemporal neighborhood. Interactions remain local at all levels of description. Cells, for instance, behave in accordance with their own internal structure and in response to the causal influence impinging upon their outer membranes. They are not directly affected by any other objects or by any global property of the system in which they participate.

## LEVELS: SOME DISTINCTIONS

Curiously, a merely incidental feature of atomist reductionism has been responsible for its success. Atomism probably would have died in its infancy had the world not been so constructed that the reductive analysis of wholes into parts could proceed by stages. Social systems are composed of individual organisms, organisms are systems of organs, organs are made up of cells, cells of molecules, molecules of nuclei and electrons, and so on. For

1 / One version of the theory of quarks violates this rule (Drell 1978).

that reason, we may talk about the world conveniently at any of several levels. Nevertheless, according to the reductionist program, the lower level of two accounts of the same system approximates more nearly to the way things are. Even though we do not yet have an assuredly fundamental inventory of ultimate particles, we may effect a reduction from one level of discourse to the next below it confident that a step has been taken in the direction where the complete truth lies.

In any discussion concerning the reduction of theories on a given level to theories on a lower level, it is essential to be clear as to which level a given sample of discourse resides on. Usage varies widely in the literature on levels of description and levels of organization. As I shall use the term "level," the distinction between parts and wholes will always decide the issue. Language that treats a composite entity as a unit, avoiding any implication as to its being composed of parts, functions on the upper level of that part–whole interface. And a story that, indirectly or by implication, assigns causal roles and other activities to the parts functions on the lower level.

One must not confuse an increase in the range or scope of a narrative with a shift to a higher level. Let me illustrate this point with some examples.

1. When a physicist stops talking about the properties of individual atoms of helium and starts talking about the doings of a swarm of atoms and of the interactions among them, the range of the conversation has been broadened, but its level remains the same, for the objects referred to are still atoms of helium. Only when the physicist leaves off speaking of atoms altogether and describes instead the bulk properties, such as the compressibility, of helium gas or the interaction of a sample of helium gas with other objects (e.g., the pressure exerted by the gas on its container) does the discourse reach a higher level, for only then are the gas and the container treated as units without regard to their being made up of atoms.

2. When a sociologist warns a psychologist that the actions of an individual human being cannot be understood without reference to the influence upon that person of many other people, the sociologist is not shifting the discourse to a higher level but merely extending the range of the conversation to include more individuals at the same level. A higher level is reached only when

the sociologist begins to speak of social groups and the interactions among them in such a way that the groups are treated as units without reference to their being composed of individual human beings.

3. Consider a jigsaw puzzle. We may say of the puzzle that it has a mass of fifty grams. None of its parts has a mass of fifty grams, so the predicate attaches to the whole puzzle. Moreover, we have neither said nor implied that it consists of parts. Consequently, to estimate the mass of a jigsaw puzzle is to engage in upper-level talk. But we may also say of the puzzle that it consists of 750 interlocking pieces. That predicate, too, attaches to the whole puzzle. However, the assertion that the puzzle has 750 pieces is not uttered at the upper level, because it refers to the entity as a system of parts. Note that an upper-level assertion about an entire entity need not imply that it is not composite; to qualify as upper-level discourse the description must merely be free of implications about the existence of parts.

4. The concept of temperature attaches only to whole systems of molecules and not to individual ones, but the history of the concept shows a transformation from the upper to the lower level. When temperature was defined merely as the propensity of an object to exchange heat with others, nothing was implied about the molecular composition of the bodies involved in the exchange; thus, the original definition of temperature was part of upper-level discourse. But in modern science temperature has come to be defined as a statistical property of the distribution of energy among the parts of an object, which distribution accounts for the propensity. So the current definition of temperature refers to the object's being made up of parts. Temperature, though it attaches to the whole system, is now a lower-level property.

5. When we make a functional analysis of a mechanism, we often designate a subassembly in terms of its function within the larger mechanism. Such a description moves within the level of the mechanism's parts but not the still lower level of the parts of the subassembly, for their presence is not implied. However, although being a feedback system is a property of an entire mechanism, it is a lower-level property. As I shall argue in chapter 4, when we call something a feedback system we imply that its parts are arranged and causally act upon each other in a certain speci-

fied way. By implying that the system has parts, we place the conversation at their level. Talk about feedback, though about whole systems, is lower-level talk.

Are the entities named at various levels all on an equal ontological footing? Are societies, organisms, cells, molecules, and subatomic particles equally real? The assumption that they are would establish an uneasy truce among the academic disciplines associated with these levels. Nevertheless, if the program of reduction has merit, such a laminar relativism will not do. According to the program, the descriptions, including the causal laws, appropriate to any upper level present a less faithful picture of the world than the descriptions proper to lower levels; thus, the entities named in upper-level theories must forfeit any claim to be listed as agents in the world's affairs.

But programs and promises are not enough. About a program as ancient as atomism it is entirely appropriate to ask whether the program fits the nature of things, whether the promises can be made good. We need an argument in support of the atomist reduction program for two reasons: First, we need to know whether to take the reductionist claims seriously. Second, because we shall shortly turn to the consideration of an assortment of antireductionistic claims, we shall require an opposing argument against which they may be tested. Put into direct confrontation with a strong argument for reductionism, the antireductionistic arguments will be able to show their strength. Can reductionism be expected to work? Let us construct an argument on the affirmative side of this question.

## ELIMINATIVE ATOMISM: A TARGET ARGUMENT

Our linguistic freedom to move at will from one level of description to another exposes us to a logical trap. We are often tempted to introduce into a narrative told at one level an agent whose native country lies at a higher or lower altitude. Rousseau, scrupulous in this respect, warns against mixing the level of description at which a state may function as a unit of the narrative with the level at which persons form the units: "In fine, States can only have other States, and not men, for enemies, because there can be no true relation between things of different natures" (1791, 1947,

p. 11). The blunder Rousseau shuns exemplifies what Gilbert Ryle has termed the category mistake (Ryle 1949, p. 16). In what follows I shall argue that any attempt to produce a complete description of the world at a level higher than the most basic one will display mysterious causal gaps that can be filled only by conscripting entities proper to a lower level, thereby illicitly relating "things of different natures." In the interests both of completeness and of logical coherence, then, we are forced to abandon each upper-level narrative in favor of a lower level.

To illustrate the category mistake, Ryle tells a story about a visitor to a university who, after a tour of the buildings, gardens, and playing fields, asks to be shown the university. Now Ryle's naive sightseer made a rather more interesting error than the kind I wish to focus on, for a university is more than just the buildings and other landmarks considered as a patterned whole; it is also a network of human conventions, intentions, and obligations. But less interesting mistakes may also be instructive. Suppose that the same obliging tourist could be induced to display his simplicity in a poultry yard. After being introduced to each individual chicken, he asks to be shown the flock. That, too, though more elementary than his faux pas in academe, is indeed a blunder. A narrative about an individual hen, or even about several hens as individuals, occurs on the hen's level, but mentioning a flock raises the story to another and higher plane. The suggestion that one hen attacked another or even several others, framed as it is consistently at the lower level, is a coherent suggestion; equally coherent is the upper-level assertion that one flock attacked another flock (though one would hardly look for such organized belligerence in poultry). But to suggest that an individual hen interacted in any way with a flock is to lapse into incoherence. Though our talk about the world may be framed at many different levels, we ought to maintain the purity of our layers; if we mix them up we breed nonsense. Hens interact with other hens, not with flocks. A hen is capable of many things, including pecking another hen; but even the most accomplished of chickens cannot peck a flock. Mixing levels in our descriptions of the world simply confuses them. To adapt one of Ryle's aphorisms, the words for hens and flocks cannot be put to roost in the same logical tree.

INCOHERENCE OF UPPER-LEVEL DESCRIPTIONS

If our linguistic practices reflect the nature of things, surely they can be pursued without threat of inevitable incoherence. Descriptive modes that produce incoherence, even if only occasionally, must be regarded with suspicion; however useful they may be, the truth is not in them. But we find in practice that the world is so constituted that our talking of flocks and other upper-level entities, if practiced without restraint, inevitably leads to incoherence. Though we may set out to describe the world consistently at a certain upper level of organization, we will encounter events involving the upper-level entities which occur in such a way that, to speak of them at all, we must drop our description to a lower plane. The linguistic strata, so the world is constituted, are not watertight. Let me cite two examples to support this claim—one fictitious and one based on reports of space travelers.

Suppose the following drama unfolds in some poultry yard (I give first a lower-level account): The assorted biddies are industriously scratching among the pebbles and seeds when a marauding fox incautiously shows its face in some nearby bushes. One of the hens happens to notice the enemy and runs for cover, squawking agitatedly. The others do not see the fox, but they know consternation when they hear it, so they all follow the first hen. Next, consider how an upper-level account of the same incident would run: The flock, we might say, relocates itself from the open yard to the shelter of the hen coop. At the upper level the story condenses to a mere headline. But how do causal influences fare at this level? What caused that unit, the flock, to move? The fox did, certainly (and here we already feel uneasy, for is a lone fox on the same logical plane as a social entity like a flock?), but how did the fox cause that event? By what mechanism or mode of interaction? Well, it allowed itself to be seen by a hen; so we might be tempted to say that the proximate cause of the flock's removal to shelter was the action of that alert hen. But note how that sentence mixes logical categories. It can be saved from incoherence only by substituting for the term "flock" a reference to all the individuals that compose it. If a chicken cannot peck a flock but can only peck other chickens, it also cannot put a flock to flight. So it turns out that, although it may suit our convenience as narrators to speak of flocks and their histories, the world will not countenance our doing so consistently. Flocks, we discover, get themselves into trouble from which only hens can rescue them. Likewise, our upper-level discourse leads us narrators into difficulties from which we escape only by abandoning the upper level. And, having relocated to the lower level, we encounter no need to rise again, except for the sake of employing a convenient shorthand. Henceforth, upper-level things, though named as units, are conceived of as collections.

My second example was widely reported when astronauts were first spending extended periods in orbit beyond the protective influence of the earth's magnetic field. Several of these space travelers reported experiencing the sensation of irregular flashes of light while resting in darkness with closed eyes. The explanation proposed for this phenomenon was that the light sensations were caused by massive and highly energetic cosmic-ray particles striking individual photoreceptor cells in the retinas of the astronauts. This hypothesis was corroborated when some intrepid terrestrial experimenters placed their own heads in the beams of particle accelerators (McNulty, Pease, and Bond 1978). Therefore, we might glibly and incautiously say, the astronauts detected cosmic rays. A visual experience, an event involving a human being, was caused by—well, we would like to say a nucleus of iron-57. But, as Ryle has cautioned us, persons and atomic nuclei do not contend for seats on the same logical bench. Persons interact with (among other things) other persons, and nuclei with other tiny charged particles. How, then, are we to describe the event in which the person and the nucleus participated? Not by clinging to the upper level, for there nuclei are not permitted to function. On that level the perceptual event has no cause. So we must relinquish our reference to persons and descend to the level of atoms; on this descriptive level the story unfolds in its completeness, without a sudden reticence imposed by logical scruples.

It would be easy to multiply more prosaic examples of this type. Cosmic rays are known to produce the familiar vapor trails in cloud chambers and are thought to trigger lightning flashes. A single X ray photon may cause a mutant eye color in a strain of fruit flies; and, to revert once more to higher levels, the action of a single person may lead to the overthrow of a state.

What can we say, then, about our habits of speaking about

upper-level entities, including persons, as units? Only, it seems, that we may continue to do so within limits and for the sake of convenience, recognizing that the world is so constituted that such talk must simply be dropped in the interests of accuracy when the occasion demands. But perhaps not merely dropped. Because incidents of the sort I outlined for the poultry yard have been familiar parts of everyday life since before the English language was formed, we have a standard linguistic device for dealing with them: We treat the term "flock" as a collective noun, to show that, though a flock may be a unity in our speech, it is a plurality in itself. We have not always regarded human beings as pluralities, but recognition of the fact is, nevertheless, of greater antiquity than the space program. The elderly bon vivant who informs us that the sluggishness of his liver is responsible for his attendance at a mineral springs resort may have stopped mixing his drinks but not his levels of description. Language is the repository of our knowledge about the world; even the structure of language reflects to some degree that knowledge. But structure changes more slowly than knowledge grows. *Flock* is a collective noun because we have always known that a flock is a collection of, for example, hens. *Iron bar* is not a collective noun—not because a bar of iron is a radically different sort of entity but because we have but lately learned that a bar of iron is an arrangement of iron atoms.

At whatever level of description our talk about the world may be set, it could not pretend to be complete unless it included some reference to causal interactions among the entities that belong to that level. The causal influence of one thing on another is, at any level, what makes our narrative hang together. Yet we find, whenever we look closely at causal actions, that the flow of upper-level narrative, when followed far enough, always vanishes into the sands, only to be recovered, fresh and broader than before, as a subterranean stream. When we characterize things and events at an upper level, what may be the nature of the connections between them is ultimately mysterious until we descend to lower strata; but when we descend we always find that the mystery begins to clarify. The connections, about which we were unable to speak coherently at the upper level, are seen to be interactions among the parts that compose the upper-level entities. All this is not to say that the ultimate result of our efforts to look into causal connections is the dispelling of all mystery; the causal interactions among the ultimate atoms (if we ever find them) cannot themselves be explicated in terms of still lower-level mechanisms, precisely because they are the ultimate particles. But surely we ought not to multiply mysteries beyond necessity. How quarks and gluons interact may turn out to be just brute fact and hence an ultimate causal mystery; but the influence of foxes upon flocks is not mysterious if we are willing to talk of hens, nor is the hereditary influence of parents upon their offspring mysterious to one who acknowledges the existence of molecules of DNA. For these reasons, an integral part of the reductionist program is the claim that all causation must ultimately be understood as physical causation.

When flocks interact with hens and persons interact with atomic nuclei, the only coherent level of description is that of the lower level: Flocks must be regarded as pluralities of hens and human beings as pluralities of subatomic particles. The causal laws we employ in upper-level discourse are either helplessly mute at inconvenient points or, if we introduce lower-level entities to patch up the gaps in the upper-level narrative, crazily incoherent. Upper-level descriptions may be convenient, economical, practical, and evocative, but they are not faithful to the way things are. Having recognized these facts, we have been forced to alter our understanding of upper-level things forever. We are compelled to admit that any upper-level entity, be it a flock of hens or a human being, far from acting as a causal agent in its own right, is more accurately described as a collection of lower-level entities arranged in some fashion and interacting according to their own causal laws.

So our ordinary, causal, explanatory talk about macroscopic objects is either superficial to the point of error or superfluous—superficial, in fact, erroneous, if it is taken as identifying the actual causal agents; superfluous in that the microscopic account does not need to be supplemented, for in mentioning all the interactions it lists both all the causal agents and their relevant properties. It is superfluous also because, if an upper-level entity simply is its parts arranged and interacting as such parts do, then upper-level laws are obtainable by means of a combination of approximation, hypostatization, and inference, according to the usual standards of what physicists call derivation.

INSUBSTANTIALITY OF UPPER-LEVEL THINGS

Things at any level endure. That is partly why we designate them as entities. I shall argue that the manner of their enduring provides an additional reason for denigrating the reality of some upper-level things, among them living organisms, whose reality we most strongly wish to uphold. Consider the following examples.

In the world as reconstructed from an atomist ontology we find collectives of quite different sorts, all of which are treated alike in ordinary speech but differ in the relation of part to whole. On one extreme we find enduring sets of atoms, such as billiard balls and rocks, whose atomic membership remains fixed or nearly so. On the other extreme we find ourselves applying names to collections whose memberships are continually changing and treating these collections, linguistically at least, just as we treat rocks. In this way we may assert that the traffic on an expressway was very dense at eight o'clock but that it had thinned out by ten-thirty, speaking of the traffic as if it were an enduring object undergoing changes in one of its properties, just as we might say that a boulder has warmed up in the morning sun. But the truth, or something nearer the truth, is that there are other and fewer cars on the highway at ten-thirty than there were at eight.

A more elaborate and instructive example may also be drawn from the highway. A line of cars is stopped at a traffic signal. The light turns green and, about a second later, the first car in line begins to move, leaving a gap between itself and the next car. The second car's driver, jolted from his or her reverie by the sight of the first car in motion, drives off as well, again with about a second of delay, and so on. At each instant there is a point along the line of cars on one side of which they are relatively far apart and moving and on the other bumper-to-bumper and at rest. This point is to be found farther back from the traffic signal as time elapses. What I have just given is a lower-level description of the phenomenon. But we can assign a velocity to the point of demarcation and give it a name: We may call it a pulse, a special sort of wave form. Describing the same process now in upper-level language, we may say that a wave or pulse of decompression moves back along the line of cars at a rate of about four meters per second. Now a line of traffic is only one type of medium in which wave motion can occur, and each medium has its own causal mechanism whereby waves form and propagate. But the traffic wave serves as well as any other example to illustrate the fact that, in an atomistic reconstruction of the world, waves are not things. In reductionistic science, just as in ordinary speech, we maintain the sort of distinction that appears on the pages of any printed drama or on any playbill: We speak of the actors, and we speak of their actions. The actors are the entities to whose existence our theories commit us; they are referred to by the nouns of our suitably purged descriptions. The story we tell, full of incident, is the story of those things. According to the atomist paradigm, it would be wrong to list waves among the dramatis personae of the cosmic drama; instead, they should be counted as activities performed by the true agents, the atoms.

This is not to say that, given our epistemological connection to the world, all waves are deliberately hypostatized processes, as traffic waves clearly are. Some waves are perceived more directly than the media in which they move, so they are taken by us, unreflectively, to be substantial entities. The ripples in the surface of an otherwise calm pool attract the eye more than does the water whose distortions they are. But as we reconstruct the world in theory this distinction disappears. Our senses, connected as they are to the causal influences of our environment, sometimes lead us to respond to such transient configurations as waves as if they were concrete things. We respond to a traveling wave just as we do to a moving swimmer, by shifting our gaze horizontally; but, when we follow a wave, the only objects engaging in horizontal motion are our eyes.

Living organisms, considered as arrangements of parts, are more like waves than like rocks. Take a single-celled organism. As the processes of metabolism proceed, with a steady importing of nutrients and exporting of wastes, not much remains at a later time of the material that once composed the cell, even if it has done nothing so drastic as to reproduce by fission. Just as a particular wave crest is composed now of one portion of the surface of the sea and later, as the crest moves on, of another portion, so an individual cell is composed now of one set of molecules and ions and later, after ingestion, metabolism, and excretion, of a distinct set of molecules of the same kinds. Each cell, and, therefore, the entire organism, is an enduring configuration in the jumble of nutrients and wastes; it is a wave or eddy in the molecular flux. An organism is a complex dance into whose dynamic pattern the atoms insert themselves for a time, performing their intricate steps until, displaced by newcomers, they move on to other actions in other places. Just as a wave is properly understood as the action of a body of water or other medium, so a living organism is properly thought of as concerted motion passed on from one group of molecules to the next. The molecules are the actors; the organism is what they do.

### UNWELCOME IMPLICATIONS

That, I submit, is in rough outline the program of reductionistic atomism. Now is there any reason to feel uncomfortable with this sort of reductionism, any reason why we might welcome mitigating considerations?

There is, and the roots of our discomfort lie deep in our concept of self. We do not mind being told that our language about the billiard table is only a rough-and-ready approximation to the truth, a convenient accommodation to our perceptual organs and a reflection of our limited interest in the events on the table. We do not even mind being told that we ourselves are made up of all manner of wonderful mechanisms, of pipes, bellows, pumps, and valves: Such knowledge in itself, taken as adding to our fund of self-knowledge, might only increase our satisfaction in ourselves, showing that we are "fearfully and wonderfully made." The trouble arises when we are told that the story about pumps and bellows is not to be added to the stories we also tell about dreams and emotions but to supplant them. We are willing to conceive of ourselves as thinking, feeling, and willing beings who happen also to be made up of cells and fluids or of atoms and molecules; what we find distasteful is the suggestion that, although we may say that we are smelling roses or basking in the sun or opening a door, these descriptions of ourselves lie considerably farther from the truth than the lower-level accounts that are to replace them, that, in short, what is really, or more nearly really, going on is to be told in some story about cells and their ways.

What it comes down to is this: As in theory we construct the world from its parts, we find ourselves greatly inconvenienced by having to record the actions of a multitude of atoms. To simplify the task of storytelling, we adopt, when possible, the expedient of attaching names to collections of large numbers of atoms, treating these groups as modules, as honorary individuals. In this way the names of the objects of everyday experience are brought back into the narrative, but they function there only as a concession to the demands of economy. A term like "the eight-ball" is now seen to be just a name we apply for convenience to a certain set of atoms, and it is the atoms, not the ball, that are concretely real. As realists about atoms we have had to become nominalists about billiard balls—and about ourselves. In fact, the situation is somewhat worse with regard to living organisms, for they turn out, on this reconstruction of the world, to be at two removes from the actual agents. Living systems, along with many other sorts of entity, are not even concrete sets of atoms. Rather, they turn out to be mere configurations or patterns in the flux of material particles: They turn out to have, in short, the ontological status of waves, of baseball teams, and of societies. Yet, one feels, if anything is concretely real—not just an abstraction—it is one's self.

According to the standard atomist paradigm, we approach closer to the way things are when we leave off speaking of a complex system and its actions and begin to speak of the system's parts and their actions. Regardless of where this process of reductive explication may end—and the end is not in sight—this general program for understanding the world commits us to the view that complex systems are not themselves the true causal agents in the affairs of the world. But this view is a source of perplexity: Human beings are complex systems of parts; and if human beings are not seen as causal agents, how can they be regarded as moral agents? If we are mechanisms in this very literal sense, then what we do is in fact merely what the atoms do as they flow through the dynamic configuration that bears our name; how, then, can we be either praised or blamed for what are simply the antics of our parts?

The conflict between atomism and our intuitions about human nature centers on the question of unity. Our concept of inner unity springs from what we experience of ourselves, yet the mechanist picture has room only for the sort of external unity

Rousseau grants to a state: "With respect to what is external to it, it becomes a simple being, an individual" (1791, 1947, p. 17).

We may be tempted to suppose that the scheme of organization of a composite system forges an inner unity out of erstwhile individual parts. The temptation arises because we tend to think of such organizational patterns on the model of human plans and designs: the blueprints for a building, the score of a concerto, the wiring diagram of an electronic circuit, the sequence of calls for a square dance. Through the creative agency of human beings, all of these patterns play an active role in constituting the systems that embody them. The atomist program rejects these analogies. Every group of particles must display some pattern or other, most of which, like the pattern of arrangement of the rocks in a mine tailing, fail to hold our interest; but all patterns, even those displayed by the atoms momentarily composing a human being, must be regarded as incidental results of the behavior of the particles. The atoms act according to their simple laws, regardless of setting, lavishly generating patterns of many sorts, none of which has any causal role to play in the world's affairs.

If we are unwilling to place ourselves at the metaphysical center of the universe—and as the heirs of Copernicus and Darwin that is just what we are unwilling to do—then we are obliged to concede to rivers, trees, and other external objects what we claim for ourselves: If we have intrinsic natures—if we are what we are in ourselves, apart from the relations we sustain with other things—then those things must have their intrinsic natures, too. But scientific realism also insists that their natures can be known. Taken together, these two assumptions mean that our descriptions of the inner natures of external objects ought to serve as models of the descriptions we apply to ourselves. But the model repels. We find on close inspection that external things are either pluralities of atoms or wavelike patterns in the flux of atoms; that they are pluralities in themselves and unities only in the way we think of them. Then, given our modest assessment of our place in the metaphysical scheme of things, what we say about the inner nature of other organisms we must say also about ourselves. That means that we too are unities only in the regard of other beings; we only appear as units. Yet our deepest intuitions of self insist otherwise.

Let us now consider what manner of reply may be made to the

argument for reduction. As I have formulated it, the argument rests on several assumptions about the nature of science, about the nature of common sense, and about the relation between our knowledge of the world and the world itself. Let me survey those assumptions more closely in order to expose points in the argument that may be vulnerable to counterattacks of one sort or another.

## ASSUMPTIONS OF ELIMINATIVE ATOMISM

1. In posing the problem, I have assumed that scientific talk about the world is of a piece with, though an extension of, our commonsense talk about the world. I have assumed that any science, and in particular physics, aims to produce a description of the way things are; this description may be more precise and more detailed than our ordinary descriptions of things, but it is intended to be a literal description.

2. The problem was posed against a background of commonsense realism, which includes a commonsense, prescientific variety of atomism. This commonsense realism is, simply, a belief in a knowable but objective world. The world is objective in this sense: What is so is quite distinct from our knowing it and from how we come to know it. The external world, in this view, is not inextricably intertwined with human aims and attitudes. Things in the world are what they are independently of what we may think of them, what we intend to do with them, or how we compare them with other things. And commonsense atomism requires us to spell out the intrinsic nature of any thing in terms of its composition and structure. In itself, a particular wall is just a group of stones in a definite arrangement. A landholder with intentions of his own put them there, so the wall is also a boundary marker; but that is nothing to that pile of stones. Local sweethearts sometimes hold clandestine meetings there, so the wall is also a trysting place; but that is nothing to that pile of stones. When we call it a trysting place we may seem, from the grammatical similarity of the two sentences, to be describing it in the same way as when we call it an arrangement of stones. But if we hold to commonsense atomism, we do not intend the two sentences to do the same sort of work at all. In calling the wall a pile of stones we tell what it is, objectively, in itself, whereas in calling

it a trysting place we are saying something about the habits of lovers in relation to those stones.

One way to say what something is is to tell what kind of thing it is. But, according to commonsense atomism, the key to any particular thing's intrinsic nature is its composition: We say what it is when we tell what parts it is composed of, how they are arranged, and what they do. For example, suppose someone, looking up into the sky, remarks that she sees what looks like a dark, undulating ribbon moving north at a considerable altitude and asks what it is. An ornithologist may inform her that it is a collection of geese flying in formation. Both parties, if they hold to the commonsense view of the objective world, would feel satisfied that the ornithologist had properly told what the object really was, in itself. He might also have called it a sign of spring, but that would have been a quite different sort of reply. The ornithologist's actual reply was not, of course, as detailed as it might have been, though detailed enough to suit the occasion. But suppose the questioner had persisted and asked what a goose is? One way to answer would be the method of Linnaeus: Tell her that a goose is a special sort of bird with a certain set of distinguishing characteristics. But suppose the ornithologist had been pressed to say what an individual goose is in itself. He might then quite properly reply that it is an arrangement of bones, muscles, feathers, and so on, acting as such things will act. This reply would show the same spirit as his reply to the question about the ribbon in the sky—he would be saying what something is by telling what composes it.

Depending upon the social circumstances, one or another method of describing a thing may be the appropriate way to say what it is. If the thing is unfamiliar but made up of familiar objects, we naturally specify these components and their arrangement. If, however, the object itself is an instance of a familiar kind of thing, we more naturally specify the kind. We naturally characterize a particular forest as a group of trees, rather than as an instance of vegetative ground cover, though usually we characterize a particular tree as an instance of its kind of tree. But the general knowledge possessed by the people who ask us what this or that object is and their intentions in asking are nothing to those objects in themselves. When we call a forest an instance of vegetative ground cover we allude to the fact that there are many other objects similar in certain respects to this one; we do the same when we call another object a maple tree. But to say that a particular forest is a group of trees arranged in a certain way and to say that a particular tree is a group of cells in a certain arrangement is to specify what those objects are in themselves, independently of our proclivities for comparing and classifying. When we identify something as an instance of a kind we choose a subset of all the things we could say about it and we liken it to other objects about which the same things may be said. We might have called the tree a vascular plant and the forest a battleground. Our choice of kind depends on our purposes in making the description. But what an individual thing is intrinsically, in all its individuality, is a certain group of parts arranged and interacting in a certain way.

3. If, according to common sense, we are able to say what things are in themselves by telling what they are composed of, and if science is continuous with common sense, then we are led naturally to a third assumption, or set of assumptions, forming part of the background of the problem I have posed: I have assumed the viability of scientific atomism as a program for spelling out the nature of things. As we continue to probe into the inner composition and structure of things, we move by degrees from what is obviously prescientific common sense to what is obviously highly scientific. What about a particular muscle? What is it in itself? We have a nearly commonsense answer to that: It is a collection of cells and intercellular fluids. And what of a particular cell? And what of that cell's nucleus? And what of a particular chromosome? And what of a particular DNA molecule? And what of a particular carbon atom? The same sort of answer is given to each of these questions. So according to this view of an objective world, the way to spell out what something really is in itself—which is not the same as telling how we know about it, or what we hope or intend about it, or what relations it bears to other things—is to say what composes it. And in the program of scientific atomism the most accurate, the most thorough spelling out of what something is must always be a statement that describes it as an arrangement of its ultimate parts, interacting in their own ways. These ultimate components form the only truly

natural kinds. One maple tree is not exactly like another, nor are any two phloem cells quite alike, but the atoms of a given kind are distinguished only by their spatiotemporal locations.

4. Finally, the program of scientific atomism admits of only one kind of effective causation: physical causation. Every instance of causal action of one thing on another is the action of ultimate atom upon ultimate atom. David Hume's indictment of causation persists even in the face of the mechanistic treatment of causes. The notion of physical necessity or causal connection remains as mysterious as it ever was. But the force of Hume's skepticism can be moderated considerably by a mechanistic philosophy. Like a savings and loan association, mechanism invites us to consolidate our doubts. The link between smoking and cancer can be clarified by the discovery of carcinogenic substances in tobacco smoke and the elucidation of the action of such molecules on living cells. The action of one molecule on another is clarified by the theory of the electron pair bond. The electrostatic attraction between protons and electrons is explained by the exchange of virtual photons between them. In this way, the causal mysteries of one level of organization are dispelled by the causal processes at the next lower level. As a result of this reductive explanation of causation, the mysteries are confined to the ultimate level of reduction, where they remain ultimately mysterious. To understand any instance of effective causation one must think of the ultimate atoms as the causal agents because that is the way things are.

## SIX REJOINDERS TO ATOMISM

This set of assumptions may be assaulted at several points, two of which lie outside the scope of this essay. First, one might attack realism by arguing, for example, that our commonsense talk about the world carries no ontological claims, that it is only a way of organizing our experiences. Second, while retaining a realistic attitude toward the world, one might reject atomism, an ontological program of concrete material particulars, and campaign for some rival metaphysical program (Campbell 1976). I shall not consider either of these lines of attack; indeed, I aim to see how well the program of commonsense realism coupled with atomistic reduction can be made to work. Third, without discarding commonsense realism or commonsense atomism, one might try to drive a wedge between science and common sense, not by modifying the realist claims of common sense but by setting limits on what science can claim to tell us about the nature of things. This counteroffensive, launched by Gilbert Ryle (1954), will form the subject of chapter 3.

Fourth, one might complain that the mechanists rest too comfortably on their laurels. The reduction of macroscopic thermodynamics to statistical mechanics, though an admirable achievement, provides no model for the reduction of such upper-level concepts as purpose, goal, and function; hence, it does not justify the expectation that they can be given reductive explications. Chapters 4, 5, and 6 will be concerned with rival approaches to the explication of goal-directedness: a reductive, cybernetic theory, originated by Arturo Rosenblueth, Norbert Wiener, and Julian Bigelow (1943); and a nonreductive, selectionist theory, proposed by William Wimsatt (1972).

Fifth, without attacking realism, or denying the continuity of scientific with commonsense descriptions, or questioning the propriety of the atomist program, one might try to mitigate reductionism by showing that there are objective, that is, non-anthropocentric, reasons for listing the macroscopic objects of everyday experience among the dramatis personae of the cosmic drama. This is the line taken by Jerry Fodor (1968; 1975) in his defense of the autonomy of psychology. Briefly summarized, Fodor's point is that the laws of upper-level sciences, formulated, of course, in terms of upper-level things, are assertions about the world, yet they are incapable of being expressed, at least in closed form, in terms of the entities of lower levels. Therefore, to exclude names for upper-level entities from our vocabulary is not merely inconvenient; to do so is to render ourselves unable to express some truths about the nature of things. Fodor's suggestion, with applications of it by David Hull (1974) and William Wimsatt (1976), will form the subject of chapter 7.

Finally, one might try to ground a defense of everyday objects, or at least of certain special things such as central nervous systems, on the holistic features of quantum mechanics. This proposed solution to the problem posed by reductionism would not threaten any of the assumptions listed above; rather, it would show that atomism, if pursued far enough, produces its own answer by justifying our treating complex systems as unitary wholes. Indeed, some interpreters of quantum mechanics see in it a radical challenge to the ontology of materialism, by way of support for mind–matter dualism. Arguments for the supposed holistic and dualistic features of the quantum theory will be considered in chapters 9 and 10.

THREE

# Reduction and Common Sense

COULD THE PROBLEM I HAVE POSED IN THE PREVIOUS chapter be only apparent? Would a right assessment of the nature and limits of the scientific enterprise show that what it tells us about the world does not, after all, clash with our commonsense formulations of the way things are? Gilbert Ryle (1954), defending the legitimacy of our commonsense view of things, suggests that reductionistic science only *seems* to challenge our common sense. Unlike the philosophers whom I shall consider next, Ryle feels called upon neither to enlist in a battle between science and common sense nor to offer his services as an arbitrator, because in his view there is in fact no feud: The notion that science conflicts with common sense could arise only from a mistaken idea as to what science is about.

Ryle's conjecture is presented in "The World of Science and the Everyday World" and its sequel, "Technical and Untechnical Concepts" (1954). In these essays Ryle offers his readers a series of examples and suggestive analogies and leaves it up to them to determine how the analogies may apply. For my purposes Ryle's allusiveness is a virtue, for it requires me to fill out his partial recipe for an argument by supplying some ingredients of my own. It allows me to raise and propose answers to several questions about the connections between science and common sense, of which possibly only one may capture Ryle's intended point, but all of which need to be aired and settled. I shall take up Ryle's challenge, then, aiming at two objectives: to test the argument of the previous chapter that scientific realism clashes with important commonsense intuitions, and to build a foundation for the arguments of succeeding chapters by spelling out how atomism can accommodate some of the standard complexities built into our ordinary talk about the world.

Ryle distinguishes the cosmos, the world we all live in, from the narrow "worlds" of specialists of various sorts. Examples of special worlds are the world of poker, the world of accounting, and the world of stamp collecting. Though certainly parts of the cosmos, these special worlds stand apart because they are the provinces of specialists with their own aims, vocabularies, and techniques. Most significantly for Ryle's case, the practice of these specialties often leads to the introduction of technical concepts, by which he seems to mean concepts that arise in the context of, and apply to, the aims and techniques of the special area of interest. Ryle offers a number of examples of what appear superficially to be clashes between claims made in the context of distinct special worlds but which are easily seen not to be clashes at all. Let us consider two of his examples.

A particular hand of playing cards may be said to contain honors in trump or a royal flush but not at the same time. Whereas either of these descriptions may be true of the hand (depending on whether it arises in the context of bridge or of poker), both cannot be true simultaneously. But that does not mean that bridge and poker conflict; it means only that one cannot play both games at once. The worlds of bridge and poker overlap, because each involves the standard pack of playing cards. In that sense the two worlds are related, but not in such a way that there could be a clash between poker statements and bridge statements.

An accountant may record the business transactions of a college library and produce a tidy and pleasing balance between the income from endowments and fines and the expenditures for books. What the accountant says about the library is or may be true—of the fiscal aspects of the library. But the accountant's truth could not clash with what an undergraduate says, for the student is concerned with the subject matter of the books, not their prices. Neither set of statements about the library need be false; yet each is irrelevant to the other.

In some such way, suggests Ryle, the claims made by scientists about objects in the world bear upon our everyday descriptions of things. Just how the analogy is apt Ryle does not say, so I shall examine in turn several ways the analogy might be applied, using hints gleaned from the two essays.

Ryle says that appearance of a clash between science and common sense does not occur on all fronts. The findings of botanists, for instance, or of astronomers, do not even seem to challenge common sense in any important way. According to Ryle, the trouble seems to arise when we consider the physics of the very small. But as I have formulated the problem, war breaks out long before the frontiers of the light microscope have been passed. Commonsense intuitions are challenged wherever science tells us that an ordinary object, as it is in itself apart from considerations about its relations to other things or to human beings, is to be understood as nothing more than a set of interacting parts, even when those parts are organs or cells. Ryle does not say whether his analogies are to be applied to sciences of all sorts or only to chemistry and atomic physics. But some of his analogies seem to me to apply rather nicely to some of the sciences he singles out as obviously compatible with everyday descriptions of reality, so I suppose he intends to suggest that the world of any science, not just the world of atomic physics, is a specialist's world. Moreover, only if Ryle's conjecture is construed in this broad sense can it serve as a possible dissolution of the problem of reductionism, so that is how I shall construe it.

How, then, are Ryle's analogies to be applied? In what respects are his examples like the confrontation, or mock confrontation, between science and everyday experience?

## SPECIALISTS' WORLDS

One feature that may distinguish a special world is its special matter. Philatelists operate in a separate world at least partly because they deal with objects of a special sort, namely, stamps.

Likewise, entomologists study insects but not snakes, and astronomers observe stars but not beetles. However, that cannot be the way Ryle's analogies are to be applied to the case at issue because, as he points out, the discipline at the center of the storm (or seeming storm) is atomic and subatomic physics, which is concerned with everything there is: rocks, insects, plants, and people. In suggesting that the claims of physics do not, after all, clash with our everyday views of the world, he does not wish to suggest that physicists are concerned only with special sorts of objects to the exclusion of others.

Another feature that sets some special worlds apart is their concern with human conventions and rules of behavior. That is clearly true of the worlds of various games. Poker is a world unto itself because the game is a set of arbitrary social conventions, a purely formal activity. Although snakes would still crawl even if herpetologists lost interest in them, inside straights would simply cease to exist if people stopped playing poker. What poker players say does not challenge our everyday experience of the world because poker talk is about a world formed by the people who play it. As poker players concentrate on the artifacts of the gaming table, so accountants deal with the artifacts of the marketplace. The way we handle money is governed by social conventions; it is something like a game. If human beings ceased to take an interest in money and contractual obligations, then, though wheat and iron would remain, debits and credits would fade away.

Could that be the way Ryle wishes us to look at science? Certainly one can find instances of this sort of thing in the various sciences: The concept of the standard deviation of a set of measurements, for example, applies to the technique of measuring, not to the objects on which measurements are made. If people gave up measuring, there would be no more standard deviations. But, unlike chess and poker, science is not a purely formal activity, and unlike accounting, natural science does not take human conventions as its subject matter. Concepts that apply merely to scientific technique are not the ones Ryle is or should be concerned about.

But there is another way that we may consider Ryle's parable of a college library as an analogy to the distinction between science and common sense. The accountant has something to say about everything in the library; what sets her world apart is not a special set of objects of interest but a special way of being interested in them. She is concerned only with the fiscal aspects of the college, with, for example, the price of each of the library books but with the literary value of none. Part of Ryle's quarrel is with a certain view of the nature of atomic physics, which, as he stipulates, applies to everything there is. So it seems clear that he wishes to suggest that, like the accountant, an atomic physicist is concerned only with some particular aspect or feature of every object in the world.

What could that special feature be? What, in Ryle's view, is the atomic physicist's peculiar perspective on the world? Again we must rely on hints gleaned from his examples, but it seems that he has in mind the physicist's characteristic preoccupation with matters quantitative. I base this guess primarily on the opening paragraph of "Technical and Untechnical Concepts." "A scientific theory," Ryle says,

> has no place in it for terms which cannot appear among the data or the results of calculations. . . . Since scientific truths are about what can carry and be carried by calculations, colours, tastes and smells which cannot be so carried must belong not to the facts of physics, but elsewhere, namely either to the facts of human and animal physiology or to the facts of human and animal psychology.
> [1954, p. 82]

Later Ryle denies the consequent of that sentence but allows the antecedent to stand. The passage quoted shows most clearly, I think, how Ryle intends his analogies to be applied, but there are other signs that point in the same direction. One of them is the fact that the accountant, in the only example that seems at all close to the case of atomic physics (as we have seen), is also concerned with a quantitative aspect of the world, with "what can carry and be carried by calculations." The accountant speaks not about library books themselves but only about their (numerical) prices. Similarly, according to Ryle, physical theorists "do not describe chairs and tables at all, any more than the accountant describes books bought for the library" (1954, p. 79). Another clue that number and calculation are the keys to Ryle's analogies turns up in a later chapter, "Perception," in which he offers to defend commonsense notions of perception from the onslaughts of "thinkers who wish to maintain the pre-eminence of mathematical knowledge over other beliefs" (p. 94). Still later, in "Formal and Informal Logic," he refers to the earlier chapters as involving "litigations" between "mathematicians and men in the street" (p. 111). Ryle seems to be saying this: Scientists perform measurements on the objects of everyday experience, thereby generating numerical data. (See, for example, how he contrasts "thermometer-temperature" and "warmth," p. 91). Scientific discourse, then, is about these numerical data and, properly understood, does not provide descriptions of the objects from which the data have been extracted. Any suggestion, then, that scientific statements could conflict with commonsense talk about objects like chairs and tables must rest on a failure to distinguish talk about the numerical artifacts of measuring from descriptions of actual things.

When we explain the fuzzy appearance of a dandelion head by pointing out that close scrutiny shows it to be made up of a multitude of tiny white filaments, we are engaged in one sort of commerce with the world, Ryle seems to argue, but when we explain the rigidity of a bar of steel by pointing out that indirect evidence obtained by means of instruments other than eyes or microscopes shows the bar to be composed of atoms arranged and interacting in certain ways, then our commerce is of quite another sort. A botanist's claim about a dandelion is an actual description, but a metallurgist's claim about the atomic composition of a bar of steel is neither a description nor a misdescription of the bar; it is, Ryle seems to say, a statement about the numerical results of measuring, just as what an accountant says is about prices and neither describes nor misdescribes books.

## CONTINUITY OF SCIENCE AND COMMON SENSE

It is not easy to assess, much less criticize or try to reply to, a series of suggestions backed up by plausible analogies. Let me, however, make the attempt by proposing some suggestions and analogies of my own.

Does the scientists' preoccupation with numerical data set their world apart? Consider this example. A physicist with a penchant for mathematical speculation and a hearty, nonmathematical cricket player are both observing a hut with one door and no windows. As they watch, three persons enter the hut, and after a short time two emerge. The physicist performs a mathematical operation on his data and concludes that one person remains inside. The cricketer runs up to the hut, peers through the doorway, and sees one person inside. Both now voice the claim that the hut contains one person. Ryle's argument, as I have interpreted it, would lead us to say that the cricketer's claim, based as it is on the sort of evidence that any able-bodied person could obtain, is about the world we all live in, whereas the physicist's claim, based on a branch of learning rightly shunned by the common man, is a claim about the special "world" of the physicist; it is about only those peculiar quantitative aspects of the world that intrigue physicists and bore the rest of us. Clearly, that is nonsense. The physicist employed numerical data as clues to what was going on in the world, but although what he said was based on the results of data gathering it was not about those data. Like the cricketer's claim, his was an actual description of the hut.

So it is, I claim, with atomic physics. The quantitative reasoning that led Dalton to conclude that the world is made up of atoms was of the same sort as, and hardly more complicated than, the quantitative reasoning employed by the physicist watching the hut. And if it is nonsense to suggest that the physicist in the parable was not talking about an ordinary flesh-and-blood person in the hut, it is equal nonsense to suggest that Dalton was not asserting a claim about the actual composition of our everyday world. Dalton reasoned from a narrow set of quantitative facts about chemical reactions to a conclusion about the world we all share. To the extent that he and his successors did their job properly, their atoms are everyone's atoms.

I suggest that Ryle has not noticed how scientists actually employ mathematics in their work. In company with many people to whom the apparition of an equation on a printed page is as paralyzing as the sight of a serpent to a sparrow,[1] he has seen the mathematical formulas but has not heard the extensive discourse that surrounds and interprets them. It is as if, in the story of the physicist and the cricketer, a bystander had noticed the physicist's scrap of paper, on which the figure 2 was subtracted from 3 but had failed to notice that the physicist's aim, in performing

1 / I do not know how Ryle felt about mathematics, but this accurately describes many of my friends.

this feat, was to describe the contents of the hut. Neither Ryle nor anyone else would claim that the physicist was merely abstracting out of the concrete situation a purely formal, mathematical structure in keeping with his professional preoccupation with "what can carry and be carried by calculations." To do so would be to mistake the physicist's means for his ends: He did not scan the world in order to pull out of it a mathematical formula; rather, he used numerical data as clues and a formula as an aid to reasoning, in order to augment his description of the world. Ryle wants to set up a contrast between the views of "mathematicians and men in the street." But physicists are not mathematicians. Ask any mathematician, or any physicist. Mathematicians and poker players make no attempt to describe the material world; physicists and men in the street do.

It seems that a mistaken view of the uses of mathematics, which would tempt no one in as straightforward a case as determining the contents of a hut, has bemused many people, Ryle among them, when they consider the less readily accessible field of atomic physics. Ryle would say, of course, that an ornithologist who interprets the sight of a black "ribbon" in the sky as a flock of geese arranged in a V speaks in the same matter-of-fact tone used by the physicist and the cricketer when speaking about the hut, but he wants to reject the suggestion that Dalton's successors used that tone when claiming that an iron bar really is a large number of iron atoms arranged in a lattice. I claim that no distinction between the tones of voice of atomic physicists and men in the street can be based on the fact that the former sometimes reason from numerical data by means of mathematical formulas.

## THEORY-LADEN TERMS

Ryle also suggests that the claims scientists make about the world are couched in a vocabulary whose meaning derives from the way its terms are used in scientific theories. Many of the terms used by scientists, he asserts, are "theory-laden," whereas our ordinary discourse about the world is not.[2] Therefore, scientific claims about the world do not stand on the same ground as,

2 / Or some, at least, of commonsense discourse is not. Ryle draws his contrast between "the technical concepts of a scientific theory and the semi-technical or untechnical concepts of the pavement" (1954, p. 91).

and cannot be made to fight with, commonsense claims. This way of avoiding a confrontation between science and common sense is independent of the argument from the mathematical predilection of atomic physicists, for, if this argument works at all, it does so whether scientific theories take a mathematical or some other form. Let us see if it works.

It is important not to confuse Ryle's claim that scientific talk about the world is theory-laden with the suggestions of later philosophers (for example, Feyerabend 1970) that all our talk about anything whatever is both theory-laden and hopelessly subjective. Ryle wishes to align himself with the man in the street; at least, he wants to defend the plain man's view that the world as we know it from everyday experience is real, not a "dummy world"—not to be relegated to the insides of our heads but really out there. The world Ryle defends is the world defended by Samuel Johnson in his famous retort to Idealism. That world is as it is, regardless of what we think about it; against it we can stub our toes and shatter our theories. Ryle, I think, wishes seriously to defend some kind of commonsense realism; he is not George Berkeley relaxing in white flannels.

How might scientific talk about the world be infected with theory in such a way as to quarantine it from our ordinary descriptions? In the absence of worked-out samples from Ryle's own pen, we must try to guess what he has in mind. The analogy he offers is the way the terms of bridge and poker are laden with the rules of those games. Of the terms of genetics Ryle says (1954, p. 90), "The technical terms of genetics are . . . laden . . . with the luggage of genetic theory. Their meanings change with changes in the theory. Knowing their meanings requires some grasp of the theory." Similarly, he suggests, knowing the meaning of "straight flush" requires some grasp of the rules of poker. But a general allusion to genetics is hardly an example. Ryle does, however, suggest two specific examples (without working them out) of what he considers technical concepts: the concept of "light wave," which he contrasts with the commonsense concepts "pink" and "blue" (p. 91), and the concept of "thermometer-temperature," which he contrasts with "warmth" (p. 88). Let us see what can be made of these hints. Ryle is surely mistaken in suggesting that "light wave" and "blue" are contrasting concepts, because a light wave is an object of some sort whereas "blue" specifies a property of objects; surely no one would be tempted to substitute one of these terms for the other. But in comparing "thermometer-temperature" with "warmth" Ryle chooses a useful example. Someone might in fact wish to suggest (mistakenly, Ryle would say) that "thermometer-temperature" does the same sort of work as "warmth" but does it better. "We can," says Ryle, "be seriously perplexed by the question whether behind the warmth of the bath water which the child feels with his hand, there does not covertly reside some grander property which he fails to detect, namely the thermometer-temperature of the water" (p. 88). But to think that there is a "logical rivalry" between the two concepts is to be mistaken in somewhat the same way as when we suppose that there is rivalry between "trump card" and "queen of hearts," according to Ryle. A given bit of pasteboard may simultaneously be the queen of hearts and a trump card, but these are two logically different sorts of conditions in which a card may find itself.

Now there is a sense, but a trivial one, in which "thermometer-temperature" illustrates Ryle's point. It is true that to understand that the bath water is fairly warm requires no grasp of scientific theory, but to understand that it is at 50°C does require some grasp of the conventions of the Celsius scale of temperature. But from these facts it emphatically does not follow that being at 50°C and being fairly warm are two quite different sorts of conditions in which the bath water may find itself. The statements, "It is at 50°C," and "It is at 78°C," though laden with conventions, are nevertheless attempts to specify more accurately the same sort of thing we specify by "It is fairly warm" or "It is very warm." The phrase "boiling hot" is made more precise but not transformed into another logical category when translated as "nearly 100°C." One's aim in uttering either sort of statement is to tell how warm the bath water is. And Ryle is simply mistaken in his suggestion that anyone would feel tempted to think that the thermometer-temperature of the water lies behind its warmth and goes undetected when we touch the water. Behind the thermometer reading lies the ability of the water to cause the expansion of mercury, and behind the warmth-sensation lies the ability of the water to cause sensations of warmth. But common sense requires us to take the thermometer reading as a symptom of the same intrinsic property of the water that warmth-sensations are clues to. The property of objects we detect and measure by means of thermometers is the same property we detect and estimate by touch. As I shall argue at greater length below, the property we have always understood ourselves to be referring to by the term "warmth" has turned out to be a statistical feature of the distribution of energy among the parts that compose warm things.

So the theory-ladenness of technical concepts like temperature does not justify quarantining scientific from commonsense talk. Not only does our employment of thermometric terms merge continuously with our use of terms like "cool," "warm," and "hot," but we have the same aim as well, namely, to describe an object by specifying a particular one of its intrinsic properties.

Let us make one more attempt to see whether the close connection between scientific terms and scientific theories may forestall possible conflicts between science and common sense. Note that, when we say that the intrinsic property of warm bodies that we detect by touch and by thermometry is a feature of the distribution of energy among the microscopic parts, our claim is only as firm as the thermodynamic theory on which it rests. Scientific descriptions, unlike those of common sense, frequently stand upon elaborate theoretical foundations; if the theory on which a scientific description is based should be abandoned, the description might likewise collapse. Is that how we should interpret Ryle's observation that scientific talk about the world is laden with theory? Would that interpretation prevent scientific terms from claiming a seat on the bench normally occupied by the terms of common sense? The following simple counterexample shows that this interpretation, too, fails to support Ryle's thesis. There are two ways in which a new planet may be discovered. One way is to look very carefully in the region of the ecliptic for a point of light whose position changes slowly with respect to the background stars. That is how the planets known to the ancients were found, and it is the way of common sense. The other way is to compare the observed motions of known planets with theoretical predictions of how they ought to move, given our present knowledge of the structure and dynamics of the solar system. Then, if the planet fails to move as we expect it to, we hypothesize that an unknown planet is responsible for the discrepancy between observation and prediction. That was the method used by Adams and Leverrier in discovering the planet Neptune, a method that is theory-laden inasmuch as it employs Newton's laws of planetary motion. Because this second method operates by means of scientific theories, I take it to be an example of the scientific way of dealing with the world that Ryle wants to differentiate from common sense.

Ryle's distinction (as applied to this example) might have looked more plausible if our belief in the existence of Neptune had continued to rest only on the perturbations of the orbit of Uranus and had not been substantiated by the telescopic observations of J. G. Galle. But who now could seriously suggest that Galle, the first person to see Neptune, and the ancient people who first noticed the wanderings of Saturn were engaged in a radically different sort of enterprise from that of Leverrier and Adams? Clearly, they were all asking the same questions and making the same sorts of claims about the world. Their employing direct visual observations on the one hand and indirect ones, supplemented by careful reasoning, on the other does not at all serve to drive a wedge between their enterprises.

In contrast to the science of Newton's day, modern science has burgeoned to such a degree that the ordinary educated person often feels shut out from the scientific enterprise. And it is true that scientists have invented techniques and concepts that are merely technical, such as the concepts of molality and of tare weight. But do the facts that relatively few persons have a confident grasp of modern science and that scientists employ some purely technical concepts in their work show that science is at bottom a technical world unto itself? Surely not. Science aims to find out what the world is like—what it is made of and how it works. And science claims, rightly or wrongly, to answer questions of ontology and of causation.

When Watson and Crick found that the DNA molecule is made up of nucleotides arranged in a double helix, they were engaged in the same sort of activity as were the early microscopists who found that living tissues are composed of cells; indeed, in the same kind of activity as were our prehistoric ancestors who learned that cattle are composed of bones, muscles, viscera, and so on. The notion of a plank steak is a butcher's technical concept and signifies nothing much about the composition of a cow. But the notion of a bone is not a technical concept—it is as everyday and commonsensical as the concept of a grain of sand. When we approach a side of beef as butchers do, bearing in mind the demands of our customers, we can see the carcass as consisting of so many steaks, chops, and roasts. But when we approach it on its own terms, carrying with us nothing of the specialist's tricks and procedures but merely asking with the common man, "What is it like?" and "How does it work?" then we find it to be made up of bones and muscles.

But what of this muscle? What is it made of? The attitude of open inquiry (common sense extended but not altered in spirit) leads us to answer that it consists of cells. And the cell? And the cell's nucleus? And the DNA molecule? And the carbon atom? All these questions and their answers, tentative though they be, are put forward in the spirit of the common man. They are not specialist's questions, even though they tend to be asked by only a small fraction of the populace. What turns discourse into specialist's lingo is not its limited popularity but the special social context in which it resides and the peculiar aims it serves. The argot of the poker player is technical talk because it acquires its meaning from the rules of the game and the aspirations of its players. But when a molecular geneticist inquires into the composition of a strand of DNA, he or she engages in the same kind of activity as one who wonders what is in the soup tonight or whether the restaurant is made of brick or stone. Nearly everyone knows the slang of the baseball diamond, and very few are at home in a laboratory of molecular genetics; yet the world of baseball is a specialist's world, and the world of genetics is everyone's.

If the business of science is the business of commonsense inquiry into the composition and workings of the world we all live in, then we may expect occasionally to encounter genuine clashes between what we believe to be true of the world on the testimony of current scientific theories and what we hold to be true on other grounds. Such a conflict is not a problem generated by the practicing of an esoteric technique; it is generated by the working out of an attitude toward the world that is part of the general outlook of Western common sense. Because the outlook belongs to everyone the problem does, too. There is real, not just apparent, strife between the ontology of reductionistic atomism, which tells us that the pieces that compose the objects of ordinary experience are the only effective causal agents, and our deeply rooted intuition that we ourselves, though material, physical beings, are as persons both causal and moral agents. We have real, not mock, warfare on our hands. These rival claims cannot be explained away; they must be adjudicated, not ignored.

## ATOMISTIC STRATEGIES

I have been able to find no support in Ryle's own examples or in my attempts to follow his hints for the thesis that, because of the technical nature of the scientific enterprise, what science tells us about the world is not a description and so could not conflict with our commonsense intuitions and descriptions of the world. I believe that thesis to be mistaken. Nevertheless, Ryle's examples and analogies raise other questions, which I have not yet addressed. Clearly, the language we employ in ordinary affairs is marvelously subtle and complex. So varied are our modes of upper-level speech that reductionism faces a formidable task; the simple substitution of atomistic nouns and verbs for the terms of common speech is but a part of what needs to be done. Indeed, the antireductionistic arguments to which I shall turn in the following chapters claim to show that there are some valid and widely used forms of upper-level language that cannot be reduced. Let me, then, conclude this chapter and prepare for the next by setting forth, more systematically than I have done hitherto, how, according to the reductionist program, the various patterns of upper-level speech are to be brought into a standard atomist format.

The descriptions we produce in ordinary conversation and in the upper-level sciences display several features, each of which presents its own challenge to the reductionist program. I am able to distinguish five such features: First, we sometimes refer to upper-level entities by their *proper names*. Second, in referring to upper-level things as instances of kinds, we sometimes characterize them by *intrinsic properties*. Third, some upper-level kinds are characterized by *relational properties*. Fourth, some of the properties we assign to upper-level entities are propensities, or *abilities*. Fifth, some of these abilities are abilities to produce *subjective experiences*. Let us consider how the atomist program meets, or is intended to meet, each of these challenges.

PROPER NAMES. Consider, first, the simplest of these types of upper-level narration. Whatever other features may be present, upper-level and commonsense talk does pick out entities, actions, and circumstances for which there are no lower-level names. Suppose the upper-level reference occurs by means of a proper name. In such a case, to replace the conventional upper-level designation for a composite object or process by an atomic specification—for example, to replace "that object" (pointing to a crystal of salt) by "those sodium and chloride ions arranged in cubic array," and so on—is to convey all the information of the upper-level formulation and more. There is no loss but rather a gain when the spelling-out of the composition and structure of an object is substituted for its proper name. In itself—that is, apart from its abilities, its relations to other things, and to our experiences of it—any individual composite object just is its parts, arranged as they are and doing what they do; nothing more.

INTRINSIC PROPERTIES. Second, when we pick out an ordinary entity as an instance of a kind whose characterizing property is intrinsic to the entity, as when we refer to the object *as* a salt crystal, then, too, explication of the upper-level term by means of the structural features and internal dynamics of the upper-level entity leads to a gain of information, not a loss. Intrinsic properties, at least according to the atomist program, can always be given a lower-level, structural explication. Thus, salt crystals are characterized microscopically as cubic arrays of sodium and chloride ions; galaxies are collections of enormous numbers of stars, protostars, planets, gases, dust, and other debris; and deuterium nuclei are neutron–proton pairs tightly bound by the nuclear force.

Now, when we replace a commonsense description or formulation by its translation into the language of the parts, we must replace the commonsense terms for kinds by the lower-level explications of those kinds. Assuredly, something may be lost in this translation. What may vanish is the set of implications and references to other pieces of the world (when the kinds are specified in terms of relational properties) and to our subjective experiences. But if our aim is to describe truly, accurately, and exactly a limited section of the world as it is in itself, *and only that sec-*

*tion*, then we need not refer to other parts of the world and to our subjective experiences, for they are not part of the intrinsic situation. Still, there are other facts that must be included in a complete description of the whole of reality, among them the truths we express in relational terms and in terms of our subjective experiences.

RELATIONAL PROPERTIES. When we describe any object or spatiotemporal portion of the world according to the standard format of reductionistic atomism we leave out those assertions about the object or piece of the world that refer to relations between it and other things. What must be done with this leftover content of the upper-level descriptions? A relational property of an object (that is, a property not intrinsic to the object and so not explicable in terms of its structure) is shown to be an intrinsic, structural property of a larger system that includes the object. This treatment of relational properties is not a technical peculiarity of the reductionistic program; it fits equally comfortably within the purview of common sense, as the following examples show. Detroit's having a population in excess of one million is a property discoverable by one whose attention is concentrated wholly upon the city itself, but Detroit's being north of Tampa, a relational property of Detroit, is simply a structural property, having to do with the arrangement of the parts, of a larger system of which both Detroit and Tampa are components. While engaged in action off the coast of Brittany, Horatio Hornblower became a father; but even those of his companions who were regarding him most closely at the time failed to notice the event. What we actually refer to in this apparent description of Hornblower is the birth of a child to a woman in England and the previous signing of a marriage contract by that woman and Hornblower. We refer, that is, to a network of causal (and perhaps other) connections in a larger system of which Hornblower is a part.

But notice that, although in these cases assigning a relational property to an object is equivalent to assigning a structural property to a larger system, the equivalence involves no shift to a lower level of description. This observation suggests what appears to be a promising lead. Unlike descriptions of objects in terms of intrinsic properties, which place the discourse on a lower level where the parts do the causal action, descriptions in terms of relational properties seem to retain the original level of description, merely broadening the scope of the discourse. They require us to add to the cast of characters without dismissing any of them. The tendency of this observation, though not explicitly antireductionistic, is at least not explicitly reductionistic. It is reasonable to suppose, therefore, that some of the laws of the upper-level sciences, stated in terms of relational properties, may resist reduction in this manner. Arguments to this effect have been proposed by Michael Polanyi, Karl Popper, and Jerry Fodor. Because these suggestions represent a departure from standard reductionist doctrine, I shall postpone a detailed discussion of them until chapter 7.

ABILITIES. Both in upper-level sciences and in our ordinary talk about the world we make free use of a mode of description that includes reference to the abilities of upper-level entities to act in certain ways and/or to produce certain effects. For example, in ascribing the property *shininess* to a bar of steel we refer to its ability to reflect incident visible light without appreciable scattering. The description "*X* is shiny" is equivalent to "*X* is able to reflect light like a mirror." A second example of a commonsense property that turns out to be a propensity is the commonsense meaning of "warmth." The description "*X* is warm" is equivalent to "*X* is able to induce warmth-sensations in a normal, suitably prepared human."

As prescribed by the atomist program, any ability must be explicated in terms of the composition and structure of the object that has it and in terms of the general laws that govern the behavior of the object's parts. To see that this prescription is reasonable and in accord with common sense, consider the following characteristics of the way we ordinarily ascribe abilities to everyday objects.

Note, first, that abilities are intrinsic to the objects that have them, because an ability is distinct from the tests by which we detect it. The ability of *X* to do *Y* in circumstances *C* can be detected by arranging the circumstances so that *X* actually does *Y*. But the ability to do something is not identical to the doing. For example, it would not be incoherent to suggest that a certain bar of steel is shiny, though it be forged, polished, and melted down again in darkness. The ability to reflect visible light like a mirror does not depend on the actual presence of visible light. Warmth, too, is an intrinsic property. Suppose I touch an object on two occasions five minutes apart and find it to be warm both times. I can then assert, possibly incorrectly but not incoherently, that it is warm also during the five-minute interval. I may even assert, again not incoherently, that another object is warm even though no one has ever felt it, even if it has never touched another object. Calling it warm is equivalent to claiming that if it had been touched it would have produced a sensation of warmth. Similar counterfactual statements can be extracted from the property *shininess*. The connection between abilities and counterfactuals is a clue that ability descriptions can be translated into lawlike, causal descriptions.

A second feature of abilities is that they are open-ended. Warmth is the ability to produce warmth-sensations in an indefinite number of human beings and in an indefinite number of circumstances; but it is (or is lawfully tied to) the ability to do many other things as well: to cause thermometers (of an indefinite variety of designs) to respond in certain ways, to transfer heat to cooler objects, and so on.

Abilities are intrinsic to the objects that have them, but having a certain structure is also an intrinsic property of a composite thing. Moreover (and still within the domain of common sense), the abilities of things are frequently linked to their structures. Consider the ability of a rattlesnake to strike. In one sense of "able to strike," every normal, healthy rattler is able to strike; yet, in another sense, only a rattler that is coiled in a certain way is able to strike. A rattlesnake has the ability (in the second of these two senses) by virtue of its being coiled. We say that the structural property (being coiled) accounts for the ability; the rattler's structure enables it to strike or gives it the ability to strike. Yet, such are our linguistic habits, we resist saying that the ability to strike in the second sense is identical to being coiled. Now, there may be good reasons for our habits in this case. The action that an object is able to do by virtue of its structure is related to that structure somewhat as effect is to cause, or at least as effect is to causally antecedent conditions. And a pervasive feature of causation is the nonspecificity of effect to cause; generally, a given effect can be produced by a variety of causes. Perhaps because of this asymmetry between causes and their effects we find a similar asymmetry in our linguistic habits: We are willing to say that to be coiled[3] is to be able to strike but unwilling to say that to be able to strike is to be coiled. It may be that no rattler has ever struck from an uncoiled position, yet we feel that unusual circumstances *might* arise such that an uncoiled rattler would be able to strike—for example, it might be supported in some mechanical contrivance or wedged between two stones.

Finally, causes occur in transitive sequences. This feature of the world, too, has its counterpart in our speaking about structures and abilities. A normal, healthy rattlesnake is able to coil itself by virtue of its muscular and skeletal structure. Therefore, we say that to have the normal rattlesnake structure is to be able to coil up. But to be able to coil up is to be able to place itself in a position to strike. Therefore, to have the normal structure is to be able to strike. So the difference between the two senses of "able to strike," noted above, is a matter of proximity in the causal chain.

So we see that talking about abilities and talking about structures that confer those abilities are both normal features of our commonsense formulations of the way things are. Therefore, the goal of reductionistic science—to account for all the propensities of the objects of everyday experience in terms of their structural features and the propensities of their parts—is not foreign to our ordinary way of dealing with the world.

But can we, merely by spelling out the composition, structure, and laws of behavior of the parts of composite systems, say at a lower level all that we say at an upper level in terms of abilities? We have seen that, in general, the ability to do something is not strictly identified with the object's structure. Nevertheless, we do habitually identify abilities with structures *under normal circumstances*. We naturally say, speaking of rattlesnakes in general, that for them to be able to strike is to have the normal rattlesnake structure. The generalizations we make about rattlesnakes and their characteristic abilities are made with the understanding that normal circumstances prevail. A wounded snake might be given the ability to strike by some prosthetic device, but when we

3 / Of course, other conditions must be added, such as being alive, awake, healthy, etc. These are omitted here for the sake of brevity.

speak in general terms of striking ability in snakes we tacitly rule out such artificial circumstances.

This point is even more obvious in the case of warmth. The ability to induce warmth-sensations (no matter how) cannot be identical to thermodynamic or statistical-mechanical temperature, for, if we are willing to consider nonstandard circumstances such as unusual states of the human perceiver, then objects in identical intrinsic states may be warm on some occasions and not warm on others. But we normally determine that warmth shall be an intrinsic, public, objective property of objects, and we carry out this resolution by setting up standard conditions under which the propensity is to be displayed. So resolved, we say that, under standard conditions, to have the statistical-mechanical property is to be able to induce warmth-sensations and to be able to induce warmth-sensations is to have the statistical property. Given the laws of physics and the standard conditions, a given object induces warmth-sensations if and only if it has that statistical property. These standard conditions include the state of the perceiver, the mode of connection between perceiver and object, and the manner of preparation of the object.

It may be that, in speaking of technical and semitechnical concepts, Ryle is referring, among other examples, to the sort of standardization I have outlined for warmth. In that process, standard conditions are specified so that our use of "warmth" can be objective, so that in describing an object as warm we can cut our ascription loose from "the facts of human and animal physiology and the facts of human and animal psychology." But is such a refined concept really technical or semitechnical? Even in ordinary speech we intend warmth to be an intrinsic property. Therefore, when a physicist or other specialist does make the effort to standardize thermometry, she is not turning a commonsense concept into a technical or semitechnical one—not, for example, giving a peculiar twist or special meaning to the concept—but merely fulfilling an obligation that binds every user of language. In this labor the physicist works on behalf of everyone.

To summarize: When in upper-level speech we ascribe an ability to an object, we mean that it is able to perform a specified action or produce a specified effect (and possibly we add a description of the circumstances under which this ability is demonstrated). The lower-level translation of this ability-ascription consists of a spelling-out of the composition and structure of the object, a lower-level explication of the action or effect, and an exposition of the laws of behavior of the parts in terms of which these lower-level explications have been formulated. From this information one can obtain, by the standard theoretical methods of the lower-level science, a statement that the action occurs or that the effect is produced under some specifiable circumstances. And when we show that there are nomologically possible circumstances under which an object performs a certain action, we have captured all that we mean to convey when we say it is able to perform that action.

SUBJECTIVE EXPERIENCES. Finally, let us consider the most recalcitrant sort of commonsense locution: descriptions formulated in terms of abilities to induce experiences in human perceivers, as, for example, "looking blue," or "being painfully hot." The standard response to this challenge proceeds by two stages. First, we argue that the fact that a state of affairs obtaining in a portion of the world out there, that is, in a bit of the world that does not include a human observer, is able to produce, under appropriate additional circumstances, certain results in the perceiver is *nothing to the object or state of affairs in itself*. Therefore, the absence of reference to potential human experiences in the atomist description of the object or state of affairs does not constitute a fault, for, though those potential experiences are of tremendous importance to the human perceiver, they are not a legitimate part of an objective description of that external thing.

Nevertheless, those references to objective experiences are presumably true and belong somewhere in a complete description of what there is. Therefore, a complete description of the world (not just a description of the nonhuman portions of it) must somehow find a way of coming to terms with those experiences. This brings us to the second stage of the standard response to the challenge. Abilities to affect or produce human conscious experiences are treated in the same manner as abilities to affect other, nonsentient objects, as outlined above for the treatment of propensities in general. Abilities to affect consciousness are explicated not as intrinsic properties of the objects that have them but as lawlike generalizations about the composition, structure, and internal processes of portions of the world that include perceivers.

But on this front the program has not progressed very far, for when the standard treatment of propensity statements is applied to abilities to produce subjective experiences we find that we need a lower-level explication of what it is to cause a subjective experience, and—at least at the moment—we are unable to produce lower-level explications of what an individual subjective experience is. We come face to face, in short, with the mind–body problem. At this juncture reductionists have proposed a variety of scenarios for the future development of the program of reduction, all of them going under the heading of *physicalism*. If atomistic reduction is to succeed, something along the lines of the physicalist theory of mind must ultimately carry the day. I shall return to that portion of the atomist program in chapter 8.

FOUR

# Teleology: Reducing Cybernetics

WHAT FEATURES DISTINGUISH LIVING ORGANISMS FROM all other things? Can the distinction be expressed in purely mechanistic terms, or does it resist a reductive analysis? Hints toward answers to these questions may be gleaned from the fact that an organism is something to which teleological concepts apply. Living things—typically, human beings—harbor intentions, seek goals, and adapt means to ends with conscious deliberation. These activities are paradigms of teleology. But we also find it appropriate to apply such teleological concepts as function and adaptation to organisms as simple as plants. Clearly, then, functionality among the parts of an organism does not entail consciousness in the whole. Nor need talk of functions imply anything pro or con about an organism's having been produced by a divine Designer. That much is evident from the way natural theology was done in pre-Darwinian times. The proponents of the argument from design drew their theological conclusion from their observations of the adaptedness of organisms. Because the adaptedness is discernible independently of theological considerations, it is logically prior to them. And biologists today speak nontheologically of the adaptations of organisms to their environment, and some even debate whether the "ultimate goal" of natural selection is the proliferation of genes or some other, higher-level result. Clearly, even a very simple organism may seek goals of its own, its parts may have functions and serve ends, and it may adapt itself to threatening or challenging circumstances. Teleological activities such as these can be recognized for what they are purely by reference to the organism's own internal structure and to its interactions with the environment. An organism is a teleological thing, simply on its own terms and apart from any possible relation to consciousness or to intelligent design.

Natural objects, then, fall into two categories, one of living things and human artifacts, which have teleological features, and another of the nonartifactual inorganic, which do not. The question arises, therefore, whether the organic sciences are divided from the inorganic by an unbridgeable gulf, so that living creatures should rate a separate and irreducible entry in our catalog of natural objects. Is a living thing merely an unusually complicated dynamical arrangement of parts, as the atomist program suggests, or does it display an utterly novel feature? Are goals, functions, purposes, and the like merely interesting examples of what atoms can do and how they can arrange themselves when they fall together in sufficiently large numbers, or are they irreducible characteristics of life, symptoms of a deep dichotomy in nature and guarantors of the ultimate autonomy of the organic sciences?

These are broad but also vague queries. We can take a few steps toward answering them by posing a narrower, more clearly defined question: Can some typical teleological concepts be reduced to standard mechanical concepts? Can we understand functions, goals, and adaptations in complex organisms simply in terms of the arrangements and interactions of their atomic parts?

## A PECULIAR KIND OF REDUCTION

Clearly, the question we have posed concerns the reduction of upper-level languages to a lower level; it lacks, however, some of the features we find in the paradigms of interlevel reduction of theories. In the standard cases, one starts with two theories that apply to the same set of objects but operate at different levels of analysis. These theories are sufficiently complete to be formulated as axiomatized logical structures, so that they can serve as sources of deductive-nomological explanations. The question of interlevel reduction can then be phrased in this manner: Can the axioms and theories of the upper level be deduced, with the aid of bridging postulates, from the axioms of the lower-level theory? The primary example of this kind of reduction is the derivation of macroscopic thermodynamics from the statistical mechanics of collections of large numbers of atoms. The reduction establishes connections between upper-level and lower-level concepts. Entropy, heat, and temperature, for example, acquire explications in terms of the statistical properties of swarms of microscopic bodies. This explication of upper-level concepts in terms of lower-level ones proceeds hand-in-hand with the derivation of upper-level theories from theories that operate at lower levels. The coherence of the entire process validates both the derivation and the explication. Whether the temperature of a gas must be understood as the average kinetic energy of its molecules or as some more subtle statistical property of the parts depends on whether such an understanding allows us to derive from the lower-level theory all that must be said about macroscopic objects in upper-level language.

Parallel to this development in thermodynamics run attempts to reduce portions of biology to the principles of physics and chemistry. When the efforts of Mary B. Williams (1970; 1973) to construct an axiom set for evolution theory gain general acceptance, and when and if successful derivations of these axioms from the laws of molecular biology are produced, then we may expect analyses of the concepts of adaptation and function to participate in the process as links between lower and upper levels. But we need not wait for the axiomatizers of upper-level theories to complete their tasks before we ask whether teleological *concepts* are reducible to mechanistic ones. Even though, strictly speaking, the issue will not be settled until the logical structures of the two levels of discourse have been formally displayed once and for all, the debate over the explication and possible reduction of teleology has produced a number of cogent arguments both pro and con. There are plenty of informal but sufficiently clear uses of teleological concepts both in ordinary speech and in the organic sciences. We may be satisfied at present, therefore, with an informal reduction and its concomitant explication of teleological concepts. Such a reductive explication, provided we can construct one, would be all that we need as we attempt to decide whether one can plausibly affirm or reasonably doubt that a living thing is anything over and above a collection of mechanically interacting atomic parts.

Attempts to generate reductive explications of teleological concepts deserve to stand alongside the microreduction of thermodynamics and the still debated reduction of Mendelian to molecular genetics as valid additions to our stock of examples of interlevel reduction. The question we shall face in this chapter does not directly concern the derivation of one well-formulated theoretical structure from another; rather, it concerns the explication of a set of somewhat murky upper-level concepts in terms of clearer concepts that operate at a lower level of discourse. We cannot measure the success of the enterprise against a stable and formal upper-level theory; rather, we must ask whether a proposed explication squares with the intuitions developed through using the upper-level concepts in informal descriptions and explanations. Intuitions are to some extent malleable, subject to modification and growth. We may expect, therefore, that our attempt to explicate teleological concepts in terms of mechanistic ones will clarify the upper-level concepts and sharpen distinctions. If the effort succeeds, we will discover what we ought to have meant all along by function, goal, adaptation, and their kin.

Philosophical analyses of teleology differ as to the degree to which they concentrate upon biology. Some, of which the works of Berent Enc (1979), Peter Achinstein (1977), Christopher Boorse (1976), Andrew Woodfield (1976), and Larry Wright (1973; 1976) are recent examples, aim at the greatest possible generality, assigning a prominent place to the way we use teleological terms in describing the activities of human beings, in contexts where there is a presumption of conscious intention or design. These analyses treat the use of teleological terms where consciousness is not implicated as a special case. Subhuman biology provides restricted examples at best; and in Woodward's analysis nonconscious teleology turns out to be defective or merely analogical. The other approach to the analytical task, of which Ernest Nagel's (1977), William Wimsatt's (1972), and Francisco Ayala's (1970) in other respects very different analyses are recent examples, concentrates on biology. Without disavowing an interest in the analysis of teleology in general, this approach draws its paradigms from function talk as it applies to the parts of simple living systems. I shall adopt the more restricted of these two approaches, proceeding from particular cases in nonconscious systems only a step or two in the direction of generality, for two reasons. First, although by focusing initially upon functions in ordinary biology we postpone a general understanding of all uses of teleological concepts, we gain thereby a greater appreciation of the complexity and diversity of uses within biology itself. Second, we would violate the spirit of the atomist reduction program if we took the analysis of teleology in mentalistic terms as a paradigm. According to this program, talk of purposes, goals and functions in human affairs must be understood in terms of the teleology of nonconscious systems; mentalistic concepts must be reducible to merely mechanistic terms, not the reverse. That reduction may turn out to be impossible, but we must not prejudge the issue. By taking the inductive approach, proceeding from function talk in simple organisms and in machines toward the analysis of teleology in conscious beings, we can give the atomist program a fair hearing, allowing it to demonstrate its full strength.

Having chosen this second approach, we face another pair of alternatives, one seeming to favor the reductionist conjecture, the other the antireductionist. The older alternative, proposed originally by Arturo Rosenblueth, Norbert Wiener, and Julian Bigelow (1943), analyzes teleology in living things and human artifacts in terms of the concepts of cybernetics. According to their conjecture, which has been developed and refined by many authors, when we ascribe a function to a part of an organism or machine we claim that the containing system is organized according to a cybernetic pattern, typically feedback; that being so organized it seeks a goal; and that the part in question contributes in some way toward the achieving of that goal. This contribution is its function. A more recent conjecture has been proposed, with variations, by William C. Wimsatt (1972) and by Larry Wright (1973; 1976). Whereas the cybernetic analysis takes human goal seeking and biological homeostasis as paradigmatic, the newer conjecture, which I shall call the selectionist analysis, draws its paradigms from human creative activity and from the theory of natural selection. According to the selectionist theory, when we ascribe a function to a part of an organism or machine, we call attention to the process by which the system came to be as it is, with that part in its present place; we also claim that the process involved a weeding-out or selection and that the part contributed in some way toward the system's surviving the selection process. This contribution is the part's function.

These rival analyses of teleology suggest at least prima facie cases for and against the reductionist program. Proponents of the cybernetic tradition analyze goal orientation and functionality in terms of the arrangements and dispositions of an organism's parts. The thrust of this approach moves inward and downward to the parts contained in the goal-seeking system, and so to lower levels of organization. Although the case must still be argued in detail, there is reason to suppose that the cybernetic theory of teleology will permit us to construct a reductive explication. That reduction would be far-reaching indeed, for William T. Powers (1973; 1978) has shown us how to subject even human behavior to a cybernetic analysis. The selectionist theory, on the other hand, points to selective systems and other processes that enclose the teleological system and, for that reason, perhaps points also upward to higher levels of organization. Again, the case must be examined in detail, and I attempt to do so in chapter 6; nevertheless, we may reasonably suppose that, if functionality in biology can be understood only in terms of selection processes and the systems that support them, our explication of teleology will convey a non- or even antireductive flavor.

The rivalry between various analyses of biological examples of teleology has sparked a vigorous debate, which I shall review below. Although Ernest Nagel (1977) has defended his version of the cybernetic theory against various criticisms, including Wright's and Woodfield's, Lowell Nissen (1981) raises additional questions, which I shall examine. But perhaps the most persistent impediment to the cybernetical reduction of teleology may be the one pointed out by Wimsatt (1971). Until we have produced a convincing reduction of a typical cybernetic concept such as feedback, we cannot place much confidence in the reductive claims of cyberneticism. And feedback has turned out to be surprisingly difficult to explicate. (See also Manier 1971.)

## CYBERNETICISM

It is necessary, then, that I attempt to establish the cybernetic theory as a thoroughly reductive alternative to the selectionist account. That would demonstrate the pertinence of their rivalry to questions about the ontological reduction of living things. I do so by proposing an analysis of the concept of feedback that extends the explications of Nagel (1961; 1977) and Beckner (1959; 1968; 1969) and showing that the understanding so achieved can be put to good use in the atomist reduction program. Having established the reductionist credentials of the cybernetical analysis, I shall, in the following two chapters, attempt to judge between it and its selectionist rival, concluding that cybernetics, and not selection, can help us to clarify and justify the only scientifically important sense in which biologists employ teleological terms.

STAGES IN THE PROGRAM. Briefly stated, the reduction strategy of the cybernetic theory of teleology calls for the following four-step program. (1) The theory asserts that an organism or other system is oriented toward a goal state just if the parts are so arranged that under certain circumstances it would act in a way that tends to make the goal state occur or more nearly occur. Within limits, the system's internal state disposes it to meet deviation from the goal by employing appropriate countermeasures. The system may be so simple that its repertoire includes just one strategy, or it may be so complex that it can shift to a more effective one as conditions change. (2) The cybernetic theory claims that the type of organization known as negative feedback is the prime example of such an internal state. In a temperature-controlled house, for example, the furnace turns on or off as the temperature falls below or rises above a certain aimed-at range. In the bodies of mammals, to take one more example, blood vessels constrict or dilate and shivering begins or ceases as the temperature of the blood falls or rises beyond the organism's normal temperature. Some special hookup of wires and switches orchestrates the furnace's benign influence on the temperature of the room, and a set of special anatomical parts performs a similar governing activity in the mammal's internal economy. These regulating mechanisms, whether human artifacts or physiological homeostats, are feedback devices. (3) In a cybernetic reduction we must specify explicitly what kind of assemblage of parts—what characteristic wiring diagram—qualifies a system as a negative feedback device. Doing this amounts to reducing a property of an entire system to relational and dispositional properties of its parts. (4) We must show how this characterization can be reduced in its turn to still lower levels of description, eventually to the level of fundamental particles. Steps 3 and 4 will occupy our attention in the remainder of this chapter; the plausibility of steps 1 and 2 will become apparent as we subsequently examine the biological employment of cybernetic concepts in teleological explanations.

OBJECTS AND THEORIES. Let us then take up the task of explicating the concept of negative feedback in terms of the arrangement and interactions of a system's parts. Here we must make a choice as to method. The obvious and straightforward way to express the explication we require is to say how the system does or would behave and how its parts interact in generating this behavior or making it possible. This analysis speaks directly about the system itself and about the objects that compose it. I shall call this an *object-referring explication*. But another, more elaborate way of formulating the explication has also been adopted by those who analyze cybernetic concepts, often without clearly distinguishing it from the first. These explications of feedback are formulated in terms of the descriptions one applies to candidate systems of mathematical variables and the functions that relate them. I shall call this second sort of explication a *theory-referring explication*. The object-referring sort of explication has the merits of simplicity and directness. But the theory-referring sort is also essential to our task for two reasons: First, we cannot characterize a feedback device simply in terms of the behavior it displays during a finite period of observation, because such a criterion would not distinguish a clever or fortuitous imitation from the genuine article. Rather, we must also specify what the system would do under a range of conditions not actually observed. We must, therefore, speak of the dispositions of the system and its parts, of their lawful behavior under conditions contrary to fact—in short, of the laws of nature that govern their activities. Although we intend our explication to express the way things are according to the laws of nature, for practical and epistemological reasons we must formulate it in terms of our best current scientific theories. Second, to complete the fourth step in reducing teleology, we must demonstrate how to obtain the descriptive statement that a system operates in the feedback mode from statements that describe the arrangements and interactions of its parts. In short, we must produce a theory-referring explication.

## FEEDBACK

Rosenblueth, Wiener, and Bigelow's effort (1943; 1950) to explicate goal orientation in purely behavioristic terms was so convincingly criticized by Richard Taylor (1950*a*; 1950*b*) that subsequent investigators who have not sympathized with Taylor's preference for a mentalistic account have concentrated on searching for an analysis in terms of internal causal mechanisms. Indeed, despite their announced determination to distinguish teleology from causality, even Rosenblueth and his colleagues allude to causal mechanisms in their analysis of feedback, stipulating that "signals from the goal are used to restrict outputs which would otherwise go beyond the goal" (1943, p. 19). Others, such as Nagel (1961; 1977), Manier (1971), and Wimsatt (1971), have spoken of causal mechanisms and of the mathematical variables and functions by which we represent them. The most ambitious and systematic effort of this sort, and the one on which I shall model the analysis to be presented below, is the explication of the concept of "teleological system" proposed by Morton Beckner (1959).

I refer the reader to my earlier essay (Faber 1984) for a more detailed discussion of the problems of explicating feedback. Here I shall simply present a summary of that argument, in three steps. First, I shall set down the intuitive desiderata of an explication of feedback. Second, I shall express my analysis of the concept in object-referring terms. Finally, I shall state the same explication more formally in theory-referring terms. As noted above, this last effort is required if we are to learn whether the identification of a system as a feedback device can be derived from its theoretical description at a lower level of analysis.

INFORMAL CHARACTERIZATION OF FEEDBACK. A thermostat in a house or an automatic steering mechanism in a sailboat performs a task that might have been carried out by the householder or the steersman. The possessor of one of these feedback devices regulates the temperature of the room or the course of the boat by proxy. The thermocouple, wires, and transformer of the thermostat, or the vane, gears, and levers of the steering mechanism are additions to the system they control. They could be removed entirely without altering the causal connections in the controllable system. The temperature of the house would still be determined by the rates of inflow and outflow of heat, and the course of the boat would still be determined by the angle of its rudder and the pressure of wind and waves on canvas and hull. In any teleologically regulated system, then, we may expect to find a distinct subassembly, the regulating device, which can be removed by breaking certain causal links. In fact, the thermostat sustains two distinct connections with the room. It *senses* the controlled property, the temperature, by means of a thermocouple or bimetallic strip, which is situated in thermal contact with the air, and it *controls* or corrects the temperature, turning the furnace on and off by means of a set of wires and relay switches. Extracting the thermocouple from the device or cutting one of the wires leading to the furnace will equally disrupt the regulating activity. Either connection may be broken without affecting the other, and each is necessary in this sense for the proper operation of the device. So the regulating subsystem senses and controls through two physically distinct causal processes. These two connections differ also with respect to direction. Through the sensing link causal influences pass from the larger, controlled system to the regulating subsystem, and through the controlling link the influences pass from the regulator back to the main system. Just as the householder's shivering or perspiring signals an excessive variation in the temperature of the room without thereby materially influencing it, so the bimetallic strip exchanges a few calories with the room without in the process materially affecting its temperature. Similarly, the furnace roars into flame as a result of a switch having been closed by the twisting of the bimetal, without thereby exerting a direct influence on the latter's shape. Causal influences pass predominantly in just one direction around the feedback loop.

To summarize: We have noted three desiderata for a satisfactory explication of feedback. First, a complete teleologically controlled system must exhibit a sufficient degree of complexity, consisting at least of a controlled system and a regulating subsystem. Second, this subsystem must be connected to the regulated system through two physically distinct or "orthogonal" causal channels. Third, the regulator must passively sense through one of these channels and actively control through the other.

Having identified certain desirable features of an adequate explication, I now set down more formally, and in object-referring terms, a set of severally necessary and jointly sufficient conditions for a mechanism's qualifying as a feedback device. I present this explication without further supporting arguments. A fuller treatment of the issue and a criticism of other explications may be found in my 1984 essay. Following the presentation I shall illustrate its import by means of a few examples not previously published.

OBJECT-REFERRING EXPLICATION OF FEEDBACK. A complex system of causally interacting parts is a feedback system if and only if the following conditions are satisfied: (1) The system consists of two physically distinct parts, a controlled main system and a regulator, both of which are subject to causal influences from an environment. (2) The controlled system has a variable property $g$, which depends causally on at least two of its other variable properties, $f_1$ and $f_2$; and these are causally independent one from the other. That is, external influences may alter $f_1$ and through it $g$, without materially affecting $f_2$, and vice versa. (3) The regulator's connection to the controlled system proceeds through a pair of distinct causal processes to the properties $g$ and $f_1$. One of these processes operates through at least one component part whose removal from the system has the effect of disrupting the regulator's influence upon $f_1$ without materially affecting either its responding to $g$ or the causal dependence of $g$ upon $f_1$ and $f_2$. Likewise, there is at least one other component part whose excision from the system renders the regulator unresponsive to the property $g$ without materially affecting the dependence of $g$ on $f_1$ and $f_2$. (4) Finally, the feedback must be *negative;* that is, environmentally induced changes in the property $f_2$ must result in smaller variations in the property $g$ when the structure is intact than would occur if either of the surgical operations mentioned in condition 3 were performed.

Our interest in the reduction of teleological descriptions and explanations leads us to ask for more than this object-referring criterion. We need to know whether a statement characterizing a composite object as a feedback system can be *derived* from a description that characterizes the arrangement and interactions of the lower-level objects that compose it. Consequently, we require a set of severally necessary and jointly sufficient conditions that spell out the characteristic features of the lower-level *description* of a teleological system; that is, we require an explication of feedback that refers to theoretical descriptions. Again, I shall simply present the conclusion of my 1984 argument; the reader may refer to that essay for details.

## THEORY-REFERRING EXPLICATION OF FEEDBACK

Let us suppose that we have a lower-level description of a certain candidate system and of relevant portions of its environment. The level may be the one at which we employ terms for bits of wire, nuts, bolts, and bimetallic strips; or it may be any still lower level down to and including that of subatomic particles. At any level we have a consistent set of explanatory laws, or at least rules of thumb, for predicting the behavior of the things named there and for describing their causal interactions and spatial relations. The issue here concerns in-principle reduction; therefore, it is appropriate to assume further that the lower-level narrative is as complete as descriptions at that level can be. I shall assume a lower-level description of the composite system that contains a complete list of the things at that level that compose the system and its environment, an adequate set of natural laws that express the modes of interaction of those parts, and an adequate set of boundary conditions that specify the spatial arrangements of the parts and their causal connections in that setting. This theoretical model serves as a surrogate for the putative feedback system and relevant portions of its environment. Theoretical operations on the model represent physically possible operations on the modeled system.

"OBTAINING." We can apply the standard methods of physical analysis to this model. In addition to strict logical inference—the deducing of theorems from axioms with the aid of natural laws and other principles—we may compute averages, define new variables, substitute simpler, approximate functions for more accurate but unwieldy ones, invent names, and the like. This procedure is a kind of inference, both logically loose and creative, and it is what physicists and other scientists mainly do when they employ basic scientific principles, natural laws, and empirical rules of thumb in explaining real-world objects and processes. "Deriving" is too narrow a word to apply to this process, so I shall call it "obtaining by the standard methods of physical analysis," or simply "obtaining."

TRUNCATING. One of the things we may do with a complete theoretical description is to truncate it, to leave out portions. In particular, we may delete some components from the list of parts and eliminate their causal connections to the rest of the members from the list of interactions. This produces the theoretical surrogate for a simpler system. For example, in the complete set of boundary conditions for system and environment we have a model from which we can obtain a subset for the system alone. These simpler boundary conditions describe the system as it would behave if causally isolated from its environment. Similarly, we can obtain truncated boundary conditions that designate what our system would be like and how it would behave if a certain part or a set of parts were absent. Because we do not eliminate any information except about the parts crossed off the list, we retain a complete set of boundary conditions and laws for the remaining, simpler system.

Obviously, this kind of operation on a theoretical model represents the physical operation of causing the part or parts to vanish instantly from the composite system, leaving the rest of it momentarily as it was before. That kind of surgery, though possibly of great heuristic value, can be expensive if performed on the object itself; that is one of the reasons why theoretical models are so useful. Because causal connections between two things are established through material intermediaries such as the wires joining a thermostat to a furnace, a suitably truncated set of boundary conditions can represent the system we would get after interrupting a causal link. I shall call such a set of boundary conditions a *component-wise truncation* of the original model.

DYNAMICAL ANALYSIS. A theoretical model may also be used in calculating what would happen in a system if one or another of its properties were affected by environmental influences. We choose a variable $x$, which the boundary conditions show to be subject to such influences, insert a number or set of numbers for the change in $x$ that we imagine to be produced by the action of an environmental factor, and calculate the changes the model shows to be entailed by this input for still other variable properties of the system.

CAUSAL ASYMMETRY. We have also noted that causal influences must pass unidirectionally between active and passive elements in the feedback loop. That asymmetry must be discernible in any adequate theoretical description. Suppose that the model of a system allows for the possibility of environmental influences on two variables $x$ and $y$ and specifies a functional dependence of a third system variable $z$ on both of them. Then the relation among $x$, $y$, and $z$ is causally asymmetric in such a way that $x$ and $y$ are causally independent of $z$ while it is causally dependent on them just if the following conditions are met. Let a dynamical analysis assign a change in $x$ (representing exogenous influences). The analysis then calculates resulting changes in $y$ and $z$ with the result that $z$ changes appreciably while $y$ remains essentially unchanged. Similarly, an input change in $y$ entails an appreciable change in $z$ and no significant change in $x$. Finally, the model allows changes in both $x$ and $y$, entailing an appreciable change in $z$, without contradiction.

DISCONNECTABILITY: PHYSICAL INDEPENDENCE. Finally, we have found it necessary to require that some of the causal connections in a feedback loop be disconnectable without breaking others, simply by the removal of some component part. This feature of the causal processes in the object system is reflected by a kind of inferential independence (i.e., independent obtainability from the model) of the relations that represent them. I shall call this independence of relations *physical independence*. I define it in terms of the boundary conditions and the standard methods of physical analysis thus: One relation is physically independent of another with respect to a theoretical model just if there is a component-wise truncation of the model such that the first relation cannot be obtained from it but the second can.

FORMAL EXPLICATION. Having established these preliminary definitions, we can now define feedback as follows: Suppose we have a theoretical model of a set of causally interacting objects and of their possible interactions with an environment, complete at some level of description. This model represents a feedback system just if the following criteria are satisfied:

1. From the model and the laws of physics or other relevant science and empirical rules of thumb, one can obtain by the standard methods of physical analysis (at least) the variables $f_1$, $f_2$, $g$, and $h$.

2. These variables are not defined as functions of the time variable, nor are they related to one another by definition or any other analytic relation.

3. According to the model, the two variables $f_1$ and $f_2$, but not the others, are available to be set into functional dependence on other, environmental variables.

4. From the model one can obtain three nonanalytic relations $G$, $H$, and $F$, such that $G$ relates $g$ to $f_1$ and $f_2$, $H$ relates $h$ to $g$, and $F$ relates $f_1$ to $h$. This requirement insures that the model represents a causal loop.

5. The relation $G$ is causally asymmetric, so that $g$ is causally dependent on $f_1$ and $f_2$ but they are causally independent of each other.

6. The relation $F$ is physically independent of the relation $H$, and both of these are physically independent of the relation $G$.

7. (Here we require that the feedback be negative.) A dynamical analysis of the model, which treats $f_2$ as an "input" variable, changing over time within a limited range, yields an output time-dependent function for $g$ which either is finite and approximately constant or varies within finite bounds. In addition, two corresponding dynamical analyses based on component-wise truncations of the model from which one cannot obtain, respectively, the dependence of $g$ on $h$ and the dependence of $f_1$ on $g$ yield other time-dependent functions for $h$ that range more widely.

## APPLICATIONS

I have applied these criteria to a variety of examples, true feedback systems and counterfeits, in my 1984 essay. Here I apply them to a different set of closely related examples, the sequence of safety valves shown in figure 1. The sequence runs from mildly complex assemblages of moving parts to an ordinary lidded saucepan. I have chosen these examples for two reasons. First, the sequence straddles the boundary that our definition marks off between teleological systems and simpler mechanisms. The examples show how the criterion of independent disconnectability can distinguish among a group of otherwise similar devices. In addition, even the most complicated of these mechanisms lies fairly close to the line; I suspect that the intuitive judgment of some persons would exclude all of them. They would be excluded, for example, by Beckner's informal requirement (1959), which he states in his preliminary remarks but does not retain in his formal explication, that the energy by which a feedback device operates must come from an internal source. I have presented my reasons for following the example of Beckner's formal recommendation rather than his informal one in my 1984 essay.

In all of these examples the protected property ($g$ in the formal analysis) is the pressure in the boiler. Its value is determined by the joint operation of two processes: the rate ($f_1$) at which steam escapes through a vent or gap and the rate ($f_2$) of influx of heat from a flame. This causal connection is best represented by an equation over time. The variable $h$ that responds to pressure changes is the position of the piston, cap, or lid. Its value is determined by the opposing forces exerted by the gas and the spring or weight. We can represent this causal connection by a graph, which would take the form of a step function for the gravity-operated devices and of an S-curve for the spring-loaded ones. Finally, the rate at which steam escapes through the vent depends upon the pressure and upon the extent to which the vent is uncovered or the gap opened, and this in turn depends on the position of the piston or cap. When we apply criterion 6, independent disconnectability, to these examples, we find that for cases *a*, *b*, and *c* of figure 1 the judicious removal of a material portion of the system leaves the causal connections represented by $G$ and $H$ intact but paralyzes the controlling action, the covering and uncovering of the vent. This piece of surgery is most easily visualized for the first device: We simply remove the rod that connects the sensing piston on the left to the sliding valve on the right. In cases *b* and *c* we find no such removable macroscopic part. However, if we cut through the metal cylinder with a saw along the plane indicated by the arrows, we will remove a material portion of the system (which will lie on the workbench in the form of metallic dust). This removal will disconnect the sensing

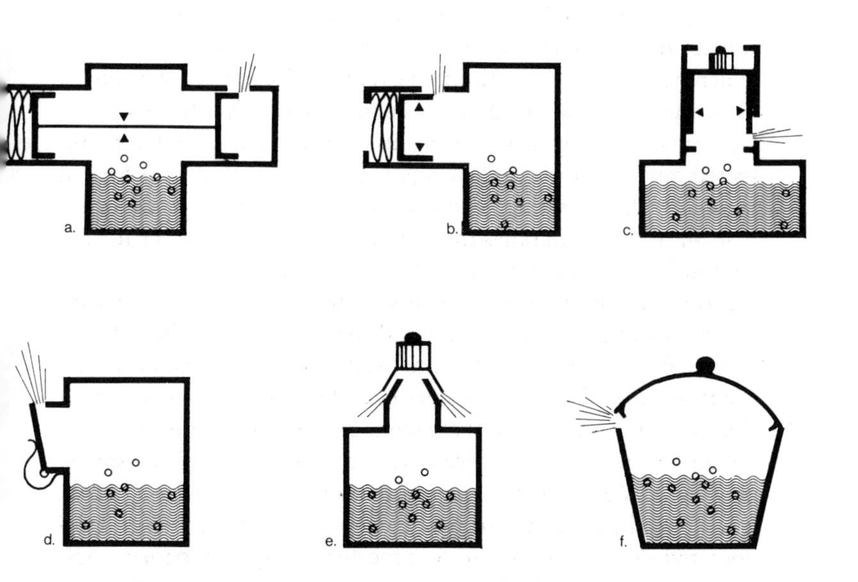


A series of pressure valves, including a pressure cooker and a lidded saucepan. These examples show the utility of the criterion of independent disconnectability. Systems a, b, and c qualify as rudimentary feedback devices because their degree of articulation is sufficient to satisfy criterion 6. Systems d, e, and f, however, do not contain a part whose removal would disrupt the controlling function while leaving the sensing function intact.

motion of the piston from the sliding motion of the valve just as effectively as does the removal of the rod in the first case.[1] Although examples *b* and *c* can thus be shown to satisfy criterion 6, no analogous surgical procedure avails for devices *d*, *e*, and *f*. In these examples, any removal of metal that halts the opening and closing of vent or gap also disrupts the sensing action. These devices have too few independent causal connections for them to qualify as feedback systems; their design is too simple.

Yet the nonteleological systems perform the task of releasing excess pressure no less effectively than do their more complex relatives. So we see that our explication of feedback commits us to the proposition that a system's being teleological is not a matter of how sensitively or efficiently it performs the task we have set for it; it is instead simply a matter of how elaborately—and with what manner of complication—it does so.

The criterion of independent disconnectability, which distinguishes among the safety valves of figure 1, also discriminates between feedback systems and a problematic case proposed by Lowell Nissen (1981) in his criticism of Nagel's cybernetic account of teleology. Nissen claims that Nagel's analysis includes the process by which atmospheric convection cools a geographical area that sunshine heats above the temperature of neighboring areas. (The same process occurs as the air around an incandescent light bulb is heated by the warmth of the lamp, rises, and allows cooler air to move up to replace it.) This system does not define its aimed-at temperature range by turning on and off at definite temperatures as an ordinary thermostat does. Nevertheless, convective cooling resembles thermostatic control in that one part of a composite system responds to the increase in temperature of another part in such a way as to reduce its extent. Shall we admit convectively cooled lamps and islands cooled by

1 / Here we see the usefulness of the atomist reduction program. While applying the saw we must view the cylinder—one of the components of the feedback system at the first level of analysis—as being itself composed of still finer parts, which the teeth of the saw can reveal to us. This illustrates the general principle we noted in chapter 1, namely, that attempts to describe a system's causal connections consistently at a chosen level of analysis occasionally must yield to the necessity of introducing entities at still lower levels. In this case, we acknowledge that a force exerted on one end of the metal rod reaches the other end by means of the actions of the intervening atoms on their neighbors.

sea breezes to the class of feedback systems? If so, then Nissen could rightly complain that our analysis qualifies almost any object in the world as a goal-directed system. But it does not qualify convective cooling. The process is not complex enough, not in the required way, for it contains no part whose removal would retain the "sensing" connection to the atmosphere—the heating of the surrounding air—while breaking the "correcting" connection—the replacement of this warmer air by cooler from below.

## ASSESSMENT OF THE REDUCTION

The aim of the foregoing analysis of feedback has been to forge a conceptual tool suitable for the mechanistic reduction of the teleological descriptions and explanations of biology. This account of teleology occupies a central place in the atomist program for reducing the organic sciences, which are distinguished by their use of such concepts and explanations, to the sciences of inert matter. I submit that the attempt has succeeded, for two reasons.

First, the analysis makes no reference to teleological processes in other portions of the world. It does not refer, for example, to the intentions of the designer, manufacturer, or employer of the feedback contrivance or to any person or containing mechanism that has selected the device according to some criterion or for some purpose. This corroborates the earlier conjecture that the general thrust of a cybernetic analysis tends inward and downward, to the parts of an upper-level thing and to their causal interactions. True, the explication does not treat feedback systems in complete isolation from other things, because it stipulates that the property represented by the variable $f_2$ be open to disturbances from the environment and that the other properties represented by the other variables be free from outside influences. Nevertheless, the outward-pointing lines lead from individual, lower-level features or properties of the system through causal channels composed of lower-level parts. For example, we have required no more of a thermostatically controlled complex of parts than that an object outside the system be able to draw heat away from it, thereby offering something for the thermostat to correct.

Second, because the explication concerns the causal influences that pass from one material thing to another within the device, the further reduction of the concept to still lower levels of analysis can proceed along well-trodden paths. Causal connections that may appear as mysterious, unanalyzed facts at an upper level of description become clearer as we descend to the descriptive mode that names the microscopic entities that mediate them.

It must be admitted that the theory-referring explication is a relative one, for it is stated in terms of physical laws and empirical rules of thumb that represent the best that physics or some other natural science can offer at the present stage of its development. These laws are of human construction, fallible, and subject to change. Nissen (1981, p. 130) seems to suggest that an explication so relativized cannot show feedback to be an objective property of systems as they stand, self-contained, independent of human desires and intentions. But our plight is by no means so dire. We have analyzed feedback in terms of human knowledge about how the world runs generally, but that fact simply places the claim that something is a feedback system on the same footing as the claim that accelerations are proportional to forces. Both are fallible, but neither imports a covert reference to human teleology into a discussion of the nonhuman world.

It must also be admitted that this reduction of feedback does not conform to the standards of logical rigor set by the reduction of thermodynamics to statistical mechanics. In that paradigm of theory reduction one proceeds by careful definition and strict implication to derive the laws of the macroscopic theory from the laws of the microscopic and the principles of statistics. The present analysis has made extensive use of what I have called *obtaining*, a logically much looser form of reasoning that proceeds by means of averaging and approximating, aided and abetted by empirical rules of thumb and all the other tricks of the applied physicist's trade. In explicating feedback I have not shown how one may *derive* a statement such as "this object is a feedback device" from statements that assign propensities and relative positions to a set of lower-level things. Rather, I have identified a certain sort of pattern of causal influences that can be found in some collections of interacting parts, identified a corresponding pattern of linguistic relations in the theoretical descriptions we make of such collections, and shown how to recognize the latter sort of pattern in any description of the same objects made at still lower levels. In short, we can obtain a characterization of a macroscopic object as a feedback device from lower-level descriptions only by exercising our ability to recognize patterns. But this admission does not in any way weaken our claim to have produced a thoroughly mechanistic reduction of this cybernetic concept. Nothing in our analysis could encourage an antireductionist in thinking that a teleological system defined in this way is such a thing by virtue of anything other than the spatial arrangements and mechanical interactions of its microscopic parts. It still appears that a teleological system is just one of many interesting patterns of activity generated by atoms as they dash to and fro. If, as I shall argue in chapter 5, to be a goal seeker is to be organized according to the feedback pattern, then the seeking of goals is just one of the things that atoms do when they happen to fall together in a certain way.

FIVE

# Teleology: Goals and Adaptations

WITH A REDUCTIVE EXPLICATION OF FEEDBACK, WE have made the first step toward reducing to mechanistic notions any concept explicable in terms of it. A cybernetic analysis of teleology is an avenue through which to draw the organic sciences into the empire of the physical. This chapter explores that road by addressing the following questions:

1. Can goal seeking be explicated by means of feedback?
2. Can an organism's or a mechanism's goals be identified by reference solely to the structure and activities of the thing itself, apart from the intentions of its employer or designer?
3. Can we satisfactorily understand the teleological ideas and explanations of biology in terms of the seeking of goals?

I respond with qualified affirmatives to these questions. I argue that biologists employ the notions of adaptation, function, and goal in two senses, a strong one and a weakly analogical one; and that the cybernetic analysis satisfactorily accommodates the former, whereas the selectionist theory fails to do so. But I also argue that an apparently important class of teleological descriptions and explanations, those having to do primarily with reproduction, do not sleep comfortably in the cybernetic bed. To understand these examples of teleological language we must look for help to the selectionist theory. Although this failure to accommodate reproductive systems may seem a fault of cyberneticism, it is in fact a success. I shall argue that cyberneticism discriminates where a scientifically significant distinction should be made, whereas the selectionist analysis does not.

If a mechanism does seek a goal of its own, the sought-for condition must be a state of affairs that the action of the mechanism tends to achieve under some possible circumstances and, having achieved it, either rests or enters a "hunting" phase around the goal state. This is a necessary condition of something's being the goal sought by a mechanism but certainly not a sufficient one: Even a pendulum "hunts" around its equilibrium position and tends to cease its activity when that state is achieved. Therefore, on observing a thermostat's actions when the room's temperature rises above a certain value and drops below a lower one, we may speculate that the device seeks a temperature within the range bounded by those two values. But the conjecture must be tested by further analysis.

Whether human contrivances seek goals or not, their designers and users certainly do. And the goal of a machine, if it has one, may not coincide with the one sought by its employer or, in the case of social machinery, by its component parts. A householder may install a thermostat in the domestic heating system with the intention of keeping the room's temperature as close to 20°C as possible; but an incandescent lamp placed too close to this feedback device, or an ice cube balanced on top of it, will soon reveal that the machinery itself, if it aims at anything at all, aims at a temperature of 20°C only for its own bimetallic strip. A similar disparity occurs higher up on the scale of teleological systems. The policy of promoting civil servants who demonstrate an adequate competence to positions of greater responsibility, and of not demoting those who perform inadequately, may be intended by the makers of the policy to achieve two ends: optimally to deploy the varied talents of administrators and to avoid the grumbling of demoted employees who are learning to cope with restricted salaries. But if this piece of social machinery has any goal of its own, it must be the state of things that the policy tends not to alter. And that state, according to the Peter Principle, distributes a moderate but considerable degree of incompetence at every level. Similarly, we may think that the machinery of representative bureaucratic government aims at the welfare of each individual citizen or the increase of joy and contentment in the commonwealth as a whole, but elected legislators in fact aim at such goals only when they lie in the same direction as their real target, the gaining of another term of office. Bureaucrats seek not so much the public benefit as the smooth operation of their own departments, following Macaulay's ironic dictum that "all is well that runs quietly." This discrepancy between the aims of the builders of social machinery and of the machinery itself accounts for a pervasive feature of modern government, namely, a continual tinkering with tax codes and the charters of regulating agencies, piling up corrective additions in the hope that this time the machine will steer straight.

Examples such as these should put us on guard against imputing too readily to allegedly goal-seeking machinery the aims of its users. Besides, there can be no doubt that in calling a machine goal-directed we stretch, perhaps too far, the range of application of a concept originally designed for human intentions, desires, and beliefs. Yet the ascribing of goals to machines seems to be appropriate in some cases. Can the concept of feedback justify this practice?

Andrew Woodfield (1976) claims that when we ascribe goals to machinery and the lower forms of life we exploit an analogy to human mental activity. The "core concept" around which all of our talk of teleology has grown up has to do with desire and belief. If the ascription of a goal to a machine is justified at all, it is only because the machine's outward behavior resembles goal-seeking in sentient beings and its inner mode of organization is like a desire in some essential feature. Without claiming to spell out the similarity in detail, Woodfield does set down a necessary but not sufficient condition, namely, that the internal state must *represent* the goal state. It is not clear, however, just how a mental image represents its object—if there are such things as mental images. Woodfield acknowledges the difficulty by not attempting to give necessary and sufficient conditions for representing. Yet I believe his suggestion may be helpful, provided we do not place unduly heavy requirements on the idea of representation. We should not, for example, require that the internal state of the machine represent the goal to the machine itself. Instead, we should merely require that this internal structure of the machinery represent the goal to us; that is, that from a knowledge of the inner workings of the machine (and perhaps of its normal environment—I shall return to this possibility below) we should be able to infer what state of affairs the machine is working toward.

Whether or not my loose interpretation of representing accords with Woodfield's intentions, the program I have adopted requires me to take issue with him over the kind of analogy that is involved in extending the concept of goal orientation from humans to simpler creatures and to machines. I must leave the question entirely open as to whether the reduction program of atomism can be carried into the traditional preserve of mentalistic concepts. Woodfield may well be correct in asserting that there is a mere analogy at work here, some shared abstract feature of the mental entities that constitute human teleological states and the physical entities that make up the internal states of goal-directed machinery. However, the atomist reduction program aims to construct an understanding of desires in terms of patterns of causal connections. I shall, therefore, leave open the possibility that, even for a human being, orientation toward a goal consists in having the nervous system organized according to the feedback pattern.

Despite his appreciation of the cybernetic theory, Woodfield claims (1976, p. 193) that the concept of feedback control cannot explicate goal-directedness for two reasons. First, the classes of objects to which the two concepts apply overlap only imperfectly. Only those feedback systems are goal-directed, he claims, that have some additional (unspecified) properties. "Feedback loops are ubiquitous in electronics, but they do not create goal-directedness wherever they appear" (p. 189). And not all goal-oriented behavior participates in a "process or a sequence, the precise unfolding of which is guided by perceptions" (p. 191). Because the kinds of things explained in terms of feedback do not overlap exactly with the things explained in terms of goal orientation, there is no "possibility of any direct reduction of one kind of explanation to the other" (p. 191).

Woodfield does not cite examples of the feedback loops so common in radio and television equipment that he disqualifies as teleological systems, but I suspect that he has accepted the engineers' very loose employment of the term. Many examples of popular usage are disqualified by the explication presented above. What is called a feedback oscillator, for example, does not satisfy the criteria; such an oscillator works by so-called positive feedback, which does not involve any sort of control by the loop.

And Woodfield is simply mistaken in requiring that, for feedback to play the decisive role in qualifying a piece of behavior as goal-oriented, the behavior must be guided in its "precise unfolding" by the fed-back perceptions. He cites the example of a cuttlefish flinging out its tentacles to grasp a shrimp: Once the muscular discharge has begun there is no possibility of correcting the aim if the shrimp should move. To this example we could add two more: A person reaches out to grasp a coffee cup from a familiar spot on the table while looking in another direction; and a spring-loaded relay switch snaps shut, turning on a furnace in response to a weak electrical impulse from a thermocouple mounted on the wall of a sitting room. In each of these examples, some kind of activity occurs that is goal-directed, in the sense that it promotes the reaching of a goal by the system that contains the active part; yet the precise unfolding of the behavior is not subject to control by perception or other fed-back information about its effects. Although the person could establish such a detailed guidance mechanism simply by watching the progress of the hand toward the cup, no feedback of this sort in fact occurs; and the relay switch, having been pushed past its balance point by a small electrical impulse, flips completely to its closed position under the force of a spring, whether or not the temperature of the thermocouple changes during this fraction of a second.

I submit that Woodfield has identified a useful distinction here, but his skeptical conclusion is unwarranted. We must distinguish between the goal-directedness of a whole system and the goal-directedness of some of the behavior and internal processes of the system. According to the cybernetic theory, a system is oriented toward a goal by virtue of its organization in the feedback pattern, and a sample of behavior or an internal process may be said to be directed toward that goal if it contributes to its achievement. Because only sufficiently complex systems can be goal-oriented, their parts and behavior earn that epithet only derivatively, only if they contribute toward the goal-seeking activity of the total system. I conclude that the freedom from detailed control of some of the achievement-promoting processes within goal-seeking systems gives us no reason to abandon the cybernetic theory. The system, according to this conjecture, *aims* toward a goal by virtue of its feedback loop or loops, and the behavior or other process *is aimed* by virtue of its participation in one or more of those loops.

Woodfield also discusses another helpful distinction, sorting teleological activity into three types: seeking, aiming, and keeping. Keeping is typified by the thermostat, which maintains a variable property within limits; aiming, by an automatic pilot or guided missile, which homes in on a target. But this, too, is a sort of keeping, because the homing occurs by maintaining a compass reading within narrow bounds or by keeping the image of a target within the sights of the tracking device. Seeking is done by certain guided missiles, which are designed to scan in various directions when no target is within their sights. This activity is also directed toward the goal of the missile yet is not itself controlled by feedback. Have we here an example of a goal-oriented mechanism or process that falls outside the territory mapped out by the concept of feedback? Again, that conclusion would be unwarranted. Imagine a machine with a scanning program that is not also programmed to begin homing when a target appears within its sights but just goes on swiveling its electric eye. We would hardly want to call such behavior seeking. Although the scanning behavior is not itself under feedback control, its connection to a feedback mechanism is what justifies our calling it goal-oriented.

Once again, an analysis of the concept of goal orientation has led back to the concept of feedback. I conclude, despite Woodfield's cautious skepticism, that we may continue to entertain the cybernetic conjecture.

Ernest Nagel (1977) reaches the same conclusion in his discussion of Woodfield's arguments, though by another route than the one I have taken above. More recently still, Lowell Nissen (1981) has criticized Nagel's position, bringing new examples to bear in support of theses similar to Woodfield's. Nissen claims that feedback is not a sufficient condition for teleology, citing cases of alleged feedback that are clearly not goal-oriented. His examples of the convective cooling of an island by breezes from the surrounding ocean I have discussed earlier, showing that it fails to satisfy the criterion of independent disconnectability in my proposed explication. As I understand them, all of Nissen's proposed counterexamples fail to satisfy this criterion; that is, they are systems of too little complexity. I conclude that the charge that feedback is insufficient as a condition of goal-directedness is still unproven. But Nissen also contends that feedback is not necessary for teleology, citing artifacts such as hammers, which, being used in the achieving of goals, have functions yet are not feedback systems. A hammer has its function because of the intentions of the person who grasps it, so Nissen suggests that mentalistic concepts such as intentions (possibly nonconscious ones) may be needed to construct a complete analysis of teleology. This criticism can be met with the same answer I proposed to a similar one of Woodfield's. We must distinguish two senses of the term "goal-oriented." An object or a dynamical process may *aim* at a goal—that is, it may be a full-fledged teleological system—or, like the hammer, it may *be aimed* by a system of the former sort. Both the system that actively aims and the one that is aimed may qualify as goal-directed by reference to a cybernetic analysis of the former.

Having cleared these obstacles from our path, I must now show that we can walk it and that it leads to a satisfactory understanding of teleology in biological systems and in human artifacts.

## IDENTIFYING GOALS

Can we extend to certain machines and to simple biological organisms the property of having or seeking a goal, without stretching the notion too far? And can we do this in such a way that the goals, purposes, and desires of human beings can be understood as nothing other than especially complex instances of what a servomechanism can do? Can we, in short, understand human teleological behavior in terms of interlocking feedback loops and of nested hierarchies of them?

Let us exclude consciousness, conceived as a nonphysical thing or property, from our discussion as a matter of policy. No harm should result from this exclusion for a wide range of goal-seeking systems, because even human beings can have goals and desires of which they are not aware. Indeed, no difficulty need arise at any stage if the physicalist theory of mind can be made to work. Let us not assume here that it will fail. And let us proceed inductively, starting with the simplest cases, namely, feedback loops, and proceeding from that base to reconnoiter the terrain of more complicated systems, glancing occasionally toward the distant ranges of human intentionality.

Consider, then, a thermostat. Does it seek a goal? I have agreed with Woodfield (1976) that a necessary condition for an affirmative answer to the question is that the system should represent (in a very loose sense) its goal state; that is, we should be able to infer the goal state from our examination of the system's anatomy and inner workings. What, then, can we learn about the state of affairs that is aimed at by a thermostatically controlled home heating system? The correcting action of the device, the opening or closing of the relay switch that turns a furnace on or off, is triggered by the rising or falling of the temperature of the thermostat's bimetallic strip. The two temperatures at which these distinct responses occur define a range of temperature. So we discover that the system discriminates between two sorts of sensory input. Does it also exhibit the plasticity that Nagel (1977, p. 272) suggests is another hallmark of teleology? Yes, but only to a very small extent. It operates less flexibly than the temperature homeostat of a warm-blooded animal, which is a paradigm of the plasticity Nagel refers to. To mild environmental threats to the stability of body temperature the homeostat responds by constricting or dilating blood vessels; and it mobilizes strategies such as shivering to meet greater threats. The plasticity, such as it is, of a thermostat consists merely in its ability to respond in two distinct ways to distinct threats. The system is not elaborate enough to command still stronger measures if, for example, heat escapes faster than the furnace can replace it. Still, we find that the thermostat aims at a certain condition of its bimetallic strip, namely, its having a temperature within the range defined by the device's two responses.

## THE CONTEXT RELATIVITY OF MACHINES

Does the thermostat seek a temperature within that range for the whole room in which it is situated? No; as we have noted above, carelessly placed incandescent lamps or ice cubes reveal that the feedback loop consisting of thermostat, switches, furnace, and heating pipes controls only its own input, which it receives by means of its thermal sensor, the bimetallic strip. The goal of maintaining the room's temperature within those limits belongs to a more complex system, namely, the householder who has installed the device. The simple loop acts in such a way that in normal circumstances—lamps and ice cubes being kept away from the sensor—the householder's goal will be realized as an incidental result of the thermostat's achieving its own.

This simple example shows how important the context may be for our attempts to discover the goals of cybernetic machinery without imposing our own intentions on them. And the context resolves other ambiguities as well, as the following examples show.

The theory-referring definition of feedback assigns the variables $f_1$, $g$, and $h$ to distinguishable positions in the loop. The relation $G$ connecting $g$ to $f_1$, $f_2$ . . . must be causally asymmetric, but we have not required that property for $H$ and $F$. The relation $F$ between $f_1$ and $g$ must be disconnectable independently of the relation $G$, but we have not required that $G$ be disconnectable without breaking $F$. Because of this unequal participation in the loop, we can in the most general case distinguish the protected variable $h_1$ from the others. Therefore, a scrutiny of the internal structure of the loop will show unambiguously that $g$ is the property at whose stability the loop aims. But special cases of greater symmetry may arise: All three relations may be causally asymmetric; all three may be disconnectable independently of the others. In such a case, the properties represented by $f_1$, $g$, and $h$ participate equally in the loop. Any one of them might be the protected variable. The ambiguity clears up, however, because the definition points to the context. The model may specify that the variable $f_2$ acts as the principal port of entry for environmental disturbances; other loci in the loop do not receive disturbances from outside. Only the $g$ property needs protection by the loop; therefore, its stability is the device's goal.

We must employ the distinction between an active device and the context in which its action occurs also within the feedback loop, because the definition distinguishes the regulator from the regulated system that contains it. Hitherto, I have applied the epithet "goal-directed," in its primary, active sense, to the entire feedback loop. But a case can be made for ascribing goals more narrowly to the regulator itself. A thermostat or an autopilot occupies the same place in its complete loop as the householder or helmsman for whom it substitutes. When the regulating is done by a person we locate the goal orientation more precisely in this organic regulator; why not treat an inorganic servomechanism as generously? Are there relevant differences between an autopilot and a helmsman?

I have required that any goal we ascribe to a mechanism must be discoverable just from an inspection of its inner workings. If we study an autopilot apart from the boat it steers, we find no clue that the reading of its built-in compass is designed to coincide with the course of the boat or that its output normally moves the tiller to port or starboard. Neither does the structure of the device alone dictate that it shall be placed only in the kind of setting for which it has been designed. Ignoring the clear instructions supplied by the manufacturer, we might reverse the output by 180 degrees, so that the device pushes the tiller to port when starboard is needed to restore the boat to its course. This would be an instance of positive feedback, not a controlling or keeping device of any sort; the system would have no goal. And other settings can readily be imagined in which the autopilot participates in a negative feedback loop whose goal is quite different from maintaining a boat on course. For example, it might be installed in an elevator so as to cause it to move up and down in step with a second one moving in a parallel track and carrying a magnet whose field the autopilot senses.

Some context relativity seems inescapable if we wish to ascribe goals to the sensor-controller subsystems. Provided we speak of goals very narrowly, that is, only in terms of the regulation of sensory input (the reading of the autopilot's internal compass, the temperature of the thermostat's bimetallic strip), we may assign the goal with the modest proviso, "relative to a context in which the device acts as the sensor controller in a negative feedback loop." If we wish to call the autopilot a mechanical helmsman or the thermostat a regulator of room temperature, then we must specify the potential context, relative to which the goal is ascribed. A simple sensor controller does not define its own context.

## HUMAN CONTEXT RELATIVITY

How does a human steersman fare when put to this same test? If disconnected from the tiller, the output arm of the autopilot will continue to push out and pull in as the compass needle swings about, but no steering is done. Yet, if we knock the helmsman's hand from the tiller he will reach out to grasp it again; if we loosen the screws that hold the compass securely to a bulkhead he will tighten them; if we lift the rudder from its gudgeons he will replace it. The internal structure of the person's nervous and muscular systems by which he performs these actions helps to define their proper context, namely, a moving boat in which the compass indicates the course and the rudder influences it. This context justifies our saying that the steersman's goal is a certain course for the boat, not merely a certain reading for the compass. And one could continue this analysis further. A human steersman contains an immensely complicated network of sensor-controller mechanisms, interlocking and hierarchically arranged. His goal is not merely a southwesterly course for the boat but arrival in Tahiti, and not merely that but living among peaceful neighbors and trees full of fruit. The autopilot cannot share the sailor's dream of an easy life or even his subsidiary goal of arriving in Tahiti. The most that we can deduce from its structure is that, provided it is connected into a negative feedback loop of some kind, it will tend to regulate its own sensory input, to maintain the reading of its internal compass within certain limits. How could we alter it so as to make it more expressive of its proper context? This question amounts to asking how to begin to construct a working replica of a human being. Clearly, we can produce only an in-principle answer, but as a first step in that direction let us ask how to complicate the autopilot's structure so that it would more nearly define its proper context as the sailor defined his in reaching for the tiller. To this small problem the answer is obvious: We add another feedback device, this one a homing mechanism that detects some optical feature of the tiller and homes on it.

But the mechanism can detect only a finite set of features. Hence, it could be fooled by imitations of various sorts, as a heat-seeking missile could be drawn toward the sun. The autopilot's new goal, built into its internal structure, is a more complicated sort of sensory input, namely, both a certain compass reading and a certain sort of stimulation of its optical sensor. And if this step is typical of the dauntingly many we could take in principle as we construct a truly interesting autopilot, then we must admit that we cannot, even in principle, make a machine that wants to sail to Tahiti. At best, we could make one that seeks the sort of sensory input that, in the normal conduct of the world's affairs (ruling out malevolent demons, etc.), could be obtained only if it had guided a boat to Tahiti.

But that admission in no way damages the plausibility of the atomist program for reducing teleology. The same difficulty applies to human beings, though more subtly. Our uncertainty over whether the machine seeks the island or merely the normal sensory evidence of being there reflects the general problem of epistemological skepticism. Surely, the cybernetic theory of teleology may be excused from trying to solve this ancient riddle. Indeed, its cropping up here, if it does anything to the plausibility of the theory, enhances it. Any goal ascription must carry some proviso about normal settings, even for human beings, the paradigms of teleology. It is, therefore, no blemish on the cybernetic theory that it, too, must make its goal ascriptions only relative to contexts.

## HIERARCHIES OF LOOPS

The voyager to Tahiti illustrates another pervasive feature of more complex goal-oriented machines, namely, that they have a hierarchical order of ultimate and subsidiary goals. This feature, too, can be illustrated with simple feedback loops. An autopilot, for example, might consist of a compass containing a fluid that is sensitive to variation in temperature and a thermostat that maintains the temperature of the compass within the range required for its proper functioning. The ultimate goal of this device is the steering of a certain course, and a subsidiary goal is the keeping of a certain temperature. We can easily understand in terms of our analysis of feedback why this kind of mutual support among feedback loops is generally possible. A given loop can act as a regulator of its *g* property only if other properties remain nearly constant. If the environment tends to perturb one of the others, a second feedback loop may be connected in such a way as to regulate it.

Intricate networks of interlocking feedback loops, each dependent for its own structural and functional integrity on the regulating actions of the others, typify the machinery of life. If the temperature-regulating mechanism in a warm-blooded creature allows its temperature to rise too far, none of its other homeostats can continue to function.

## FLEXIBILITY

The goals of these keeping mechanisms remain with the organism throughout its life, and the material elements whose causal interactions make up the feedback loop are permanent components of the organism's body. But some organisms are able, also, to acquire and discard temporary goals. They do this by connecting themselves through external sensors and effectors to causal loops that extend partly outside their bodies. In these feedback loops the $f_1$ property, for example, may belong to an external object, and the causal connections of sensing and effecting may be broken by actions of the organism itself. This ability of the organism to complete various feedback loops by taking on the role of the sensor controller, and to disassemble them again, is typical of the higher organisms, especially animals. But the presence of mutually stabilizing self-contained internal feedback loops is typical of life itself.

## SURVIVING

A pattern of mutually stabilizing internal feedback loops on a large and intricate scale is one of the two general and distinguishing characteristics of living things. The other one is reproduction. Of the two, only the active maintaining of structure can be called an essential characteristic of life, because a sterile organism may be very much alive, but one whose feedback loops have lost their mutually supportive integrity lives no more.

A living organism endures as a structure in an extraordinary way, unparalleled except very partially by such things as William Ashby's (1960) homeostat. Even a gnat that lasts as a stable structure for one day compels our admiration more than an ocean wave, which may last as long, and more than a spiral galaxy, whose lifetime as a recognizable pattern extends to millions of years. The organism teeters always on the brink of chaos, battered from all sides by structure-destroying forces. The concept that helps us make sense of this active "keeping" is feedback. Such a mode of enduring requires a name to distinguish it from the enduring of the eternal hills and of the spiral galaxies: Let us accept the standard biological idiom and call it *surviving*.

Surviving, then, is the one goal that unifies almost all of the other, subsidiary goal-seeking mechanisms in a living thing. Survival is what the internal homeostat that regulates blood sugar is there for; survival is the ultimate goal also of the external feedback loops by which the animal tracks its prey or eludes those that would prey upon it.

## FUNCTIONS

"Function" is a term even more widely employed by writers on teleology than "goal," for even those who reject the goal theory of teleology concern themselves with the meaning and justification of function ascriptions. What do we mean, for example, by saying that the function of the heart is to pump the blood through the veins and arteries; and how can we justify singling out that activity of the heart while we pass over others, such as making thumping noises and preventing the left lung from touching the front of the rib cage?

The standard cybernetic analysis of function ascriptions is an explication in the full sense of the word: both an unpacking of the meaning of the concept of function as it has been generally employed and a critical recommendation for its purer use in the future. When we ascribe a function to a portion of an organism or a machine, this is what we do or ought to do: We call attention to the fact that the containing system tends to maintain some variable property within a narrower range than would otherwise obtain, and it does so by means of a peculiar sort of pattern of causal connections, namely, negative feedback. This "keeping" of the protected property is to be called the goal of the causal loop or of the regulator, and only those things and processes that contribute to the normal operation of the loop (whose removal would impair or halt it) have functions with respect to that goal. The function of a member of a feedback loop is simply what the part contributes (not by happenstance but in the regular causal chain) toward the goal embodied in the loop.

However, an acceptable theory of function ascriptions must establish some continuity between its own technical explication of functionality and earlier, more intuitive usages. The concept of negative feedback has a relatively short history, whereas biologists at least as early as Aristotle have ascribed goals and functions to living things and their parts. How, then, can a cybernetic theory claim to provide an analysis of functionality as it has been used traditionally in biology? I submit that the concept of survival provides the bridge between the traditional and the cybernetical uses of goal and function. It is possible, even for one who does not include negative feedback in his stock of concepts, to recognize active surviving, no matter how untechnically discerned, as something that distinguishes living things from dead matter generally and to assign functions on the principle that the function of a part is its contribution to the survival of the organism. And we have seen how surviving can be understood more exactly in terms of the active maintaining of structure by means of negative feedback.

I have analyzed function ascriptions as a special kind of explanation. They enlighten because when we ascribe a function to a part or a process we attribute to its containing system a certain sort of dynamical structure, and we locate the functioning part within this structure. In his discussion of functional analysis in general, Robert Cummins (1975) calls this the "analytical strategy" of explanation. Christopher Boorse (1976) suggests the term "operational explanation." When we employ this strategy in science we explain the capacities of a containing system in terms of the capacities or dispositions of its parts and of their mode of organization. Cummins, aiming at a general analysis of all functional language, suggests that a functional analysis of a complex system will be more or less approximate as the "program" according to which the parts act is more or less "sophisticated" (p. 764). This analysis of functional explanation shows it to be especially well fitted to the program of atomistic reduction; for, if we can demonstrate how the teleological capacities of living things are sustained by the simple dispositions of cells or molecules acting in certain patterns of organization, then we will have satisfied the three conditions that Cummins suggests make for a high degree of "explanatory interest": The analyzing dispositions (e.g., attractions and repulsions, or tendencies toward chemical bonding) will certainly be "less sophisticated" than the goal-seeking proclivities they account for; the analyzed dispositions will be different in type from those that explain them (teleological vs. simply causal); and the organizational pattern (feedback or interlocking networks of mutually supporting feedback loops) could be called sophisticated.

In order to achieve generality, however, Cummins must sacrifice precision. The concepts of organization and of sophistication, which are central to his analysis, are necessarily loosely defined. What kind of organization of parts can justify our talking of functions? Will any type do provided only that it is sophisticated? And what shall we mean by sophistication, beyond mere complexity?

Consider, for example, the proton cycle for the nucleosynthesis of helium-4. Here is a process of considerable complexity, and of an interesting pattern as well, because the sequence of causal interactions can be diagrammed as a cycle. The individual links in this cycle involve simple attractive and repulsive forces, yet the mechanism partially accounts for the presence in the universe of an abundant element. The cycle is certainly more complex than the simple processes it incorporates, so it could be called more sophisticated. Yet the nuclear processes that support it do not merit teleological language. To take another example, suppose that some accidental rewiring of the temperature homeostat of a warm blooded animal turns that subsystem into a positive feedback loop, so that deviations from the normal temperature range are abetted rather than counteracted. We could now explain the capacity of this organism to generate increasingly higher body temperatures, to go into convulsions and eventually to destroy itself in terms of the organizational pattern of positive feedback and the simple physical properties of the component parts. This explanation would also meet Cummins's three requirements of explanatory interest, because capacities for simple attractions and repulsions are both different in type from and less sophisticated than the capacity for self-destruction, on any understanding of the term "sophisticated"; and positive feedback, I should think, has precisely the same degree of sophistication as negative, for the two patterns are identical save for a reversed sign in a mathematical function at one point in the loop.

I do not claim by these examples to refute Cummins's analysis; I merely point out the incompleteness of his program and recommend the inductive approach I have adopted here. Clearly, function ascriptions are justified by the fact that the functioning parts are organized into a system of some kind. But not every organized system is a functional one. According to what special type of pattern must the parts be connected in order to qualify their containing system for teleological language? Proceeding inductively by cases, and limiting ourselves to natural objects, we have found one such pattern, negative feedback, and a natural extension of it, a network of mutually supporting feedback loops. This pattern and its extension explicate, respectively, the capacity of an organized system to seek goals and the capacity of an organism to survive.

Are there other types of organization that would also justify function ascriptions? And would a systematic study of these types allow us to flesh out Cummins's concept of sophistication? Possibly so, but I submit that the two cybernetic patterns so far discussed are general enough to cover the scientifically interesting cases. Supplemented by the concept of selection to be discussed in chapter 6, they will prove adequate to make sense of all the usages—even the weakly metaphorical ones—of functional language for natural systems.

Whether or not we have exhausted the variety of organizational patterns that can justify functional explanations, we have studied enough to make a tentative, yet confident, reply to the skeptical questions raised in the opening paragraphs of chapter 4 about the atomist program for reducing teleology. Even if the concepts of feedback and of networks of feedback loops do not accommodate the whole range of teleological systems, they may nevertheless be taken as typical of the analytical concepts produced by the class of what Woodfield (1976) calls internalist theories. And we have seen both how some (at least) of our teleological descriptions and explanations may be explicated in terms of cybernetic concepts and how some of these concepts may in turn be reductively explicated by reference to mechanical parts and their interactions. William Wimsatt (1971) and Christopher Boorse (1976) have warned that the concepts on which the cybernetic analysis of teleology rests might not be objective properties of natural things but merely projections of human intentionality. If so, the cybernetic theory would not be a reductive analysis, and the physicalist program for understanding human intentionality in terms of cybernetic concepts would be twisted into a vicious circle. However, as the preceding arguments show, those doubts may now be laid to rest.

APPLICATIONS

Next, let us inquire whether the narrowly focused analysis of teleology I have presented above can shed any light upon four questions much debated by philosophers who take an interest in the use of teleological concepts in both human and nonhuman contexts.

TYPES OR TOKENS? Do we ascribe functions primarily to kinds of things or primarily to individuals? Berent Enc (1979, p. 361) explicitly requires that functions be ascribed to individual parts of individual organisms only secondarily, that is, only on the basis of what parts of that sort normally do in organisms of that kind. And other philosophers, Wright (1973), for example, also place primary emphasis on such things as the function of hearts in general in vertebrates in general. Obviously, this approach to functionality comfortably accommodates biology's traditional concern with natural kinds. In contrast, the cybernetic analysis I have been defending requires us to assign functions in the first place to individual parts of particular organisms or machines and to build up inductively to kinds of parts and kinds of systems only secondarily, only when such generalizations are possible. Suppose, to fetch an example from afar, that an improbable intervention during the development of a chick embryo causes the tissue that would otherwise develop into a beating heart passively to allow the passage of blood, and the tissue that would have developed into the aorta now contracts and expands rhythmically, pumping well enough to keep the chick alive for a day or two. A cybernetic analysis of this aberrant case would assign the blood-pumping function to this unique expression of the aortal genes. Its inductive character indicates the superiority of the cybernetic approach, for how could one assign functions to a type of thing prior to discovering functions of individual tokens of the type?

NECESSITY. In what sense, if any, can we say that a functional part is *necessary* for the goal-seeking behavior of the containing machinery? According to Carl Hempel's (1965) analysis of the syllogistic form of a functional explanation, one premise concerns the necessity of the functional part for the proper working of the system. Enc, too, implies necessity of a sort when he stipulates that "only the kind of thing *X* is will do *Y* in all *W*'s" (1979, p. 349). Certainly, the sense of "necessary" here, and as other philosophers use it, is not a strong one, because artificial hearts or kidneys could in principle perform the functions of those organs in every living organism. In calling a functional part necessary, we suggest not that it can have no substitutes but only that the allegedly necessary part makes a certain causal contribution to the goal-seeking activity and that no other thing in fact makes that contribution to this system. The theoretical model of the system, from which alone we obtain our assertions of counterfactual conditionals, shows that if the part did not perform its function the teleological activity would not occur. But necessity, in this sense, is not a necessary condition of a given part's having a function, because many functional parts operate in parallel. On this understanding of "necessary," neither a single kidney nor a single islet cell in the pancreas would be necessary for the proper operating of its containing homeostat, for in the absence of that organ or cell the function would be performed by the other kidney or the other islet cells. Each makes the same kind of contribution to this system, and that *kind* of contribution *is* necessary. Removing all of the parallel parts would halt the operation of the loop, and removing a sizable fraction would seriously impair it. Thus the pair of kidneys is necessary in this sense for the purifying of the blood, and the absence of a pancreas without substitution would indeed entail the end of the blood-sugar homeostasis. The various consequences of what any part of a mechanism does can be read out of its theoretical model; some consequences contribute to the regulating activity of the containing feedback loop or to the stability of a surviving network of loops; some do not. The former are the functions of those parts.

SYSTEMATIC ASSIGNMENT OF FUNCTIONS. Can we codify the way we identify functions? We have established that feedback loops exhibit teleology in its most rudimentary form and that mutually supportive networks of them are fully teleological systems, mechanisms that actively survive. And, speaking loosely, we have said that a function is some sort of contribution to this goal-seeking activity. It remains to stipulate more precisely how we are to assign functions in a teleological system, once we have identified its goal. I recommend the following four rules, just one of which requires extensive justification, for ascribing functions to the parts of a goal-seeking system.

1. Because functions are effects of causal activity, only a causal agent—that is, a material component of the machine or organism—can have a function.

2. The part must be present in the system and participate in its activity *as if* by design; that is, the part's presence in and causal interactions with the rest of the system must be in a certain sense arbitrary or special, not merely an incidental effect of some other functioning part, not the result of mere physical necessity inherent in the controlled system itself. This point is made repeatedly by George C. Williams in his suggestive analysis of biological adaptation (1966, pp. 11–13, 261, e.g.), and Steven J. Gould and Richard C. Lewontin (1979) have sounded a similar warning, with especial vividness. In Williams's example, even though a flying fish's survival depends on its returning to the water after a brief flight through the air, and though the various parts of its body contribute to this necessary process by their gravitational attraction toward the earth, we do not say that the drawing downward is a function of the body as a whole or of its parts acting in parallel. No special arbitrary mechanism is involved here: What goes up must come down. All the special, functional mechanisms of the fish labor in the opposite direction, keeping the organism aloft for a while.

A functional part must be a gratuitous addition to the system, superimposed upon mere physical necessity. Its arbitrariness can be recognized with the aid of the criterion of independent disconnectability, as the following examples indicate. According to the theoretical model, the regulating subsystem can in principle be disconnected from the rest of the feedback loop by removing material parts, in such a way that an integral, controllable system remains. The subsystem is, therefore, a physically contingent addition to the system it controls.

3. The function of a part is something that it does, or causes to occur, that is necessary as defined above—either individually, as with singular parts, or in sum, as with those that operate in parallel—for the regulating activity of the feedback loop or for the active surviving of the organism.

4. In sufficiently complex structures, goals and functions may be arranged in hierarchies. The goal-seeking or goal-achieving

activity of a feedback loop will normally have a further, functional effect in its containing organism and, as Williams (1966) points out, the loop's own goal may be connected with the surviving of the organism only incidentally or statistically, with respect to prevailing conditions. In Williams's example (p. 269), a timing mechanism in a fruit fly adjusts the insect's activities to diurnal variations in illumination; thus, the goal of this regulating mechanism is the matching of activity to the cycle of day and night. But the activity contributes to the organism's survival because, under normal conditions, variations in illumination correlate well with variations in humidity, and the latter environmental factor, rather than the amount of light, has a direct bearing on the organism's proper functioning. The function of this mechanism, the adapting of activity to humidity level, differs from its goal. It is not even a direct causal consequence of achieving the goal but a merely statistical correlate of it, because changes in humidity and light intensity are produced by a common causal process.

There is an undeniable degree of arbitrariness in these rules for ascribing functions. For example, whether or not a component of a feedback loop has a function depends in part on whether its presence is an arbitrary or physically contingent addition to the controlled system, and that in turn depends on where we choose to draw the line between the regulator and the controlled system. Consider a thermostatically regulated house. The causal chain in this instance has enough links in it for us to make this division at any of several points. We may choose to consider the furnace to be part of the sensor controller and the regulated system to be simply the building itself with its empty rooms, heated by the sun and cooled by conduction through the walls and windows. On that choice, the furnace is there by design and has a function in the loop. Or we may consider the furnace to be part of the furnishings of the house and so a member of the controlled system. In that case it is not an arbitrary addition to this system and, hence, not a candidate for a function ascription.

Although the atomist reduction program cannot tolerate an element of conventionality or subjectivity in the drawing of a boundary between teleological and nonteleological systems, it can quite comfortably accommodate a certain amount of arbitrary choice in the assigning of functions to parts. What matters for reductive atomism is that a thing's being a goal-seeking system be entirely an objective property of the system itself, with no trace of human intentionality being impressed upon it from outside. Once this point is made clear, it does not greatly matter how we condense the complete causal story that might be told about the operation of the feedback loop, whether we picture the interactions in intricate detail or paint with a broader brush, or just which link in the causal chain we name as the controlling action of the sensor controller. And where distinctions matter the cybernetic analysis does not fail us. In the light it sheds we can distinguish the functional contribution of the screws that hold the bimetal strip in its place in a thermostat from the ordinary, nonfunctional participation of the windows through which heat escapes; we can see that the gudgeons that hold the rudder in place on the transom of an automatically steered sailboat have a function, whereas the transom itself, being part of the controlled system, does not; and we find that the islet cells and the connective tissue of the pancreas, as well as the insulin molecules it produces, play functional roles in the blood-sugar homeostat, whereas the glucose, part of the regulated system, does not (although glucose does indeed function in other feedback loops).

GENERALIZING. Can we produce a *general* analysis of teleological language, speaking with one voice about the application of teleological concepts to human beings, to their artifacts, and to natural objects? This is a question I have set outside the bounds of this book, but it is appropriate to ask at this point whether the inductive strategy I have adopted can make any contribution to this more general philosophical investigation.

In the most general case, when we ask what a part in some artifact is there *for*, the answer can be obtained only from its designer. The function of the small hammer that hangs from a certain sort of fire alarm may be guessed by anyone endowed with a modest acquaintance with human affairs or with the ability to read the message inscribed upon the appliance, but it cannot be strictly inferred from a knowledge only of the causal connections internal to the device. The function of the hammer is determined by what the designer and users of fire alarms intend for it. However, in other cases, the intentions of the designer do not settle the issue. If some inept fabricator assembled a thermostat by inadvertence, intending to make some other sort of contrivance, all his protestations to the contrary would not overrule our claim, based on an analysis of how the device operates in fact, that the function of the relay switch is to turn the furnace on and off and the function of the bimetallic strip is to sense the temperature of the room around it. We have in the cybernetic analysis, then, a way of pinning down for some artifacts and for all biological systems what it means for a part to confer some good upon its containing system, to have what Peter Achinstein (1977) calls a service function. The service or the good conferred is, in the type of mechanism that can be said to survive, a contribution to the internal processes that constitute surviving, the maintaining of structure by means of negative feedback.

SIX

# Teleology: Selectionism

THE SELECTIONIST ANALYSIS, LIKE THE CYBERNETICAL, attempts to stretch the complex of teleological concepts far enough to cover both human purposiveness, the source of our essential paradigms, and examples of rudimentary means–end connections in simple biological systems. We have seen that the cybernetic theory identifies teleology at the human end of the scale with goal seeking, of which the helmsman is a prime example, and at the other with homeostasis, such as the regulation of temperature. The selectionist theory, on the other hand, points at the upper end of the scale to the sort of conscious, purposive selecting that goes on in human problem solving and other creative activity and at the lower end to the Darwinian process of natural selection. On the issue of reduction, the two theories pull in opposite directions. The cybernetic theory directs us inward and downward, finding the source of teleology inside the individual mechanism, in the workings of its inner parts. The selectionist theory, on the other hand, seems to "reduce" upward, finding the source of teleology in more inclusive, higher-level systems, in the selecting agent and its criterion. Let us try to test the value of the selectionist theory as an analytical tool. We must be careful, however, not to stretch the concept of selection farther than it can go, not to mistake for conceptual unification what is in fact merely an attractive but false analogy. Let Darwin's own example, a flight of fancy the literal sense of which he explicitly disavows, put us on our guard:

> It may metaphorically be said that natural selection is daily and hourly scrutinising, throughout the world, the slightest variations; rejecting those that are bad, preserving and adding up all that are good; silently and insensibly working, *whenever and wherever opportunity offers*, at the improvement of each organic being in relation to its organic and inorganic conditions of life.
> [DARWIN 1859, 1872, chap. 4, para. 6; emphasis his]

Can teleological descriptions and functional assignments explain why a functioning part of a natural system is there? Can they, as Wimsatt (1972) and Wright (1973) suggest, tell us anything about the *origins* of teleological structures? These philosophers propose to connect teleology with two concepts that are as characteristic of biological thinking as homeostasis, namely, natural selection and adaptation. To demonstrate the initial attractiveness of the selectionist theory of teleology, I shall show that, although the cybernetic theory is capable of accommodating some of the biological applications of the prima facie teleological concept of adaptation, it fails to make sense of others, equally firmly entrenched in biological thinking. In order to deal with these applications we shall have to give the selectionist theory a hearing.

The concept of natural selection contributes to teleological descriptions of living things in two major ways: It gives us a reason to interpret some facts as evidence of functional design, and it leads us to think of "adapting" as a process that occurs over many generations in a line of descent. Let us first examine some symptoms of functionality.

We usually do not ascribe functions to things by following formal rules; we get along quite satisfactorily with intuitive rules of thumb, which are considerably less formal and possibly less controversial than the rules I have proposed in chapter 5. In most practical instances we are content with a plausible case.

Williams, too, for all his cautious skepticism about function ascriptions, employs partial but suggestive clues in his search for adaptations. Two sorts normally count as prima facie evidence of functionality: The first connects with cybernetics, and the second with selection.

The first and more obvious kind of clue is behavior that seems to happen in response to a challenge from outside and to be directed at maintaining stability within the organism. When we see that fruit flies adjust their periods of activity and inactivity to correlate with daylight and darkness, we may plausibly speculate that the behavior is directed at some proximate goal and search for a cybernetic structure that generates the observed behavior.

The second and more subtle kind is the presence of some peculiar, seemingly arbitrary structure within the organism. The eye, for example, is such an odd and intricate organ that it cannot simply be an incidental or extraneous feature of its containing system. Up to this point, but not beyond, the modern biologist treats the evidence just as did William Paley, the champion of divine design (Williams 1966, p. 259). If a system is the product of a conscious designer, then any elaborate part that might have been left out must have cost its maker some effort. A rational fabricator expends effort parsimoniously. Therefore, the part probably was put there to perform some function, so that it repays its cost to its maker. The modern biologist reasons nontheologically, yet the argument is curiously like Paley's. Without presuming that the system was produced by conscious design, one still is able to speculate about costs and benefits in evolutionary terms. The cost is the effort required to maintain the purity of a genetic line through generations of copying, despite tendencies toward degeneration. Natural selection takes the place of the conscious designer in speculating about natural systems, and instead of a presumption about rational parsimony one adopts an analogous principle about sweeping out the errors that accumulate in the genetic copying process. As Williams says: "Any [biological] system will degenerate to the extent to which there is a relaxation of selection pressure for its maintenance" (p. 266). Consequently, when we discover an apparently gratuitous yet intriguingly complicated part of an organism, such as the human pineal gland or vermiform appendix, it is reasonable to speculate that the structure contributes something to the health and stability of the system. The clue is not infallible, of course; after careful study we may conclude that the appendix serves no function at all, even though the organism faithfully constructs it according to an ancient blueprint.

Besides helping us to view gratuitous complexity as a clue to functionality, the concept of natural selection also suggests a peculiarly evolutionary sense of the term "adaptation." Williams's use, I believe, is typical of the careful employment of this concept by evolutionary biologists. He distinguishes two sorts, facultative and obligate adaptation (e.g., 1966, p. 81). In the former, the organism responds to varying extents and in several ways to environmental stimuli so as to counter the harm they would otherwise do. The thickening of the skin in places that receive repeated and frequent friction illustrates such a facultative response; it is an adaptation in the primary sense of the term, an active mobilizing of the inner processes of the system to meet some external threat and so to preserve the structure of the organism. In this process there are, according to Williams, "sensing and control mechanisms whereby the nature of the response can be adaptively adjusted to the ecological environment" (p. 82). The cybernetic analysis of teleology in terms of feedback has an obvious application here. But biologists also recognize fixed or obligate adaptations, an example of which is the thickening of the skin on the soles of the feet, which begins already *in utero* (p. 79). How is it possible to employ a single term both for speaking about the genetically fixed characters of organisms and for those they develop in response to the exigencies of living? The theory of evolution by natural selection provides the framework that seems to justify this unification. The callus on a farmer's hand develops in response to pressure from the handle of the hoe; similarly, the thickened skin now found on the soles of human infants developed as our ancestral species responded to the pressure of selective forces. Clearly, the term "adaptation" is used in different senses. I shall call them cybernetical adaptation and evolutionary adaptation. The theory of natural selection suggests that the concepts can be treated as one by reason of an analogy between responsive changes within an individual organism and mutations in a line of descent.

Attractive as the analogy may be between the response of a species to selection pressure and the response of an individual organism to various environmental opportunities and threats, we do not need selection to justify our ascribing functions to many obligate adaptations. Even if we knew nothing of Darwin's accomplishment, we would still be able to determine the function of the vertebrate retina or of the walrus's blubber by following the prescription of the cybernetic theory: We would search for the contribution the structure makes to the survival of the individual organism that bears it. There is a considerable area of agreement, even of redundancy, therefore, in what we learn from an analysis of functions in terms of adaptations, in the primary sense of that term, and what we learn from an analysis based on the notion that species adapt to the exigencies of natural selection. Almost anything that promotes the survival of an individual organism also promotes the spreading of copies of its genes among the population.

If the areas covered by the cybernetical and evolutionary understandings of adaptation coincided exactly, an atomist could fairly choose the former, on the grounds that it fits better than selectionism into the reduction program of atomism. But the two areas do not wholly overlap, as the following examples demonstrate; therefore, our choice between the two theories cannot be made merely according to preference for the atomist program.

Some cases of what is conventionally called adaptation fall within the circle of selectionism alone. All the cases of this type that I am aware of consist of the structures and strategies of reproduction, and every such structure belongs to this type. Cybernetical adaptations are, of course, abundant within the reproductive process; for example, the mechanisms that regulate the levels of sex hormones in the estrus cycle. But let us inquire about the functions of the estrus cycle itself. To this question the cybernetic theory responds with silence, at best. The cycle does not contribute to the active, delicate balance by which the organism survives. This finely tooled submechanism, though it fully satisfies the rule that a functional part must be a gratuitous addition to the organism, has just no function discoverable by a cybernetical analysis.

In fact, the cybernetic theory of functionality treats reproductive structures even less hospitably than this example suggests: It pronounces them to be maladaptive, dysfunctional. Think of the enormous amount of effort devoted by a nesting pair of wood warblers to the raising of several broods each summer, effort that might have been spent in building up their own bodies in preparation for the fall migration. This dysfunctionality can be seen even more readily in the Pacific salmon, whose body virtually disassembles itself to produce energy for its mighty effort to reach the spawning beds upstream, a journey that ends in death for the organism (Williams 1966, p. 174). Only in an evolutionary sense of adaptation could Williams call such an extreme subordination of individual survival to reproduction "clearly adaptive": A cybernetical analysis would dictate the opposite judgment.

Here is a crisis of sorts whose magnitude remains to be assessed. We have found a class of structures to which teleological language has been applied since before Darwin's day and of which the cybernetic theory can make no sense. Has the contender that was to have been the champion of atomistic reductionism been unhorsed?

Let us be clear as to the precise location of the contest. It is not being conducted within the laboratories of the Biological Sciences Center; the neo-Darwinian theory still seems capable of explaining the origins of all these allegedly teleological systems. Rather, the battle is a skirmish between reductionism and antireductionism for control of the territory of human desires, beliefs, and goals. If cybernetical concepts can be reduced atomistically and if the teleology of machines and simple living systems can be understood in cybernetical terms, then the case for the mechanistic reduction of human intentionality, though not of course proved, is rendered decidedly plausible. But if the teleology of a natural object can be understood only in terms of still larger teleological systems that enclose it, then the possibility of a reductive explication in terms of the system's parts seems to be blocked. We would have no paradigm on which to model our reduction of human teleology, and that undeniably real and characteristic property of human life might turn out to be irreducible.

Having struck this block in the atomist road, we can choose among three possible paths. We can try to produce a cybernetical analysis even of the mechanism of natural selection; we can revamp our explication of functionality univocally along selectionist lines; or we can decide that teleological terms as they are used in biology divide irreconcilably into two camps, one grouped around cybernetical adaptation and the other around evolutionary.

## NATURAL SELECTION AS CYBERNETIC MECHANISM

The first option, the speculation that natural selection may operate as a kind of negative feedback process, is proposed by Michael Ruse (1973) and by J. L. Mackie (1974) and is dismissed with a brief mention by Cummins (1975). As we have noted above, the term "feedback" is widely employed in a variety of rather loose senses, most of which are only marginally related to the concept whose explication and teleological interpretation I have attempted to produce. Certainly some of the looser, nonteleological senses of the term may fit the case of natural selection. But Ruse takes the conjecture seriously enough to discuss a sample evolutionary mechanism and to argue that it qualifies as a goal-directed system under Nagel's (1961) explication of feedback. The mechanism Ruse discusses is the evolutionary process by which the number of eggs laid by a typical nesting plover is maintained at a stable value of four, for the great majority of females in a population. Four is the optimal number for plovers, because three or fewer young is too small a number to replace birds lost through predation and disease, and fledglings raised in a nest of five or more overtax their parents' capacity to care for them. On the face of it, then, this process has the appearance of a "keeping" mechanism that maintains a system in a beneficial goal state. Let us see how this process works, describing it as nearly as possible in a form congenial to the analysis of feedback I have presented above.

The changes we shall try to view as cybernetical adaptations occur not in individual birds but in a population over several generations. Following the model of our analysis of feedback, let us distinguish two subgroups in the system, two distinct lines of descent, one of which is to be the regulated system and the other the regulator. Tendencies to deviate from the optimal clutch size will enter a portion of the total populations of plovers because of accidental mutations that dispose the birds that carry the novel genes to lay, let us say, five eggs or, in other mutations, three.

Here, then, is an exogenous disturbance of the system, a "force" that tends to push it away from its goal state. Because all lineages within the population compete for limited supplies of food, nesting sites, and other resources, a variation in one lineage that affects the competitive keenness of its members will have a causal effect on the members of the other lineages. In response, these "other birds do things which they would not have done had the original disruption (that is, mutation) not occurred" (Ruse 1973, p. 180). Clearly, this analysis of the mechanism leads us to try to fit it into the feedback pattern by identifying the lineage in which the mutation occurs as the protected system *S*, the other birds as the regulating subsystem *C*, and the competition between the two as the causal link by which *C* senses the original disturbance. But we can push the plover's story no farther into this mold. The "correcting" connection, by which the other birds are supposed to react upon and counteract the original deviation, consists of more of the same competition. This "correction" is not, therefore, an independently disconnectable causal process; it is, in fact, identical to the "sensing." Worse still, the effect of this "adaptation" by the putative regulator on the system it is supposed to regulate bears little resemblance to a protective correcting or maintaining of some beneficial state of the regulated system. Indeed, the activity of the putative regulator, its response to the initial disturbance, does nothing whatever to restore the deviant lineage to the "goal state" of producing four-member clutches. Rather, the other birds (and let us add the creatures who prey upon plovers, and other species who compete with them for resources) respond by outperforming the bearers of the mutant gene in the race to reproduce and to appropriate food and territory, driving that lineage toward lower numbers in the population and eventually to extinction.

This simple but representative example of how natural selection works is just not complex enough to qualify as a teleological process in the cybernetic sense. Neither the species itself nor the species taken together with its environmental hazards admits of analysis into two subsystems, one of which regulates the other according to the model of negative feedback. A species or species-environment complex is not a mechanism that adapts in the way that the pancreas adapts to an increased level of glucose in the blood. The conjecture that natural selection can be subsumed under a cybernetical analysis does not seem promising.[1]

Let us consider, then, the second option, writing a univocal explication of teleological concepts along entirely new lines, giving the concept of selection rather than that of goal the pivotal position.

## UNIVOCAL SELECTIONISM

In their independent and, for our purposes, highly consonant analyses of function ascriptions and functional explanations, William C. Wimsatt (1972) and Larry Wright (1973) aim at nothing less than a complete account of all uses of teleological terms. Thus, they rightly devote their attention largely to the context of human purposiveness. However, when they discuss the use of function terms in biology they attempt to establish connections with the theory of evolution by natural selection. In the following discussion of their two versions of selectionism, I shall concentrate on their treatment of simple biological systems, inquiring how these versions of selectionism fare in comparison with the cybernetical approach.

According to the selectionist conjecture, in ascribing a function to a member of a system we imply a special sort of explanation (Wimsatt 1972, p. 67; Wright 1973, p. 154). That much may be said also of the cybernetic theory as I have interpreted it. But, whereas the latter views a function ascription as an implicit assertion about the mode of organization of the containing system and of the part's place in it, Wright's theory interprets a function ascription as a claim about the origins of the part—about how, or why, or for what reason it came to occupy its present place. "Saying that the function of *X* is *Z*," Wright suggests, "is saying at least that *X* is there *because* it does *Z*." In this formulation the term "because" has "an etiological force" (1973, p. 157); it calls our attention to the causal origins of *X*. The doing of *Z* by *X*

1 / The failure of one supposed example does not, of course, refute the conjecture. I refer the reader to my 1984 essay for additional and equally unsuccessful attempts to confirm it. I believe, however, that the failure of these examples robs the conjecture—interesting though it is—of whatever initial plausibility it may have had.

figures in the story we must tell about how *X* came, through a series of causally connected episodes, to its present situation in the system that contains it. Wimsatt makes a similar claim but refers to past performances of *Z* by possibly other things than *X*: A function ascription "implies . . . that the past contribution to the end promoted by a selection process of similar or other functional entities has resulted, via the selection process, in the presence and form of the functional entity in question" (1972, p. 67). Following Wright's prescription, we query the designers of a motor and discover that they were not interested in generating a flash of blue light or any other electromagnetic wave; they included a switch in the total design because it turns off the motor. It is there because it does that.

How do these two variations on the selectionist theme connect teleological ideas to natural selection? In Wright's theory, the relation is established by means of two useful distinctions. First, Wright distinguished two types of etiology. The first is a simple causal story, such as the explanation that oxygen is present in the blood because it combines chemically with hemoglobin. The second is an "evolutionary-etiological" story, for example, the assertion that oxygen is prevalent in the blood because it produces energy (1973, p. 160). Second, Wright distinguishes between two senses of the term "selection." Whether the selection is performed by a conscious, deliberating agent or by a nonconscious mechanism, we must distinguish "mere discrimination," where the choice does not serve some purpose but is done as it were on a whim, from "consequence selection," where the choice is made by virtue of "some advantage that would accrue from" the selected object. Only the latter is teleological. Either sort of selecting can be done by selectors of any degree of consciousness. In the case of nonconscious selecting mechanisms, the teleological sort of selection is done by virtue of an advantageous consequence of the selected part's presence; that is, natural selection is consequence selection: "When we explain the presence or existence of *X* by appeal to a consequence *Z*, . . . *Z* must be or create conditions conducive to the survival or maintenance of *X*" (p. 164).

Wimsatt expresses some doubts about the connection between natural selection and his selectionist analysis of function ascriptions but suggests how a bridge might be built between them. He speculates that "'natural selection' in biology and . . . trial and error learning processes justify talk of purposes and teleology" only if some additional condition is satisfied (1972, p. 17). This extra factor may be "phenotypic complexity," something analogous to the hierarchical organization of genes, cell, and soma that we find in living things (1972, p. 17n; 1974).

A selection process is teleological, in Wimsatt's view, if the criterion by which it discriminates can qualify as a *purpose*; and the criterion will so qualify if it specifies a property or state whose attainment is promoted by some entity and if this promoting "help[s] to explain why the functional part is present and has the form that it does" (1972, pp. 67, 70).

Let us apply these conjectures to a biological example that the cybernetic theory cannot accommodate. Consider the constellation of base pairs in a firefly's genome that "codes for" the apparatus by which the mating insects emit and recognize their characteristic pattern of flashes. As we have seen, the cybernetic theory permits us to attribute functions to various parts within this machinery, relative to goal-directed mechanisms that enable the insects to seek each other, perform their mating routine, and so on. But the theory can find no function for this machinery as a unit within the organism. The selectionist theory, on the other hand, easily assigns a function to the reproductive system. According to Wimsatt's version, base pairs very like those in the firefly we have caught in our bottle promoted the ability of this insect's ancestors to find mates; this fact helps to explain why their descendent is here with the sort of genome it has. Consequently, the genes in question (and by the same token, the somatic apparatus that expresses them) have the function of promoting reproduction. And it is easy to see that a similar line of reasoning assigns exactly the same function, this same "ultimate goal of genetic survival" (Williams 1966, p. 221), to every functioning part of an organism. Even the survival of individuals is functional only insofar as it promotes the proliferation of copies of the survivors' genes, as the self-sacrificing Pacific salmon reminds us.

The selectionist theory has received a considerable amount of critical attention. I shall not review all of this discussion here but shall simply assess those of the theory's strengths and weaknesses that bear upon our chief concern, the atomist reduction of human teleology.

Two admissions must be made to the credit of the selectionist theory. First, it gives us a principled way of attributing a function to the reproductive machinery of living things, something the cybernetical approach fails to do, apparently to its discredit. This appears to be an important achievement for selectionism because self-replication by means of specialized submechanisms is almost as characteristic of life as is survival by cybernetic processes. Our praise should be modulated, however, because neither the ability to reproduce nor the possession of a pedigree is a logically necessary characteristic of life. We do not deny a place on the tree of life to a sterile hybrid, and we would not hesitate to graft onto the tree an organism that appeared, if it were possible, by spontaneous generation. Yet the fact remains that selectionism makes sense of reproductive functionality, and cyberneticism does not.

Second, the selectionist theory paints a unified picture of biological functions, because every component part of an organism promotes the achievement that stands at the pinnacle of the hierarchy of means and ends, the copying of the organism's genes in subsequent generations. The cybernetical picture offers a narrower perspective. According to it, the ultimate goal is the survival of the individual organism, let future generations stand or fall as they may.

Third, the selectionist account resonates strongly to certain paradigms of high human purposiveness, namely, those involving conscious, deliberative choosing. Cyberneticism resonates to a different but equally attractive paradigm.

Last, the selectionist approach accords with certain terminological habits of biologists, with regard to genetical "survival," as the following lines from Williams show:

> The smallest protist is an endlessly intricate machine, with all parts contributing harmoniously to the ultimate goal of genetic survival. . . . When a biologist says that a system is organized, he should mean organized for genetic survival or for some subordinate goal that ultimately contributes to successful reproduction.
> [1966, pp. 221, 255–56]

However, on the debit side must be listed several grave defects. Let us consider some that are peculiar to Wright's version of selectionism, some that inhere in Wimsatt's, and some that weaken both. From the first two categories we get some hints of the flexibility of the basic conjecture, from the third an indication of essential flaws.

First, Wright's version attributes functions to living systems too lavishly. Certain cave-dwelling species of fish have sightless eyes, yet they are present in the organism because generations ago eyes like these contributed to ancestral vision. Wright's account explicitly allows a component to have *Z* as its function even though it does not do *Z*; hence, the fact that the lens and the muscles that swivel the eye no longer contribute to the receiving of visual signals in the fish's brain does not let us escape from the conclusion that focusing light and moving the eye are their functions still. Wimsatt's version avoids this problem by requiring a present contribution as well as an ancestral one.

Both versions distribute functions too stingily, however. When a mutation occurs that would count as a function under a cybernetic analysis, the selectionist theory must withhold the epithet until the mutant genes become established in the gene pool as a result of natural selection. Selectionism cannot accommodate spontaneous novelty. Wright recognizes this limitation but does not consider it to be a defect (1973, p. 165).

Wimsatt's version acknowledges, as Wright's does not, that continuous change may happen in the evolutionary development of a functional part; Wimsatt stipulates that the putative function of the part in question must have been performed in the ancestral organism by "similar or other functional entities" that contribute to the same end as the present one (1972, p. 67). This stipulation, faithful though it be to the biological facts, raises intolerable difficulties for the theory. According to what principle shall we identify the ancestral organs that are similar (or not!) to the entity in question? Only, I submit, by the fact that they perform the same function. But whether or not these parts perform functions at all is precisely the point that remains to be decided. We seem to be launched upon an infinite regress.

Both versions place the evolutionary history of an organism squarely in the center of the complex of facts that justifies function ascriptions. But one can usually discover the function of an anatomical feature simply by examining how the machinery works here and now. Therefore, an evolutionary interpretation entails a conceptual break with biologists of the past, because they attributed functions without suspecting the evolutionary origins of living things and (although some held it) without employing, either, a belief in divine origins.

Both Wright's and Wimsatt's versions must distinguish between purposive and nonpurposive selection and, in order to do so, employ concepts connoting purposiveness. According to Wright, evolutionary selection is purposive only because, when we explain "the presence or existence of *X* by appeal to a consequence *Z*, the overriding consideration is that *Z* must be or create conditions conducive to the survival or maintenance of *X*" (1973, p. 164). The concepts of survival and maintenance, or others very like them, are crucial to the distinction Wright's and Wimsatt's theories need. But how are we to understand them? I have shown how they may be given a cybernetic explication. Wright offers us none. Wimsatt speaks of selection processes that serve a "purpose" or "end" (1972, p. 67) and tells us that the criterion of selection qualifies as a purpose if a part's helping to meet the criterion "constitutes a teleological explanation of its existence and form" (p. 67), and he explains further that a teleological explanation is one that explains "why the functional entity is present and has the form that it does" (p. 70). Wimsatt's attempt seems to carry no farther than Wright's toward understanding what the right sort of selection is. In this respect, I submit, both versions suffer in comparison with the cybernetic theory, which does have a clear set of criteria for distinguishing purposive machinery from nonpurposive. But more can be said in favor of purposive selecting, and I shall return to the topic below.

The most radical and, to my mind, devastating criticism that can be leveled against the selectionist theory is that even if we could formulate the required distinction, under no plausible understanding of the division between purposive selecting and mere discrimination can natural selection be placed on the teleological side of the fence. And if natural selection is not selection at all in any remotely teleological sense of the term, then the selectionist theory entirely fails to connect function talk in human affairs with function talk in biology. No extension of the concepts from their mentalistic paradigm is possible. The cybernetic theory may fail to grant a function to the reproductive system, but selectionism fails more grandly, rejecting all nonconscious teleology.

To demonstrate the justice of this charge, let us construct several examples of selection processes that include some extra quality, something that lifts them above the class of mere sorting operations; and let us then compare these standards of purposive selection with the way natural selection works.

Looking first to the source of our teleological paradigms, human purposiveness, we can find a clue to the difference between selecting and mere discriminating in one of Wright's examples—paradoxically, in what is omitted from it. When a conscious designer has produced the mechanism, Wright says, the statement that "*X* was designed to do *Z* simply entails that *X* is there because it results in *Z*" (1973, p. 165). But only in special cases would *X*'s actually doing *Z* be one of the causal antecedents that have brought *X* to its present situation. The etiological story may or may not include that performance, but it must include the designer's expectations that *X* will do *Z*. We may take that explanation for granted if we assume, as Wright seems to do (p. 164), that the designer's expectations are infallible, but even then we cannot leave it out of the etiological picture (Woodfield 1976). *X*'s doing *Z* in the past *may* have contributed causally to the designer's expectation, and so to his choice as well, but not necessarily; the expectation may have been based on theoretical calculations instead. What matters is the expectation, not any actual instances of *X*'s having done *Z*. In contrast, if the designer selected the part for inclusion in the design without any expectations of its performance, the selection would be simply whimsical, mere discrimination without a purpose. It would be like the running water that sorts the grains of sand and other material in the beds of streams according to their size and density. So does the swirling water in a prospector's pan; but the discrimination that takes place in the pan is purposive because it is built into the causal interactions of a highly complex selector, a person with a disposition to employ the nuggets in the pursuit of high living in Dodge City. The conjecture I draw from these examples is this:

Purposive selection differs from mere sorting in that the selecting agent or mechanism has some internal orientation toward the selected object's performance in the future.

Can this conjecture, that an orientation toward the future is the additional ingredient that converts mere discrimination into purposive selection, be extended to nonconscious selectors? The following example shows that it can. The sensor in a heat-seeking missile is a device that responds in one way (an output signal) to sources of infrared radiation and in another (no output) to all other things. The sensor discriminates, therefore, between these two classes of objects. Let us place the sensor in its position in the feedback mechanism that guides the missile toward its targets but disrupt the loop at the causal relation *F*, the effector connection. Of this defective mechanism the most we can say is that it discriminates. Now let us restore the integrity of the feedback loop. Equipped with an internal state that disposes it to pursue the objects it has identified, the missile now may be said to select them in the teleological sense of the term. Generalizing the moral we have drawn from the paradigm, let us stipulate that a necessary condition of purposive selection is that the selector perform its sorting with an orientation toward some end or goal. I do not suggest that the combination of discrimination with future-orientation amounts to a sufficient condition, but it is necessary. The distinction Wright draws between purposive and nonpurposive selection is crucial to the selectionist analysis of teleology in natural objects; hence, this necessary condition must be satisfied somehow by the evolutionary process if the selectionist theory is to fulfill its promise.

But natural selection is not oriented toward the future. We have learned that much by watching neo-Darwinism win out over Lamarckian ideas. An organism's need for a mutation does not guarantee that it will happen; even those needed changes that save a species from extinction are simply lucky accidents. No anticipation of any sort influences the *character* of a mutation. Nor need present or future play any part in determining the *rate* of mutation. An individual organism, faced with danger of an unusual sort, will accelerate the rate at which it tries and discards possible solutions; but a species in analogous circumstances possesses no mechanism for stepping up its genetic experimentation. On this account natural selection does not support function talk.

The same negative judgment with regard to the alleged teleological character of the evolutionary process can be reached by a parallel and simpler route. Consider the following weaker and even more obvious condition. A selection process is teleological, not mere sorting, only if it involves at least two distinct things, a selector and a selectee. This condition may seem so self-evident as not to need explicit mention: How could a process be called selection if there is not a selector selecting something? But Wright discounts this possible objection. Natural selection, he admits, "is really *self*-selection, nothing is *doing* the selecting; given the nature of *X*, *Z*, and the environment, *X* will *automatically* be selected" (1973, p. 164). Wright seems to claim that natural selection's only peculiarity is its occurring automatically, but that selecting does happen, nevertheless. But how could there be a doing that nothing does?

Sorting can be reflexive, of course; a group of antelope fleeing from a lion sort themselves into front, middle, and rear ranks by their own actions. And perhaps in special circumstances a selector and the thing selected can be but one thing: The selector must be capable of being both the subject and the object of its own purposive activity. For example, the president of a faculty senate may select himself for appointment to an ad hoc committee. I do not know what would be the smallest number of simpler cybernetical circuits required to build an automaton that could select itself. It would, I surmise, have to be a goal-seeking machine which, like the heat-seeking missile, is able to establish causal connections with external objects, so completing an overall feedback loop. It would be able, second, to discriminate between these objects and others by means of some detected property. Third, the automaton would be able to detect that same property in itself and respond in the same way as it normally does to external things. I suspect, lastly, that the capability for this double participation in a purposive activity would be rooted in a high degree of organizational complexity—that, for example, any organism that could select itself could also laugh at itself. Could any organism less complicated than a human being attain this rank? It seems doubtful; yet the selectionist theory, according to Wright, must have self-selection at all levels of the evolutionary process. But certainly an amoeba falls far short of the ability to stand in for external things as the object of its own purposive activity. Certainly, too, the molecular replicating mechanisms that triumphed over their competitors in the primeval soup were too simple to be called self-selectors. Applied to the typical evolutionary etiology, *self*-selection is just a misnomer. Volunteers do not *select* themselves; they put themselves forward to be selected by the commanding officer. The teams that participate in the world series have not *selected* themselves; they have climbed to the top of their respective heaps during the regular season, from which pinnacles the commissioners of baseball, following the rules of the leagues, select them for the series. Nor have the many extant organisms that adorn our planet *selected* themselves; rather, the ancestors of contemporary living things have done better than their competitors at generating copies of their genes. Darwin's romantic metaphor of selection by Nature is much less faithful to his facts than Alfred Russell Wallace's unsentimental "struggle for existence."

The selectionist theory errs by focusing on the wrong comparison. Paradigms from human goal seeking can be connected to homeostasis by a natural extension of the concepts of goal, adaptation, and survival. Paradigms from conscious choosing, however, can be carried over to natural selection only by stretching the concept of selection to the snapping point. What is left in our hands is a lifeless metaphor.

The conceptual key to understanding the teleology inherent in living things and their evolution is not selection but survival. To get our thinking straight we need to look in the right place for the source of means–end relations. Selectionism points to the environmental context of the organism's evolution. But nature is in no way like a kindly but nonpersonal Luther Burbank. Consider a swimming coach who selects her team by throwing the entire freshman class into the pool and signing up those who float. The coach selects, because she expects her charges to win a few swimming contests, but the pool only sorts. Nature does not select either; it does not look beyond the present scene of carnage and starvation (see, e.g., Williams's eloquent paragraph on this theme, 1966, p. 255). If we would find teleology in that scene we must look where the cybernetic theory points: not at the grand scheme of things but at the individual strugglers. There we find goal seeking with an obvious kinship to our own, survival actively sought, and adaptation obviously directed at ends.

As John Dewey saw clearly enough,

> Interest shifts from the wholesale essence back of special changes to the question of how special changes serve and defeat concrete purposes; shifts from an intelligence that shaped things once for all to the particular intelligence which things are even now shaping. [1910, p. 15]

What Dewey seems not to have noticed, however, although it was obvious already to William James, is the radically mechanistic flavor of Darwin's work. The concrete and individual purposes to which post-Darwinian biology directs our attention are simply special modes of interaction among material particles.

## ADAPTATION AND "ADAPTATION"

What does the collapse of the selectionist approach signify for our efforts to understand teleology in the rest of nature and in human affairs? In particular, what sense can we make of selectionism's very own paradigms, learning by trial and error and conscious, deliberative choosing? With one possibly important exception, the indications are that we can do very well with an unalloyed cyberneticism. I have discussed one favorable omen, namely, the heat-seeking missile that can be said to select targets purposively, because it is organized as a goal-seeking mechanism. Indeed, far from being useless for the analysis of selection mechanisms, the cybernetical approach provides the only means we have found for distinguishing sorting processes that serve an end from mere nonpurposive discriminating. Many other examples can be found in Powers's cybernetic analysis (1973; 1978) of human behavior of all sorts. But difficulties may arise with regard to conscious choosing, the highest, most essentially teleological of our paradigms of selection. It will prove refractory to a cybernetic analysis if we insist that the act of choosing must introduce objective novelty into the course of events. If real choices are undetermined by the events that precede them, if radical freedom is part of the essence of deliberative choosing, then cyberneticism fails to make sense of it, for the cybernetical analysis stands firmly on a mechanistic-deterministic view of the world. We have constructed the cybernetical explication of orientation toward goals in terms of rigid causal mechanisms. Of course, not everyone would consider its marriage to determinism to be a serious fault of the cybernetical analysis. I simply note the fact here and set aside the general question of novelty until I return to it from a different direction in chapter 11.

Where does selectionism's failure leave the alleged functionality of the reproductive system? With no credentials whatever. That may seem like an unsatisfactory way to treat genetic survival, around which the evolutionary process is organized as if it were a goal. We must find a way to grant a function of some sort to the mechanisms that copy genes, if only because in some respects they hold the upper hand, ruling the kingdom of life often from behind the throne but sometimes—in the Pacific salmon, for instance—with ruthless power. I recommend the last of the three options I listed above; let us divide the uses of teleological concepts in biology into two distinct groups. On the one hand we place uses that are justified by the concept of goal orientation extended from human purposing, and on the other we set the unabashed anthropomorphisms that we generate by treating natural selection metaphorically, as if it were more than mere sorting. In one column go the cybernetical concepts of goal, goal-directedness, individual survival, adaptation in the facultative sense, and function, all understood according to the cybernetical models. These are the truly teleological concepts. In the other column we collect the concepts of natural selection, criterion of selection, genetic survival, adaptation in the evolutionary sense, and (again) function, explicated in the neo-Darwinian sense. Because natural selection does not qualify as teleological sorting, the coat of arms of the second family of concepts displays the bend sinister. These are the merely metaphorical uses of teleological terms. A robin selects a bit of string for a nest; Nature has "selected" the shape of the robin's beak. A cat's irises adapt to varying levels of illumination; the frontal orientation of its eyes is "adapted" to its predatory life style. An oak survives for a hundred years; the pattern of its genes "survives" for millions.

Disdainfully now, we squint through inverted commas at some of modern biologists' favorite locutions. What, if anything, can be said in their favor? We can point out this: The sense of "function" that we apply, for example, to the tail of the peacock or to the atrophying of the Pacific salmon's digestive tract, though weak, is justified *subjectively*, because of a legitimate interest we take in those mechanisms and processes. We have good reason to pay more attention to the fact that the peacock's display often leads to the production of peachicks than we do to the fact that it also tends to distribute bits of bright color about the lawn. We mention the connection with the next generation when we explain how approximate copies of these intricate and decorative mechanisms get constructed year after year. The etiology is not purposive, as we have seen, but the outcome of the process and the mechanisms by which it occurs are always wonderful and sometimes bizarre. If we use the honorific term "function" to distinguish the causal connections that lie within such a sequence, who can blame us?

This classification of the machinery of reproduction resembles the way one would study the inventions of the cartoonist Rube Goldberg. In a typical cartoon much activity goes on: A ball rolls down a plank into a bucket balanced on a seesaw, the motion of the seesaw ignites a match that burns through a string that has been supporting . . . , and so on. But the rolling ball generates sound waves as it moves, it bounces out of the bucket and continues to roll along the floor, and so on. Why do we lose interest in the ball after it has caused the seesaw to move—why do we want to call its action upon the seesaw its *function*? There is a twofold reason, neither part of which alone would justify the term. First, the line of cause and effect that passes through the ball to the seesaw, the match, and beyond leads to a spectacular or entertaining result, whereas the later career of the ball affords only scant amusement. Second, we presume that anything so elaborate must have been invented by an agent with a purpose and a capacity for amusement like our own. The machine originated in a purposive context; its inventor must have put the ball in the machine *in order* to move the seesaw.

Mitosis is an even more complex chain of cause and effect, and one that branches out at many points as well. Every branch but one fails to grip our attention, and that one seems almost miraculous. So the first reason for ascribing functions to the parts of a Goldbergian machine applies even more strongly to reproduction. But does the second? Does cellular replication serve some larger, objectively identifiable purpose? If someone or something *had* put this machinery together for a purpose, replication it certainly would have been. But at this point our intellect loses its grip on our instincts. Intellect follows Darwin, who has shown us how this machinery could have been assembled purely by the operation of blind, undirected processes. Consequently, the purposive background is missing, and teleological terms are not appropriate. But instinct sides with William Paley. We can scarcely find words to distinguish the interesting sequence of events without using language that suggests a choreographer directing the quadrille of the chromosomes; we fall into teleological language. Darwin did, too, though he disavowed any serious intent behind his use of such metaphors. So do modern biologists. But let us be clear about what they mean when they call the replication of DNA "survival" and the generation of progeny an "ultimate goal." They know better. These terms are merely convenient and colorful ways of distinguishing from all others what we consider to be the interesting thread in the causal tangle, the one that leads to an astounding result. Unlike the application of the terms "function" and "goal" in homeostasis, the application here is purely, in fact emptily, metaphorical.

Cyberneticism distinguishes just where a clarifying line should be drawn. Univocal selectionism does not. We need the line, for we speak too readily of evolution in teleological terms. Because careful management of stud farms, the most assiduous selecting, and infinite patience would be required of generations of animal breeders in order to convert *Eohippus* according to prescription into the modern zebra, we easily forget that Nature did the job with its eyes closed. Individual cats, cockroaches, or earthworms are indubitably goal-seeking, end-directed systems; must not, therefore, the system that produced them be at least as teleological as they? How could purpose grow out of unpurpose? In those questions lie the seeds of the argument from design and the romantic view of nature. But the central achievement of Darwinism is to show how just such a thing can happen mechanically. Individuals with their eyes on the future can be constructed by a process utterly blind.

The selectionist conjecture fails to do justice to teleology at either end of the scale. Human selecting is purposive only when incorporated into an effort to achieve a goal, and the "selection" done by nature on evolving species is not teleological at all. But with cybernetical concepts we have constructed a thoroughly mechanistic, hence reductive, explication that accommodates all teleology, from human purposes to means–end relations in the simplest living things. To be sure, the arguments I have presented do no more than establish the plausibility of this claim. The promise of the cybernetical program can be fulfilled only by scientists working at all levels in the hierarchy of teleological systems. But arguments for plausibility will carry us a long way as we try to evaluate the world view of atomistic reductionism.

Is it reasonable to believe that a human being is nothing more than an especially complicated example of what cells (or genes, or atoms) can do when they fall together in a certain way? The fact that humans entertain purposes, make deliberate choices, and pursue goals gives us in itself no grounds for rejecting the proposal.

SEVEN

# Nonreductive Physicalism

THE STANDARD REDUCTIONIST POSITION CLAIMS THAT theories that treat composite things as the actors in the cosmic drama can be justified only by their relative manageability, not by their fidelity to facts. But if such theories could be justified on grounds more solid than that of mere convenience, the entities they pick out might be rescued from obsolescence. The modifications introduced by Jerry Fodor (1975) to our understanding of reductionism and the related suggestions of Karl R. Popper (1972), of Michael Polanyi (1968), and of Donald T. Campbell (1974*b*) are interesting in their own right, because they reveal complexities in the program of theory reduction. However, I intend to examine them strictly in order to see whether they can help us restore a measure of ontological respectability to the objects of common sense, organisms especially.

Their strategy commands our attention because of its audacity: They concede to the atomist program more than seems possible without also surrendering unconditionally; yet they claim to establish an autonomy for the upper-level sciences and their designated causal agents. Taking a stand deep in territory usually thought to be held by reductionism, these theories maintain that certain mechanisms, though composed of nothing but material parts, nevertheless refuse to be reduced to their level.

As a matter of strategy I defer consideration of more radical proposals, scrutinizing first those lines of defense that leave the general program of scientific materialism untouched. The theories I wish to examine here deserve attention because they do not challenge the materialist program, yet they hold out the promise of mitigating considerations. Let us turn first to Fodor's analysis of the relations between the special sciences and physics.

## TOKEN PHYSICALISM

Scientific laws and theories make generalizations about kinds or types of entity. A natural kind, according to Fodor, is a set of objects which are "tokens" (individual examples) of a type that figures in a scientific theory. The theories generalize by grouping together things, events, or processes that share some characteristic property. Each science, to the extent that it produces lawlike generalizations and not mere catalogs of facts, recognizes and names its own natural kinds. Fodor argues that the natural kinds of psychology cannot be explicated in terms even of the natural kinds that belong to neurophysiology; hence, a fortiori, psychological kinds are irreducible to those of physics.

Fodor builds his argument on the observation that the things, situations, or processes grouped together as tokens of a single type by an upper-level or special science are often radically disparate with respect to the types that figure in lower-level theories, including the theories of physics. This position is justly called physicalism, for two reasons. First, Fodor stipulates that every token of an upper-level type exemplifies some physical type or other; yet he claims that in many interesting cases the types mentioned in upper-level theories "cross-classify" types of lower-level things (1975, p. 26). The tokens of an upper-level type cannot be characterized by a single lower-level predicate; some of the instances of a single upper-level type belong to one at the lower-level, some to another, so that they share no characterizing lower-level property. Second, Fodor stipulates that the lower-level theory may explain why each token of a lower-level type is also a token of the upper-level one, but it does not explain the upper-level generalization as a whole.

Its proponents see this analysis not just as an interesting observation about the variety and complexity of the reductionist program but also as an investment that offers to pay ontological dividends. Fodor intends to justify the special sciences by showing them to be necessary, for reasons that go beyond the merely epistemological. Unlike his own, the usual reductionistic justification of the special sciences, he says, is

> entirely epistemological. If only physical particles weren't so small (if only brains were on the outside, where one can get a look at them), then we would do physics instead of paleontology (neurology instead of psychology, psychology instead of economics, and so on down).
> [1975, p. 24]

Fodor offers a justification that goes beyond considerations of utility and brevity: "There are special sciences not because of the nature of our epistemic relation to the world, but because of the way the world is put together" (p. 24). It is clear, too, that Fodor offers his theory partly as an answer to the reductionist attack on upper-level entities; that is, as a reply to philosophers who consider psychological theories as "apt for dehypostatization" (p. 26). David Hull (1974) finds a similar disparity between the type-terms of Mendelian genetics and their lower-level counterparts in molecular genetics. And William Wimsatt (1976), who uses Hull's analysis to support his own treatment of theory reduction, also wields interlevel type disparity in defense of upper-level entities. Given this richer understanding of reduction, he says, "upper-level phenomena are seen neither to be eliminated nor to be 'analyzed away'" (p. 13).

Fodor's "token physicalism" may be summarized in the following five theses:

> 1. Every specific instance of a real thing or process is thoroughly physical; that is, nothing happens in any process that is not compatible with basic physical law or not in principle predictable by means of these laws from antecedent physical conditions.
>
> 2. Nevertheless, there exist upper-level laws, such as the generalizations of biology, psychology, and economics. These laws refer to types of entity and process that "cross-classify" physical types. That

is, some upper-level laws pick out and group together into types certain sets of thoroughly physical things that share no characterizing physical property. These sets constitute biological or psychological or economic types but not physical types.

3. The upper-level laws and generalizations are not special cases of lower-level laws or approximations to them. Thus, the upper-level laws cannot be translated into statements and generalizations cast in lower-level language. To be sure, each specific occurrence covered by the upper-level law is also explained by some lower-level law or other. But the many instances of the single upper-level law are covered by many different lower-level laws.

4. Yet the regularities expressed by the upper-level laws are there in the phenomena. Not to notice them is to miss something objectively true about the world. A complete description will, therefore, include these generalizations and thus will refer to upper-level types of entity.

5. Because the term for an upper-level kind cannot be translated into any finite set of terms for lower-level kinds, we must admit that the exemplars of the upper-level kinds contribute to causal activity with just as much ontological respectability as do the tokens of the lower level. For example, we must say that condominant gene pairs, states of cognition, and monetary systems are just as irreducibly real as electrons, protons, and neutrons. In short, our talk about human beings and other commonsense objects cannot be "dehypostatized."

What qualifies as a lower-level kind? On this point, Fodor makes an impossible demand on the lower-level account by specifying that the lower-level kind must be a *natural* kind at that level; that is, it must figure in a proper law at the lower level (1975, p. 16, 25). This requirement is unreasonable because we distinguish levels according to the part–whole relation; lower-level laws qualify as such because they refer to the parts of upper-level things. Therefore, a natural kind at the lower level must necessarily be only a part of an upper-level thing. According to this requirement, no lower-level kind could possibly be coextensive with an upper-level kind, and Fodor's thesis would be trivially true. A more reasonable criterion of what counts as a lower-level kind is this: It must be characterizable in the language of the lower level, that is, in terms of lower-level things, their arrangements and causal interactions.

Can the theories of a special science, applied to physical

things, classify them into nonphysical categories? On the face of it this question seems to demand a negative answer, for if kinds are picked out by their characteristic properties, the question would be equivalent to asking whether merely physical things can have nonphysical properties. And if something has nonphysical properties, how can it be said to be a merely physical thing? But Fodor's argument cannot be refuted so glibly, as a few simple examples will show.

The upper-level term "meteorite" classifies rocks according to a shared type of origin, a common historical setting. The term "impurity atom" (as in a semiconductor) collects its objects by virtue of their being surrounded by atoms of a different chemical kind. Is there some physical, chemical, or structural property possessed by all meteorites and only them? Possibly not. There may be rocks lying about that are in fact meteorites but are not recognizable as such because they show no trace of their history. And there is nothing about an antimony atom in itself that qualifies it as an impurity atom. Following Fodor, we can say that the kind "impurity atom" covers some but not all antimony atoms and some but not all arsenic atoms; and "meteorite" cross-classifies several physical-chemical kinds of rock.

Fodor discusses two scientifically important ways in which an upper-level type can cross-classify types of a lower level. First, he suggests that the tokens of a given psychological or biological type may share a common behavioral consequence or make the same functional contribution to the organism. What turns bimetallic strips and tubes filled with mercury into temperature sensors is the manner of their incorporation in larger systems. Second, following Hilary Putnam, Fodor suggests (1975, pp. 18 ff.) that an entire system may be characterized as a token of a psychological type by an abstract feature of the way it is connected together, by what I shall call, borrowing and stretching a term from electrical engineering, its wiring diagram. Computing machines and nervous systems may embody the same wiring diagram yet be built of quite diverse materials, ranging from gears and levers to semiconducting chips to living cells. Therefore, the members of a homogeneous organizational or structural type may be heterogeneous as to their description in terms of hardware.

I shall consider these two suggestions separately, asking about each whether the indicated mismatch between the types belonging to upper and lower levels provides a basis for the autonomy of the upper-level theory and a firm ontological footing for the things the theory names. Can token physicalism rescue the objects of commonsense experience?

My answer will arrive in two stages. First, I shall argue that the generalizations we make about objects characterized by relational properties, including the abilities to generate behavioral consequences and to perform functions, are implicit in the generalizations we make about the structural properties of the systems in which those objects play their parts. If that is so, then the second of Fodor's categories of upper-level entity swallows up the first. Next, I shall ask whether the atomist reduction program can cope with generalizations about systems characterized by their wiring diagrams. Fodor is not alone in suggesting that atomism must fail in this respect; his argument resonates with some speculations of Popper, Polanyi, and Campbell. I shall argue, in reply to all of these speculations, that generalizations of this sort are implicit in lower-level descriptions in a peculiar, though thoroughly reductionistic, way. Consequently, although we may indeed encounter disparities between types residing on different levels, the disparity does not justify enrolling the entities named by upper-level theories alongside the atoms on our roster of the world's players.

## CAUSAL CONSEQUENCES

Let us examine first a simple example that Fodor does not discuss. Catalysts and enzymes fit his category of entities that contribute to the internal economy of an organized system. Take the type of substance that can catalyze the oxidation of hydrogen. Quite likely it is impossible to specify a class of chemical types, such as ketones or Lewis bases, so that all of these and only these substances are able to catalyze the reaction.

The upper level appropriate to this example refers to chemical substances like oxygen and water as the causal agents. The lower-level theory, quantum chemistry, applies the laws of quantum mechanics to arrangements of electrons and atomic nuclei. In a reductionistic reconstruction of the world from basic physical theory, substances would be identified as catalysts by applying quantum mechanics laboriously to the theoretical model of a mixture of oxygen, hydrogen, and the prospective catalyst and finding out from the theory whether the candidate substance would catalyze the reaction. At the descriptive level of quantum chemistry, the world consists of atomic nuclei and electrons in shifting arrangements, and all the world's processes are seen as actions performed by these agents. The predicate "catalyst of the oxidation of hydrogen" does not play a role in quantum-chemical explanations, simply because quantum chemistry is concerned with individual catalysts (and noncatalysts), not with the class of catalysts as a whole.

Yet the predicate is certainly discoverable in the quantum-chemical treatment. Someone whose entire store of information about the world's affairs was conveyed in the language of quantum chemistry would be able to form generalizations about the catalysts of this reaction as well as someone whose knowledge was limited to such things as flasks and reagents. The quantum-chemical picture of the world can substitute for the world itself as inductive support for upper-level generalizations. We have, therefore, no reason to think that the lower-level theory leaves out facts that are expressible only in upper-level language. Besides, only quantum chemistry, which treats electrons and nuclei as the causal agents, can explain the catalyzing action; hence, quantum chemistry lies closer to the truth about this portion of the world than does any upper-level theory that treats chemical compounds as causal agents and leaves their interactions unexplained.

Catalysis has all the interesting features of Fodor's analysis of theory reduction. There appears to be a complete mismatch between the upper-level type, the catalysts of the reaction, and the various categories of chemical species. The example also illustrates Fodor's observation that the lower-level theory explains in each specific instance why a chemical substance is or is not a catalyst of the reaction. Yet the lower-level theory unquestionably approaches more nearly to the truth. Catalysis is a counterexample to the claim that the disparity between types at upper and lower levels protects the upper level from reduction to the lower.

## PROPERTIES OF GENES

Arrangements of nuclei and electrons that can catalyze a given reaction are characterized by their potential consequences, by what might ensue if they were incorporated into a given context. In contrast, the Mendelian predicates Hull (1974) discusses are contextual predicates that refer to actual consequences. Hull suggests that no correspondence can be established between certain Mendelian predicates and predicates for kinds of molecular mechanism unless one correlates the Mendelian term "with the entire molecular milieu" (p. 42). This expedient produces such a far-reaching reorganization of Mendelian concepts that what was intended to be reduction becomes replacement. Wimsatt (1976), however, insists that we have here a fairly typical case of interlevel reduction, an example in biology of Taylor's and Fodor's suggestions that upper-level types have no neat correspondence with lower-level types, hence that generalizations employing these recalcitrant predicates cannot be replaced by translating them into the language of the lower level.

Let us take a closer look at this argument. Mendelian genetics, because it deals with macroscopic phenomena, refers to genes as hypothetical bodies characterized by their effects in the phenotype. But definitions of the form "*x* is the agent that produces effect *E* in system *S*" are wildly open-ended. The definition carries no guarantee that *x* will lie on the same level of complexity as *S* or *E*, and there is little reason to expect that the various agents that in fact produce a given kind of effect will have enough structural similarity to be distinguished by a common intrinsic character. Similar effects do not necessarily result from similar causes.

Perhaps the early geneticists who worked with the concept of dominance as a relation between genes hoped, first, to characterize those hypothetical bodies and, second, to find that dominance was a matter of direct causal action of gene upon gene. But, if so, surprises were forthcoming in both endeavors. The gene turned out to be molecular in size, breaking through the neat separation between phenomena at different levels of organization. And dominance proved to be not at all the direct action of one gene upon another but the ultimate outcome of an exceedingly complex molecular process. One might once have said that gene *A* dominated over gene *a*, but now we say, for example, that the phenotypic effects of *a* are not noticeable in the presence of those of *A*. The story of gene transcription, activation, and suppression is long and complicated and must be told at the molecular level.

The contrast between thermodynamics as an upper-level theory and Mendelian genetics as a putative upper-level theory is instructive. In both cases the early workers expected a microreduction to be possible, but only in thermodynamics was it possible to restrict the theory to the upper level, that is, to develop generalizations that quantified over macroscopic bodies only. Temperature was defined by its (potential) effects, with no assurance it would turn out to be a property of whole bodies, though it did turn out to be so. The risk was greater in genetics because not just a property but a causal entity, the gene, was defined in terms of its macroscopic effects. Later developments showed it to be a microscopic entity. Thus, the hope (if anyone ever did hope) that Mendelian genetics might be self-contained on the macroscopic level came to naught; because the gene is a molecular entity, any genetic theory that refers to genes inevitably resides on the molecular level. In fact, molecules, and something like the idea of macromolecules, began to occupy the thinking of evolutionists at a very early stage. Hugo De Vries (1889; 1910) speculates that

> The visible phenomena of heredity are . . . the expressions of the characters of minutest invisible particles. . . . These pangens . . . [are] of quite another order than the chemical molecules . . . [yet are] composed of innumerable such molecules.
> [P. 194]

And Darwin (1890), on the nature of his hypothetical carriers of inheritance, suggests that "probably many molecules go to the formation of a gemmule" (pp. 374–75).

Replying to the antireductive arguments of Hull (1974) and Ruse (1973), William K. Goosens (1978) argues persuasively that the program of genetical theory allowed from the beginning that the gene might have a chemical structure governed by the laws of physical chemistry. For this reason, the relation between molecular and Mendelian genetics cannot be viewed as interlevel reduction. Goosens terms the reduction "whole-part reduction" (p. 91). Thermodynamics applies only to macroscopic bodies, and statistical mechanics deals with their microscopic parts; thus, statistical mechanics is appropriately situated vis-à-vis thermodynamics to be its reducing theory. But molecular and Mendelian genetics both recount the activities of (macro)molecules;

hence, they cannot stand in the relation of lower- and upper-level theories. Molecular genetics is not a microreducing theory for Mendelian; it is, rather, the natural development of Mendelian genetics as it was transformed from a theory with one foot unintentionally at each level to one that stands squarely on the lower one.

## LAWLIKE GENERALIZATIONS

The scientifically significant upper-level predicates are those that we can employ in expressing general theories and laws. Let us consider three sorts of lawlike statements: generalizations about objects defined by their spatial and causal connections, about parts defined by their functions in a goal-directed system, and about whole systems characterized by their wiring diagrams.

SPATIAL AND CAUSAL CONTEXTS. The spatial setting and causal connections of a part of a larger system do not disappear from the story as we descend to lower levels of description. Spatial relations remain without change, and causal interactions that may appear mysterious at the upper level begin to lose their mystery as the lower-level narrative introduces the microscopic mechanisms that establish the connections. Therefore, reducing a description of a contextually defined individual object presents no problem to the atomist program.

Generalizations about such objects, however, require some attention. I submit that interesting and projectable generalizations about things designated by their spatial-causal setting are grounded on the lawlike character of the entire setting. Let me support this claim by adapting a stock example.

The generalization "All the objects now residing in my pocket are made of nickel" will not support the counterfactual "If *x* were in my pocket now it would be made of nickel." Yet the generalizations "All the objects now residing in my pocket are traveling north at 20 km/h" and "All the objects now residing in my pocket have volumes less than 600 cubic centimeters" do support the corresponding counterfactuals, simply because my pocket (along with the rest of my person) is traveling north at that speed and because my pocket has a volume less than that amount. Counterfactuals like these are supported, if at all, because of some background facts about the context and the principles that govern them.

In each case there is a reason why the generalization holds. It is a condensed version of a more complete story, which when fully told will be found to refer to the whole contextual situation. The generalization, therefore, applies to a class or type of system, defined by its pattern of organization. Such a generalization will be reducible if the pattern is.

FUNCTIONAL CONTEXTS. Next, consider entities defined by their functional contribution to an organism. Insofar as the contribution is a causal consequence, this category merges with the one just considered. But, as I have argued in chapters 5 and 6, ascriptions of functions imply that the system containing the functioning part is organized in a goal-directed way, either as a simple feedback system or as a nested hierarchy of them. Composite systems such as organisms and automatons are characterized by the patterns in which they are organized. Reducing lawlike generalizations about functional parts, then, requires the reduction of descriptions that characterize systems in terms of their organizational patterns. We have seen how to do that for the special case of goal-directed mechanisms. Let us look at the task more generally.

ORGANIZATIONAL PATTERNS. Scientists of all sorts, though initially concerned with how certain objects happen to be put together, eventually broaden their investigation to include abstract patterns of connections. They do so because much of the behavior of the objects they study can be understood by reference to their wiring diagrams, without regard to the particular material realization of them that in fact obtains. A hydrodynamicist studying the action of wind on the surface of water finds that the wave motion can be explained by reference merely to certain abstract features of the composition and structure of liquid water and that these features, represented by a differential equation, are shared by a wide variety of other media. Wave motion in general becomes an attractive field of study.

To the extent that biologists and psychologists merely catalog the behavior of insects and people, or merely discover how these things happen in fact to be put together, their generalizations about Hymenoptera or *Homo sapiens* are not projectable to life in other regions of the universe and are not meant to be (Smart 1963). If their scientific activity is limited to such cataloging, there is no question of reducing their laws to physics, because they produce no laws.

But they do more. Their interest in patterns of connections leads them to distinguish *kinds* of system characterized by their wiring diagrams. In this way biologists and psychologists make generalizations that are projectable, just as physicists do who theorize about wave motion. If a psychological state in humans is characterized by the way the parts of the organism are put together, without regard to the inner structure of those parts, then what we say about such a state can be applied to robots whose transistors and switches have been wired according to the same diagram.

A law associating properties or behaviors with a wiring diagram explains them without mentioning the detailed connections by which the diagram is realized. This kind of explanation floats freely above the level of the parts. How, then, can we obtain it from a description framed at the lower level? In chapter 4 we saw how to solve this problem. There we produced a prescription for discerning the presence of the feedback pattern in a lower-level description of a system. I submit that the explication of feedback serves as a model for the general task of reducing patterns of causal connections.

I have examined Fodor's analysis from a narrow perspective, conceding that it points out a significant complexity in the program of theory reduction but questioning whether it makes good its claim to rescue organisms and other mechanisms from losing their standing as causal agents by default to their parts. The lower-level account explains each specific instance of an upper-level law. This fact, conceded by Fodor to be a general feature of token physicalism, proves generally fatal to the attempt to mitigate reductionism by showing the upper level of description to be irreplaceable. Each specific instance is allowed to be nothing more than an arrangement of particles, and the causal connections in each instance are explained only by reference to them. Hence, the particles, not the tokens of the upper-level type, perform the causal activity. In order for Fodor's theory to work as a defense against the atomist attack described in chapter 1, it would have to provide a reason for treating individual composite things, not merely classes or types of them, as causal agents. But it fails at this point, because it must allow the lower-level theory to be nearer the truth in every individual case.

## SIMILAR CONJECTURES: POLANYI, POPPER, AND CAMPBELL

Fodor is not alone in suggesting that references to wiring diagrams in our upper-level descriptions protect them from attack by reductionistic analysis. Michael Polanyi (1968) presents an independent argument for the irreducibility of composite systems characterized by their patterns of organization (in Polanyi's terminology, their boundary conditions or, simply, their boundaries). Any wiring diagram is "extraneous to the process it delimits." Of machines he says, "Their structure cannot be defined in terms of the laws they harness" (p. 1309). And Polanyi makes the same claim about the structures of living organisms. Nevertheless, he concedes, this observation by itself does not show machines and organisms to be irreducible to physics.

Polanyi distinguishes two sorts of boundary conditions. The first is typified by the shape impressed by a saucepan on the soup it contains and by the arrangements of particles studied in geology and astronomy. This sort, he concedes, can be reduced to physics. Of the other sort, such as the patterns of connections in machines and in living organisms, he claims irreducibility.

Does the distinction capture an objective difference? Polanyi seems to give two answers to that question. At one point he says that the nature of our interest in the system determines whether the pattern is of one sort or the other. If we are interested in the material, we have the first sort; if in the shape or structure impressed upon the material, the second. In the kitchen we care about the soup, not the saucepan; but in a sculptor's studio interest focuses on the shape, not on the marble itself. Polanyi is quite definite about it: "By shifting our attention, we may sometimes change a boundary from one type to another" (1968, p. 1308).

Robert Causey (1969) has turned this account of boundary conditions decisively against Polanyi's main argument. If the first kind of boundary can be reduced, and if the second kind may be made over into the first merely by thinking differently about it, Causey argues, then both sorts are reducible.

However, Polanyi's second way of distinguishing the two sorts of boundary escapes this criticism. At another point in his essay he says that organisms and machines are systems "under dual control" (1968, p. 1309). "Can the control of morphogenesis by DNA be likened to the designing and shaping of a machine by an engineer?" he asks, and answers yes, because DNA "acts as a blueprint." So what distinguishes the irreducible sort of wiring diagram is its having been impressed on its material by some organizing agent. In machines the ultimate active principle is the human mind: "The mind harnesses neurological mechanisms and is not determined by them" (p. 1312). But in living organisms there is a hierarchy of active principles, "each level of which relies for its workings on the principles of the levels below it, even while it itself is irreducible to those lower principles" (p. 1310). The "blueprint" action of DNA is one of these principles, but above it lies "a system of causes not specified in terms of physics and chemistry, such causes being additional both to the boundary conditions of DNA and to the morphological structure brought about by DNA" (p. 1310). As an example of one of these higher causes, Polanyi cites the "integrative power . . . which guides the growth of embryonic fragments to form the morphological features to which they embryologically belong" (p. 1310).

Polanyi's suggestion that processes at a given level are controlled by organizing principles at higher levels seems to echo an idea expressed earlier by Karl R. Popper in his Compton Lecture of 1965, published later in *Objective Knowledge* (1972). Popper is concerned not directly with the question of the reducibility of natural laws but with the freedom of human reason and will; yet, like Polanyi, he argues that higher principles control lower-level processes. Popper sees in organisms "a hierarchical system of plastic controls" in which the lower functions "are constrained and controlled by the higher ones" (p. 245).

Donald T. Campbell (1974*b*) advances a similar argument in the context of the theory of natural selection. Campbell identifies himself as a reductionist; yet he warns against a simplistic reductionism. He argues that a complete explanation of biological systems cannot be accomplished by physics and chemistry alone but "will often require reference to laws at a higher level of organization as well." Campbell terms this action of higher-level principles upon the processes of lower levels "downward causation"; by this he means "causation by a selective process which edits the products of direct physical causation" (p. 180).

These examples of human activity seem to demonstrate the patterning of raw materials by a patterned causal agent. Nonhuman examples may also be found: The feet of birds leave their impressions on the damp sand of a beach, and a seed crystal causes a saturated solution to copy its ordered structure in the process of crystallization. Something like the Aristotelian idea of formal cause seems to be appropriate here, as a useful and enlightening supplement to our account of events in terms of efficient causes. But at issue is the adequacy in principle of an explanatory scheme based solely on efficient causes.

This talk of controlling, harnessing, and editing derives its intuitive appeal from a picture of engineers assembling materials according to the preexisting design of a blueprint, of sculptors making their materials conform to an idea previously conceived in the imagination, and of publishers applying literary standards to hapless manuscripts. But the analogy, though attractive, is surely false.

Systems composed of many parts necessarily display some pattern or other—even the stars are grouped in triangles, Latin crosses, half-circles, and so on. But nowhere in nature do we find a pattern that arises other than as the outcome of the actions of the particles carrying on their small affairs according to their individual natures. Even negative feedback, a pattern characteristic of both living systems and machines, can be found in the lower-level description of an organism or machine and its context, as I have shown in chapter 4. Moreover, as I have argued in chapters 5 and 6, natural selection lacks an essential feature needed to make it analogous to an editing process.

But Polanyi, Popper, and Campbell have criticized mechanism at its weakest point, for there is a certain question that no mechanist theory can answer, even in principle. Consider the strongest mechanical theory, Newtonian mechanics.

The laws of mechanics are laws of development. In the mechanical philosophy of Newton and Laplace, the world's state at one time completely determines its states at all other times, past and future. Therefore, in principle, the entire history of the universe may be read out of its present condition, given the basic mechanical laws. Nevertheless, even in this tightly connected universe an indelible mystery remains. At some point any explanation of the world must assume some arbitrary facts, namely, the state of the world at some definite moment. Such starting assumptions are usually called initial conditions, and they are one example of what Polanyi refers to by "boundary conditions." There is no explanation for such facts. Even in a Laplacean universe a large measure of arbitrariness permeates the foundations. The world is the way it is today because of the way it was yesterday, but why were yesterday's conditions as they were? Because an infinite number of world trajectories are possible, the question remains, Why this one? An explanation by means of efficient causation, therefore, leaves much unaccounted for. For this reason, an explanation employing formal causation seems to fill a need. The marvelous and puzzling structures in the actual world, we feel, might be explainable by patterning agents impressing their forms on passive matter.

But the mechanistic explanatory scheme based solely on efficient causation needs no such help, or at least not yet. Clearly, its work will remain far from complete, but we can catch a glimpse of what sort of answer to expect in the work of Ilya Prigogine and his collaborators on dissipative structures (Glansdorff and Prigogine 1971). As they have shown, a mixture of chemicals, formed by pouring various solutions into a container without any additional constraints on initial and boundary conditions, may sort itself out and begin to act as a rudimentary feedback system (see the discussion of the Zhabotinsky reaction in the appendix of Faber 1984). Making an optimistic extrapolation from their work, we may expect eventually to be able to understand how the complex networks of cybernetic systems that characterize life could arise out of the dissipative processes present in the prebiotic earth. The extraordinary phenomenon of life will then be understood as the consequence of any one among a wide range of initial conditions that are themselves quite ordinary. If this reductionistic program should be successful, it would still be possible to retort that a physical-chemical explanation of life is merely an explanation of today's boundary conditions by reference to yesterday's, which remain unexplained. Nevertheless, the antireductionistic thrust of that reply would be effectively parried if today's conditions, because of their remarkable complexity, demand an explanation; and yesterday's, being unremarkable, call for none.

Popper, Polanyi, and Campbell, though their arguments differ in many respects, seem to agree that a physical-chemical explanation of life is incomplete *as a causal explanation*. "Control," "editing," and "downward causation" all convey the flavor of causal factors that supplement the ordinary causation of physics and that must be adduced as additional explanatory principles if we are to give an adequate causal explanation of the phenomenon of life. But physics/chemistry is eminently successful at what it sets out to do; namely, to trace the present, by means of laws of development, from the past. Prigogine's program has a good prospect of success.

EIGHT

# Mental Events in Prequantal Atomism

## RADICAL ANTIREDUCTIONISM

IN THE PRECEDING CHAPTERS I HAVE CRITICIZED ONtologically conservative remedies to mechanistic reductionism. Against the claim that the objective picture of the world produced by science is just one of many socially conditioned ways of constructing a "world," I have urged that the disinterested stance of science is a privileged one for the task of understanding things as they are in themselves, on their own terms. True, the scientific way of relating ourselves to matter is one of several possible attitudes toward things. Technological exploitation is another, and more popular at that. But scientific objectivity is just as much to be preferred for this task as is the posture that anthropologists recommend for understanding another culture: We must resist the temptation to incorporate the object of study into our own economy, values, or concepts. We must concede to it its own internal economy, its nature, which it is our task humbly and respectfully to inquire into.

And diagnoses of weakness in the atomistic program, of inability to wrestle with the complexity of living organisms, likewise fail to produce a cure. Against the assertion of an irreducibly hierarchical structure in our theories and in nature itself, I have urged that none of this complexity refutes the reductionist thesis that living things are determined by, without in any sense determining in return, the natures and activities of their atomic parts.

I want to suggest that these proposals have not located the center of the disease. They prescribe for specific parts of reductive science, but none is designed to strengthen the metaphysical frame on which we flesh out the atomistic story.

In this and the following chapters I shall offer a remedy based on another diagnosis—of a metaphysical ailment. I shall defend the thesis that reductionism's general picture of the world suffers from a pinched ontology, whose restrictive influence can be felt in several vital areas. Getting an adequate inventory of the kinds of things that carry out the activities that occur in the world must be our first order of business as we search for a reply to reductionism. Ontology holds the solution because by formulating it we stipulate what we are willing to recognize as real. The recognition extends both to the things that act and to the activities they perform: Not even the most whimsical of mathematicians could imagine how the Cheshire cat's grinning could continue without the cat being there to do it. Suppose that someone claims to have discovered a new phenomenon—a deviation of the motion of a planet from Kepler's laws, say, or extrasensory mental powers. Unless we have an ontological framework on which to hang the alleged novelty, we will be reluctant to accept the claim at face value. Without a picture of the world that allows room for additional astronomical bodies, or that offers a hint as to what agents might carry knowledge to the brain without going through the senses, we will prefer to try to explain away the new alleged phenomenon in terms of a tried and trusted ontology.

Science has a generally trustworthy way to make sense of new phenomena, but it also imposes limits on the imagination. In the standard protocol, an explanation must be composed in terms of material particles and their causal interactions. Even if the evidence for astrology were much stronger than it is, the scientifically proper attitude toward it would be one of skepticism unless we could plausibly propose a mechanism by which the planets exert unique influences on individual human lives. Without such a hypothesis, responsible scientists would look for flaws in the evidence or try to find another interpretation of it. Similarly, depending on what metaphysical system we employ, we may or may not be able to concede that moral and aesthetic judgments or mystical experiences make contact with reality. Limited by an ontology of atomistic materialism, we are obliged to account in mechanistic terms for ethics, aesthetics, and religion. We must say, for example, that such experiences are nothing more than the workings of neurological mechanisms hard-wired into the central nervous system by natural selection or programmed into it by school and family. With a more elaborate metaphysics, however, more realistic appreciations of these matters become possible; they need not be explained away.

Some have sought to defend the validity of mystical or aesthetic experience by recommending a more flexible epistemological stance, claiming that scientific objectivity is only one of several complementary ways of knowing the world. But this epistemological diagnosis cannot stand by itself. It needs ontological support. If the world must indeed be approached in ways that supplement scientific objectivity, then the other approaches are needed because of the nature of the world itself, because of the variety and complexity of the things that are to be known.

Physics is a metaphysically laden enterprise. It applies the ontological program of atomism to the broadest possible range of experience. Metaphysical programs, the highest of all high-level heuristics for research, are not tested by crucial experiments; they stand or fall with the progression or degeneration of their broad prescriptions for making sense of our experiences. Hence, the success of atomistic science, especially in molecular biology, reflects favorably upon the atomistic ontology. By the same token, if atomistic attempts to explain important features of experience should fail, then suspicion would settle upon the mechanist philosophy.

The ontological program of particle physics formalizes a universal activity that grows as we deepen our understanding of the world. Early in life we become conscious of ourselves as individual beings, distinct from other existing things even as we interact with them. All these things have their own existences, independently of one another, even though causally they are interdependent. Partly by contrast with our experience of other persons, we learn of the equally independent (though causally interconnected) existence of still other things, which are not persons. Material, nonpersonal beings also become the objects of our attempts to understand. Ultimately, in physics we extend our attempt to reach behind our subjective experiences to the things that underlie them and cause them. Other persons exist, certainly, but also, we speculate, some material, nonpersonal entities. We have found that these exist in large number; we call them particles. The reaching behind experience is not done experientially. We do not experience persons as we do smells or sounds, and we do not experience atoms sensuously, either. The reaching is done intellectually. It is a grasping performed, hypothetically and tentatively, by speculative reasoning. The successes of atomism have impressed reductionistic thinkers so strongly that many are willing to look for particles behind even our experiences of persons. Indeed, atomism *requires* a reduction of personhood along such lines. A strong case can be made for it, and I have tried to do it justice in the preceding chapters.

However, I shall attempt no appraisal of ethical, religious, and aesthetic judgments here. Alternatives to the reductionistic treatment of those topics can be entertained only grudgingly unless the ontology of atomism is shown to be faulty. Therefore, I shall skirt those important but tangled areas and concentrate on just two portions of the mechanist world picture that connect closely with current scientific theorizing. Not everyone has been visited by a numinous experience, but everyone has conscious experiences of the ordinary, sensory kind. And, although many entertain doubts about the objective validity of ethical judgments, the scientific community places much confidence in quantum mechanics, the currently accepted universal mechanical theory. I shall argue that the phenomena of consciousness and the puzzles surrounding what is called the measurement problem in quantum mechanics both reveal the inadequacy of an ontology of material particles alone; both pose problems that can be resolved by enlarging our inventory of the world's furniture to include minds as well as particles.

Episodes of consciousness are like the Cheshire cat's grin:

Something must be doing them. Traditional dualism says they are done by minds. Atomism says that nothing occurs that is not carried out by material particles. In this chapter I shall argue that, little as we yet know about the material substrate of sensory episodes, we already know enough to conclude that no portion of the human anatomy performs them: Atomistic materialism has banished the "cat." Therefore, we must choose either to deny the grinning or to take up dualism and recall the cat. In chapters 9 and 10 I shall show that quantum mechanics reveals a causal activity for which atomistic materialism can name no agent. Again, dualism promotes a likely candidate. Such an eminently dubitable metaphysical platform requires more than one prop. Without support from atomistic science the intuition-based argument of this chapter would seem inconclusive; and, in the absence of a prior skepticism about the physicalist theory of mind, enlisting dualism to make sense of the quantum theory would look like bringing in a *mens ex machina*; but, taken together, the two arguments complement each other.

But would a dualistic cure be worse than the reductionistic disease? Many philosophers of mind would say so. Certainly, dualism introduces many puzzles of its own. Without slighting them, I shall suggest in the final chapter how we might learn to live with the new problems while enjoying the curative effects of a more generous ontology.

## THE GRAIN OBJECTION

To prepare the way for an extended discussion of the interpretative problems presented by the quantum theory, I shall first establish a connection between the atomist view of the nature of things and the claims of Cartesian dualism. The case I shall present pivots on a discrepancy between what we know about mental events by direct introspection and what atomism reveals of the essential features of any brain process. The argument is, I believe, the same in essence as one proposed by Paul E. Meehl (1966) and criticized by Michael B. Green (1979). It differs in detail and manner of exposition, however, in that it makes full use of the reductive claims of atomism as to the formal structure of any process that occurs in a composite thing.

I agree with Green's observation that the mere fact of sentience casts suspicion on the thesis of mind–brain identity and, indeed, on the entire atomistic world picture that requires us to postulate the identity. Monistic materialism chokes on sentience because there is no room for it in the atomist picture. Other puzzling phenomena do not embarrass atomism: Why do living things exist? Why does the goldfinch's bill have its peculiar shape? How do displaced pets find their way home over unfamiliar territory? Puzzling though they are or have been, atomism has a plausible story to tell about these questions, or at least a plausible prescription for the *sort* of story one hopes eventually to tell or would be able to tell with superhumanly detailed knowledge. But there is another class of alleged or imaginable phenomena for which atomism cannot produce a plausible prescription for an understanding, for example, alleged cases of precognition or of telekinesis. And because we cannot even imagine an atomistic account of such things, we quite properly doubt their existence. Sentience falls into this second category. No one has proposed, no one can imagine a story, no matter how speculative, that would be recognizable as an atomistic account of sentience. How, for example, did it first arise? Because the primordial soup certainly did not and bacteria probably do not sustain conscious episodes, and we do, the ability to undergo or generate the kind of episode typified by sensory experiences, according to materialism, must gradually have arisen during the course of evolution. Hence, an acceptable explanation of how such an extraordinary thing could come to exist in the animal kingdom must conform to the standards of evolutionary theory. But natural selection can pick out only life-preserving or reproduction-promoting features, and sentience offers nothing of the sort. Unconscious automatons with nervous systems as complex as our own would perform as well in the struggle for survival. We might speculate that sentience is an incidental but physically necessary side effect of some other feature that does promote survival—the most likely candidate being the ability to behave intelligently. But that conjecture seems most unlikely, because most of what goes on in the brain occurs without any hint of consciousness, even some intricate examples of intelligence. Tales abound of mathematical or scientific problems solved by the sleeping brain, the answer delivered whole and polished to consciousness in the morning. The solution to a chess problem or an anagram may spring suddenly into the conscious mind, obviously having been worked out by intelligent but nonconscious mechanisms. C. S. Forester (1964, pp. 65, 66) tells of elaborate portions of the plots of his novels being presented to consciousness by such hidden factories. Clearly, the mechanical brain can handle mathematical, logical, and creative tasks without the aid of consciousness; what biological function, then, can it have? Why should not every brain process, from the least to the most intelligent, proceed equally mechanically? Indeed, considering the extreme youth of brain science, we have little reason to doubt that plain neuronal mechanisms, not varnished over with sentience, can account quite well for the overt behavior we see in other persons. How, then, could sentience have come to exist in the course of evolution? And how could that ghostly hanger-on have given to the survival-promoting behavior of the animal an extra feature that natural selection could have laid hold of? Yet there sentience is—a reproach to the Democritean ontology. All we can do is gesture vaguely toward the youthful science of neurophysiology and voice the pious hope that something will turn up.

Although considerations such as these fuel skepticism about the identity thesis, they can do no more than prompt us to seek a definitive argument. Green doubts the possibility of formulating a convincing rebuttal of the identity thesis based on Leibniz's principle. Such a rebuttal would establish a clear discordance between the known properties of a typical mental episode and those of any cerebral process with which it might plausibly be identified.

Green presents a sympathetic outline of what he dubs "the grain objection" to the mind–brain identity thesis but finally rejects the objection on the grounds that "intersubjective structure, though mind-independent, does not have a perspective-free focus which permits it to be declared either 'grainy' or 'smooth' *tout court*" (1979, p. 586). Now, I think this skepticism is unjustified. Green seems to assume that our various scientific and commonsense levels of description are quite arbitrarily chosen, that the macroscopic overview we may take toward a composite thing, in which we lose sight of its atomic constitution, is neither less nor more faithful to the way things are than a microscopic description. Both, as Green seems to evaluate them, are merely "perspectives" that we adopt for one reason or another. Such an egalitarian assessment of these modes of description might be justified if each brought to light some facts that the other obscured, if each were merely a partial account of the nature of things that needs to be supplemented by the other. I have criticized that sort of laminar relativism in my discussion of Ryle's defense of the language of common sense against the claims of atomic physics. There I argued that the atomistic, lower-level description in principle obscures nothing, hence always legitimately claims greater in-principle fidelity to objective truth than any upper-level account can boast. The subsequent discussion of functionalism was designed to make good that reductionistic claim for an especially challenging example of upper-level discourse. According to the atomist reduction program, there is somewhere, waiting to be found, a perspective-free account of the way things are. In fact, to deny the possibility of such a description (denying that we can be sure that we have finally achieved it is, of course, quite another matter) is to renounce the program of objective science. Having argued for this understanding of the scientific program above, I shall simply assert here that I take the aim of fundamental science to be an understanding of material things that accepts them on their own terms, not bending them to particular designs we may have on them, not treating them as adjuncts of our own concerns, not viewing them from this or that subjective and limited perspective, but accepting them as they go about their own affairs largely heedless of ourselves, as they also moved and interacted before human beings strode onto the world's stage. Green's criticisms of the grain objection are not fatal ones.

In fact, the objection is especially appropriate to this discussion of atomistic reduction. I shall, therefore, present a version of the argument but with several alterations I consider essential for clarity and effectiveness.

## RESTRICTIONS ON THE ARGUMENT

OTHER MINDS. Considering its unique topic, it should not be surprising that the argument presents several unusual features and raises some peculiar difficulties of exposition. Three distracting issues must be separated from the one at hand. First, there is the question of whether we can know that other minds exist. The answer is trivially *yes*, if we have already established that minds are identical to brains, but otherwise the answer is not so obvious. So we must pose the question of mind–brain identity in a way that does not assume such an easy answer to the question of other minds—otherwise, we would beg the question at issue here. Let us assume no more than is held in common by the competing theories about other minds. However much they may disagree about the possibility of access by other persons, the competitors both assume that the person has access to his own mental episode. Hence, we get this decidedly peculiar feature of the grain objection: It must be addressed personally to the reader; I must ask you to consider your own mental episode. Because at this stage we cannot fairly speculate about the experiences of a third party, each person must apply the argument to his or her own experience.

TOPIC NEUTRALITY. The grain objection cannot be stated without rejecting J. J. C. Smart's (1962) proposal to cast the question in "topic-neutral" language. Smart invites us to treat a mental event as whatever goes on in ourselves (we know not what it is) that is causally responsible for pain behavior, verbal reports of an inner state, and other manifestations of mentality, including overt behavior and covert tendencies to behave. If we should accept this invitation, we would have to locate mentality within the network of physical causes, for those hidden springs of human actions are likely to be revealed by neurological experiments as firings of nerve cells. And Smart asks more than that. In his view, one mental event can be compared to another only by our noting differences and similarities in the verbal and other expressions they impel us to make. Expressing all that we know about a mental event, one would say, in topic-neutral language, "Something is going on in me that is like what is going on when I look at McIntosh apples, blood, a sunset, and so on. How do I know that it's like those other goings-on? I find myself responding in the same way." If that is the only sort of access we have, then as owners of mental processes we know no more about them than what we hear ourselves saying in audible utterance or internal monolog; hence, we are in essentially the same epistemological position as is an external observer to pronounce on what they are like. For the owner, too, mental events are then the hidden causes of overt behavior or tendencies to behave, events to which he has only indirect, inferential access. However, the grain objection stipulates that the owner has knowledge that supplements what is obtained by the clinical psychologist or the physicist. Is that a plausible assumption? Here the reader must decide for himself or herself. Speaking for myself, I find that the experience of redness is both well known and peculiar, quite unlike the unique experience of yellowness or of a toothache, and that all of them are richer than my verbal utterances have ever indicated. I do indeed know what the smell of nitrobenzene is like, independently of the comparisons I hear myself drawing between it and other experiences. I conclude that topic-neutral language is not issue-neutral in this case, and I shall decline the invitation to use it.

SPURIOUS SPATIALITY. Compared with these fundamental restrictions on the argument, the final modification I wish to make seems trivial, but it does, I submit, promote an important increase in clarity. It is a tempting and misleading error to draw our examples from visual experience, as many authors, including Meehl and Green, do. The problem with vision as a proving ground for theories about mind–body relations is that it is so closely connected to spatiality. The connection leads us to take uncritically the commonsense belief that space as we experience it is an objective stage or container for the activities of the material objects that do the world's work. That assumption bestows upon vision a false aura of objectivity. As experienced, space-time belongs primarily to the phenomenal realm. The most we can do to reach beyond it to the world of objects is to interpret phenomenal space-time as a manifestation of intrinsic limits in the causal interactions that take place among the material objects of our knowledge. We may try to subdivide the round red patch of an afterimage into smaller red wedges and begin to feel confused as to just how far to carry this mental counterpart of rock smashing. Time, on the other hand, does not similarly steer us into byways, because temporal cross-sections of enduring objects do not count as component parts even within the material sphere. Whatever parts we may admit must be themselves enduring things or activities carried out by enduring things, not temporal slices of them. Space, not time, exerts the attraction toward befuddlement. Therefore, as a prototype of a "raw feel" I shall adopt the sort that is not normally connected to spatiality: not a visual but an olfactory sensation.

A smell sensation, though it lacks spatiality, nevertheless has an idiosyncratic richness of its own, all the more useful for our present purpose because it is not overlaid with automatic conceptual interpretation, at least not to the degree that visual and auditory sensations are. Much more easily than when experiencing these others, we can attend to the smell sensation itself without "looking through" it to its source in the world.

## CHARACTERISTICS OF SENSATIONS

I now set down, as axioms, three characteristics of sensations in general and one of smell sensations in particular. I take them to be self-evident. Whether they command universal assent or not, they are essential to the argument that follows.

First, an experience is not a thing, such as a neuron; not a property of things, such as electric charge; not a relation between things, such as spatial contiguity. It is, rather, a concrete episode in the life of a sentient being. By "episode" I mean a temporally extended doing or undergoing, engaged in by one or more enduring objects. One period of a hockey game, a cat smiling, and a gas exerting pressure during a three-second interval: these are episodes in the histories of the active entities. An episode is not the doer apart from the activity, or the activity in the abstract (neither the cat itself nor its disembodied smile); it is, rather, a concrete instance of something doing something. Now, if the atomist reduction thesis is correct, any episode of a composite thing is the concurrence of the individual activities of its parts, the simple sum of the component episodes. The gas pressing against its container, for example, is nothing more or less than the molecules of gas and bottle battering one another. A composite thing, according to the atomist thesis, is run by its parts; anything it does is done by them, any episode it undergoes is a bundle of their episodes.

Second, I shall assume that a sensory episode preserves at least some formal and numerical characteristics of what underlies it, however it may differ from the object in other respects. Philosophical traditions diverge widely as to how much we know about the intrinsic nature of an external event, but all that stand this side of utter skepticism agree that we can know at least the formal structure of the external world. The twoness of Alice's experience of Tweedledum and Tweedledee accurately reflects a real twoness in her perceptual apparatus and in the Tweedle family itself, however unlike the subjective and objective occurrences may be in other respects. No doubt more elaborate structural isomorphisms also obtain, but this simple matching of component episodes will suffice for my argument. Multiplicity in an experience imitates (according to dualism) or is identical to (according to materialism) a multiplicity of processes in the cerebral cortex.

Green, however, denies this claim. He suggests that a structural fit between a mental episode and the external object of knowledge might be achieved in some cases by a chain that merely conveys the structure without itself embodying it at each intermediate stage. He supports this conjecture with an analogy, the conveying of the structure of a poem by a message that encodes merely a page reference and the Library of Congress call number for a book in which the poem is printed. But this analogy is unconvincing, because even in this case the structure is in fact conveyed not by the reference alone but by it in conjunction with the book, which does embody the structure. Examining the entire mechanism, we find that the causal chain does convey a structure by exemplifying it. And, be that example as it may, the alternative Green proposes could not arise under the identity thesis, simply because there is then no question of a cerebral process conveying anything to consciousness, with or without exemplifying it; the cerebral episode just *is* the conscious episode and hence must exemplify its (own) structure.

Third, because the grain objection concerns known characteristics of mental episodes, it is necessary to be clear about the nature of our knowledge of them. I shall assume that, although we can think about sensations objectively, we cannot scrutinize them with the same degree of detachment that we bring to bear upon other objects of knowledge. That kind of separation is impossible because the attention we pay to a sensation is integral to the experience itself and helps to determine its quality. There are not two activities, the undergoing of a sensation and the undergoing of an awareness of it, but just one. This episode differs from other, truly double activities we may engage in, such as the combination of stubbing one's toe and undergoing a pain sensation. We cannot split a mental episode along the lines of the distinction between object and appearance. When we "look" at, not through, a sensation, the object includes its own awareness. Suppose, for example, that a person untrained in the appreciation of fine wines savors, at the beginning of a course of study, a glass of Lafite '23. Years later, more learned in the lore of the vine, she samples the vintage again, now noticing much more about the same wine. But would it be correct to claim that she notices more about the same experience? I take it as an axiom that the answer is no; the later experience is a new one, richer and more complex than the earlier. At the time of the first sampling there was much about the wine that the novice failed to notice, but nothing went unnoticed in the experience.

We cannot apply to the special case of conscious experiences the otherwise useful distinction between appearance and reality. We cannot say, for example, that a subjective experience only appears to be simple but is really full of unsuspected complexity, for to do so would introduce one stage too many in the progression from things to their appearances. The mental event is, by definition, the proceeding that makes up the last stage in the sequence. We have appearances of things but not appearances of appearances: They are not viewed, imperfectly, by a lurking homunculus. The experience is what it appears to be. For the same reasons, I shall reject the hypothesis proposed without much enthusiasm by Green as a possible interpretation of some statements of Feyerabend (1963), namely, that a mental entity has all the properties required by the identity thesis, and those properties are in fact experienced, but our speech and other "tokening" mechanisms subvert us into uttering less than the truth, so that we make false claims about unitarity and smoothness. According to this hypothesis, we come to believe that mental processes are radically different from physical ones through listening to these deceptive utterances, or attending to the interior monologs that precede them. I reject this conjecture because it seems to me obvious that speech, overt or internal, does not make experience but, rather, follows it. First we have an experience, richly and self-consciously; then we search for words to express it. The expression is usually far from perfect, but we can criticize it by holding it up against further experiences. It does not insinuate itself between us and our mental events. No veil of any kind hangs between us and our experiences.

## THE COMPLEXITY OF SENSATIONS

Finally, let us inquire as to the complexity of an olfactory sensation. What are the component parts of such an episode? Imagine a quite unprecedented smell experience, as might be had by a chemist who has just synthesized a new organic compound. How many parts has it? One feels initially at a loss as to how to divide such an episode into parts of any kind, but we may attribute this initial bafflement to the nonspatial character of olfaction and our unreasonable bias toward geometry when we speak of parts. However, if parts there must be, we may perhaps identify the occurring of certain *qualities* as components in the single smell episode—qualities of the sort that usually go unnoticed in ordinary experience and that wine tasters and perfumers invent names for. How many qualities make up a single smell episode? That depends on the experiencer's attentiveness, skill in discriminating, and state of health. I am inclined to claim that the smell episode experienced by an untrained perceiver is absolutely unitary, so that such an olfactory experience consists of exactly one part. But this version of the grain objection will stand if I concede more in the direction of multiplicity than even the most discriminating oenologist might require. Let us say, extravagantly, that in the nostrils of an expert some smell experiences may consist of the simultaneous going-on of 100 discriminated qualities, 100 component episodes.

Just what are we aware of when we pay attention to the qualities of an odor? According to monistic materialism we are making direct contact with a cerebral episode, an activity performed by a part of the brain. Normally, we know such things only indirectly, by the mediation of a sensory apparatus that generates other cerebral episodes, which are themselves not identical to the smell experience and which we must interpret by means of the concepts and theories of science. But here in this combination of qualities and attentiveness to them we have the process itself, bare, unmediated by the sensory organs or by conceptual interpretation—not a mental construct of another thing but the thing itself. For how could it be otherwise? If all we had were an appearance of the smell experience, then the identity thesis would have to apply to this new image, and the sorting out of appearance and reality would recur endlessly. No, the process of generating a sensation must terminate in a perfectly definite episode that reveals itself utterly.

Nevertheless, our mediated, sensory knowledge of this same episode, hypothetical and indirect though it be, does preserve the formal, quantitative facts, or so we must believe if we accept the reduction program of atomism. Among those facts is this: A typical conscious cerebral episode consists of many thousands of neurons simultaneously firing, of hordes of neurotransmitter molecules passing between cell membranes, of countless migrating ions of potassium and sodium. But let the argument proceed a fortiori: let us take the absolute minimum conceivable for any cerebral event that might be identified with a conscious episode, a single nerve cell firing. A neuron firing is not a unitary event either; even this episode is composed of the simultaneous running of the individual activities performed by each material part of the cell. And by a conservative estimate the parts number not less than about ten to the fifteenth power. So any neuronal event consists of at least that many concurrent individual episodes.

Here is a glaring discrepancy: From the physical description we get a count of fifteen powers of ten or more; from the subjective experience 100 or much less. Can the atomist hypothesis tolerate that discrepancy? A lack of accord over some features of mental and physical episodes would, of course, be consistent with the identity thesis. We cannot expect the physical description of a process, the view from outside, as it were, actually to convey its inner reality. Let us allow a very wide margin for that sort of discordance. For all we know to the contrary, what we conceive of from the outside as a certain potassium ion diffusing through a neuron's membrane may just be, in itself, the unique gustative episode that wine tasters refer to as the sensation of "flintiness." But there is one sort of mismatch that the identity theory cannot tolerate because it would entail abandoning the atomist program, namely, a disagreement as to formal structure. An essential element in the formal structure of an episode is the number of the component episodes that make it up. In order to discover a discrepancy over this element of form we do not need to make any questionable assumptions about what a physically characterized episode is really like on the inside; all we need to do is count. And the result is this: A cerebral episode consists of a myriad of individual doings and undergoings by a scarcely imaginable number of material objects, whereas the experience consists of a fairly small number of component episodes, namely, the temporary occurring of a few olfactory qualities.

Let us try to explain this discrepancy. First, we might question the alleged multiplicity of the cerebral episode. Can we trust the physical description? Sometimes we err in counting, skipping over an item while reciting the integers. It is at least thinkable that some important facts about the material episode have escaped our notice. Therefore, the physical episode may be more elaborate than the physical story makes it out to be, but it cannot be less so. Or, second, if we think of the mental episode as a mere result of the brain process, and thus not identical to it, then we might expect the effect to be less complex than the cause; information is usually diminished as a message is transmitted from one structure to another. But this rejoinder succeeds only by abandoning the identity thesis, because a result is distinct from its cause. Third, we might try to identify each component episode of the olfactory experience with a natural grouping of the components of the brain event, identifying the occurring of one quality, for example, with the firing neurons in one small region of the brain and another with the goings-on in a neighboring region. But we progress not at all by this stratagem. We still have a multiplicity in the physical episode that exceeds by far the multiplicity (in fact a singularity) of the mental one. The physical episode cannot be less complex than neurophysiology or chemistry pictures it, and the mental episode cannot be more elaborate than we experience it to be. Hence, the allegedly identical episodes differ with respect to a formal, essential property. None of these apologies will work.

We have uncovered a dilemma at the core of the materialist reduction program. Atomism requires us to adopt the identity thesis, but we have seen that an experience, which must be the naked fact of the physical episode, fails to conform at a crucial point with the picture we have formed by following the program of atomistic science. Either objective science utterly misrepresents the one feature of material processes that it must not miss—

their formal, numerical structure—or the experience falsifies itself. Either the ontological program of science fails to deliver the goods, or an appearance is not as it appears. The first horn would empty the identity thesis of its ontological content. Of what significance would it be to assert the identity of mind to matter if we cannot trust what science tells us about the nature of the right-hand side of the equation? And, as I have urged above, the second horn is necessarily false. Neither alternative is acceptable; hence, the identity thesis is demolished. Hence, the mental episode is not carried out by material particles. Because no physical object presents itself for that task, I conclude tentatively that it is a distinct activity, done by a distinct performer. The world is made up of two basic sorts of stuff.

## FURTHER PROBLEMS

By no means does concluding for dualism put an end to puzzlement. It opens out, in fact, a tangled field for exploration. We already have a fairly large set of unexplainable givens about matter, such as the basic structure of mechanics, the fundamental laws of interaction, and arbitrary facts about the numbers and kinds of particles that compose the world. Now we must add some basic, equally unexplainable facts about mental entities: what they are, how they participate in causal interactions among themselves and with material particles.

Some profound questions plague the dualist conjecture, and we do well to face them, even if we must leave them largely unresolved. They are made more difficult because, in attempting to think about the mental as a distinct ontological category, we have a powerful temptation to draw analogies from what we know of the material realm and force them upon our embryonic understanding of the mental. It would be a mistake, for instance, to try to translate the entire program of atomistic analysis into mental terms. As a preliminary attempt to avoid that error, let us take the unitary mental entity to be a mind and classify smells and afterimages not as component parts of minds but among the activities that minds perform. But even this plausible supposition leaves much unsettled. What, for example, could an activity amount to in a mental substance? We know how to answer that kind of question for material things. Any physical process ultimately consists of just two sorts of occurrences, motion and transmutation, which are exemplified by the flight of a muon toward the earth's surface and its decay into an electron and a neutrino. Internal processes in composite things consist almost without exception of realignment of the parts. But these examples can do nothing to aid us here.

Perhaps the most perplexing question is this: How can we understand the causal interaction between minds and particles? What conceptual apparatus can we hammer together—for, clearly, the concepts of force and motion provide no help—to make sense of the ability of a portion of the brain to cause a mind to perform a sensation? And how, if at all, can a willing, choosing mind affect the mindless surging of particles? Can a mind push upon a particle, causing it to swerve out of the path it otherwise would have taken? Most of the universe has no traffic with consciousness, or any need of it. How, then, is it possible for the mind associated with a human brain to influence the course of events in the cerebrum? For example, by what means can the speech mechanism of the brain be caused to report a mental event? How, if matter runs on its own without interference from another sphere of being, could the idea of that other sphere become encoded in the connections of the neurons?

As we shall see, a dualistic interpretation of quantum mechanics thrusts these questions under one's nose. However, as I shall attempt to show, it also hints at the possibility of a new kind of answer to some of them, an answer not imaginable within the conceptual framework of Newtonian physics.

NINE

# Potentiality in the Quantum Theory

HOW CAN WE PROVIDE THEORETICAL SUPPORT FOR OUR deep-seated intuition that macroscopic objects—human beings especially—participate in the world's affairs as unitary agents? The task looks difficult because of the portentous successes of atomistic science, which claims to account for the causal activity of any composite thing as nothing other than the concerted activities of its parts. In the early chapters I have ignored possible answers that would challenge a materialist ontology. Though not all of the antireductionistic arguments considered there were advanced by adherents of mechanistic materialism, all are conformable to it. Quantum mechanics, however, opens a new line of inquiry.

Two features of the quantum theory seem to require us to face radical questions about the place of mind in a world of atoms: The first is the theory's unprecedented treatment of probability; the second is a uniquely quantum-mechanical phenomenon, commonly called the reduction of the wave packet, associated with observation and measurement. In addition, whether or not allegations of mentalism can be substantiated, a third, closely related challenge to atomism still would stand: some expositors of quantum mechanics find in it a novel sort of interconnectedness among the parts of composite systems, a feature that deserves to be called quantum-mechanical holism. Let us see, first, how references to probability in a fundamental theory might raise a formidable barrier to the atomist reduction program.

The mechanistic picture of the world entails the physicalist theory of mind, which identifies a conscious experience as no more than a process highly placed on the reductionist ladder. The ultimate truth about such an experience, like the truth about any other upper-level event, is to be told in a story about atoms. In our present state of understanding, we must narrate such stories in the language of the quantum theory. Quantum mechanics, unlike the Newtonian variety, assigns probabilities to the possible outcomes of experiments; it does not determine definite results. But talk of probability in a fundamental physical theory raises a problem for the atomist program.

According to one common interpretation, probability ranks the degree of confidence with which a rational observer expects the event to happen; according to another, probability measures the consonance between a proposition and its evidence. Now, if probability must be understood in terms of knowledge, expectations, or the making of propositions, hope for a coherently atomistic understanding of consciousness fades away. Consciousness, treated as an upper-level event, would be explained by a story about atoms and the probabilities of their being in certain states, and these probabilities would turn the explanation back to items of human thought. Taking quantum mechanics as the basic theory of matter, we would find that consciousness lies at the heart of reality, not at the periphery as the reductionist program requires. Therefore, so this argument goes, the materialist program for dealing with sentience suffers from vicious circularity.

This threat to atomism rests on three assumptions: that atomism builds on a realist view of physical theory; that quantum mechanics, except for possible refinements, speaks the final word about physical reality; and that probability entails issues of thought and logic. As science stands, we could not abandon realism without giving up atomism, too, nor do we have at present a serious contender to displace quantum mechanics from its fundamental position in the edifice of natural laws. However, an atomist might speculate about alternative interpretations of probability without endangering the core of the program. Werner Heisenberg (1958) elects this defensive gambit, suggesting that in quantum mechanics probability represents a real property of external objects, possessed by them independently of what we may know or say about them. According to Heisenberg, the concept refers not to items of knowledge or to relations among propositions but to multiple possibilities objectively present in material things. This interpretation retains an important feature of scientific realism, because possibilities that obtain objectively would contribute their plurality to the structure of the world apart from human consciousness; thus, the theory would apply in principle to epochs that antedate the appearance of life on the planet, as any objective theory should.

However, Heisenberg's objective interpretation of probability invites a second mentalistic challenge (see, e.g., Wigner 1961). If possibilities exist objectively, then any reduction in their range, of the sort associated with the process of measuring, is also an objective event. Heisenberg calls such events transitions from potentiality to actuality. But the cause of them has been the subject of controversy among interpreters of quantum mechanics. A suggestion made by Erwin Schroedinger (1935) places the responsibility for the transition on the action of mind; Heisenberg attempts to produce a purely mechanical account of the process. I shall argue below that Heisenberg's attempt does not succeed.

With fortunate consequences for the length of this chapter, the philosophically germane issues raised by quantum mechanics can be exhibited mainly by describing typical phenomena, with little or no reference to the mathematical structure of the theory. Accordingly, I shall present the theory by means of paradigmatic experiments, showing that they require us to bring a novel concept of possibility to bear upon the physical world. This, I shall urge, is the way to employ Heisenberg's notion of potentiality.

After introducing Heisenberg's general strategy as part of a program to interpret probabilities realistically, I discuss the behavior of single atomic particles, principally in the double-slit experiment. These phenomena challenge us to find a coherent language for describing quantum phenomena. To meet the challenge, I recommend a modal logic that employs Heisenberg's potentialism and that I interpret by means of physical possibility. I turn then to a uniquely quantum-mechanical phenomenon, the transition from potentiality to actuality, which is alleged to occur in the course of a measurement, illustrating it with another paradigm, Schroedinger's thought experiment concerning a cat placed in perilous circumstances. Finally, I describe the Einstein/Podolsky/Rosen "paradox," in which a pair of atomic objects undergo correlated transitions to actuality, exhibiting the puzzling phenomenon of nonlocality.

My review[1] of the paradigms of quantum mechanics sets the stage for the principal business of chapter 10, namely, assessing antireductionistic arguments based on the nature of the theory. I consider three features of quantum mechanics that seem to challenge the premises of atomism: nonadditivity, nonseparability, and the alleged intrusion of consciousness into the measuring process. I argue that, highly speculative though it is, only the last promises to deliver a satisfactory answer to atomism's attack on our intuitions about human causal agency. Chapter 11 concludes with some cautious speculations about the place of mind in the order of nature, thereby demonstrating what is permitted (though certainly not required) by the quantum theory's unprecedented treatment of consciousness.

Nature almost completely hides from us the multiplicity that Heisenberg sees toiling behind the scenes. Even the best-designed experiments reveal the objective coexistence of alternative possibilities only indirectly, because each trial of an experiment ends in a definite, singular result. Our most nearly direct evidence

1 / Throughout this chapter I make no effort scrupulously to attribute ideas to their originators; that would require a historical study, something foreign to my purposes here. Rather, I attempt to marshal relevant portions of the physics community's quantum-mechanical lore around the central problem of this book. References, therefore, will serve merely as convenient ways of identifying certain arguments and as evidence that they deserve our attention. Hence, the reader should not infer from the absence of an attribution that an idea originates with me (one may be confident that it does not) or even that it receives its clearest exposition here. In addition to the sources cited in the text, however, I must mention two very helpful works: Abner Shimony's article, "Role of the Observer in Quantum Theory," in the *American Journal of Physics* 31 (1963): 755–73; and Bernard d'Espagnat's book, *Conceptual Foundations of Quantum Mechanism*, 2d ed. (Reading, Mass.: W. A. Benjamin, 1976).

comes from carefully contrived experiments in the diffraction of particles, commonly electrons or neutrons, which are sent through a narrow aperture or a crystal lattice to be detected at a surface. There they bring contrary possibilities into direct confrontation, producing the characteristic patterns of interference. These experiments tip Nature's closely held hand, showing as it were that Nature has been playing with more than the regulation number of cards. I shall outline the salient features of two diffraction experiments.

## THE DOUBLE-SLIT EXPERIMENT

The conceptually simplest version of the double-slit experiment transpires in a device resembling a television video tube. At the narrow end a source of particles (an "electron gun") sends a narrow beam toward a fluorescent screen at the large end, where each arriving particle generates a flash of light as it strikes one of the microscopic crystals that coat the inner surface. (A permanent record of these arrivals could be recorded on a photographic emulsion, which also consists of many microscopic crystals.) If their journey were unimpeded, the electrons would produce a focused spot of light at the screen, but they can reach it only by passing through two narrow openings in an intervening metal plate. After squeezing through, the originally well focused beam spreads out; the narrower the openings, the broader the spread. This effect, called diffraction, occurs at each slit.

When either of the slits is blocked, the arriving particles, having passed through the other one, build up a uniform spread of light at the screen. But when both are open, so that each electron has a "choice" as to route, the flashes of light build up a regular pattern of alternating light and dark bands or spots. Now that the opportunities are doubled, the particles shun half of the places that they freely moved to when given only a single way to get there. This phenomenon is called interference, and the pattern of light and dark is called an interference pattern. Contrary to commonsense intuitions, interference occurs for individual particles—it is not the result of interactions among them. This strange conclusion follows from the fact that the experimenter can reduce the intensity of the beam to such a low level that, aside from rare exceptions, each particle makes a solo flight between the source and the crystal that detects its arrival. That expedient keeps the particles from jostling one another as they move toward the screen.

This is a curious result: Our ordinary notion of an objective world leads us to expect that an electron that travels from the source to the detector must pass either through one opening or through the other. And whether the one it did not move through was open or not, its chances of arriving at any detecting crystal should be the same. For how could the mere existence of another possible route alter the manner of arrival by the path actually followed? This result makes trouble both for determinism and for an indeterminism of the ordinary, prequantal sort. According to prequantal determinism, the possibility of the other path exists only in the observer's mind and means nothing to the electron itself. The road not chosen never was an objective possibility from the moment the electron left the source; hence, the mere presence of an untraveled alternative path could in no way affect an electron passing along the one actually taken. And ordinary indeterminism pictures a past event as settled, definite, and single, however pregnant with potentialities it may have been while we awaited it. In either of these views, each electron that hits the emulsion arrives there by passing definitely through one slit or the other. Opening up an alternative path to the detector should merely permit the passage of more electrons without making any possible point of arrival less popular than formerly.

## THE OBSTRUCTED DOUBLE SLIT

Particle detectors, such as fluorescent microcrystals or Geiger tubes, wire loops, et cetera, can be inserted immediately behind either or both of the slits. The microcrystals trap the particles, and they go no farther. A loop lets the charged particle pass, but not without inducing a pulse of current by means of the magnetic interaction. Most of the particles sent into the apparatus by the source stop at the plate that surrounds the slits, but some are recorded by the detectors at the two slits, in roughly equal numbers. If a detector blocks either or both slits, no interference pattern can be produced, of course; but, even if the detectors let the particles pass, they arrive at the final plane in a uniform distribution, with no hint of the interference bands that mark the standard experiment.

## THE DAVISSON/GERMER EXPERIMENT

Long before physicists achieved the conceptually neat but technically difficult feat of making material particles diffract through a pair of slits, C. J. Davisson and L. H. Germer (1927) had recorded the interference pattern made by a beam of electrons that had scattered from a crystal lattice. The story of how the interference pattern occurs in the double-slit experiment applies in its essential features also to this one, so I shall not describe it in detail, except to note two suggestive points of difference. (1) Instead of being diffracted by passing through empty slits, the beam of electrons is spread by the crystal because of collisions with its atoms. (2) Instead of offering only two possible paths to each particle, this experiment offers billions, one for each of the possible collisions that contribute to the final pattern.

Since 1927 the diffraction of material particles by crystal lattices has become a standard laboratory procedure: So commonplace is it that electrons and neutrons are both now used as probes to analyze the structure of unknown crystals. Interference has also been observed in scattered beams of helium atoms. The collisions in electron diffraction occur by electrical repulsion, and those in neutron diffraction by the short-range and far stronger nuclear force.

The double-slit and the Davisson/Germer experiments pose the same vexatious problem: How can we speak coherently about the simultaneous occurrence of two (or many) mutually exclusive events? I shall propose a solution, drawing examples from the conceptually simpler double-slit experiment. The experiment of Davisson and Germer will prove useful below, in testing some proposed interpretations of quantum-mechanical probability.

## THE LOGIC OF POTENTIALITY

The image of a particle passing definitely along one or the other of the two paths must contain a serious flaw. We can scarcely find words to describe these experiments, much less explain them. I shall treat the double-slit experiment as challenging us to find a way to assign truth values to the two propositions *A* and *B*:

*A*: The particle passed through slit *A*.
*B*: The particle passed through slit *B*.

Because we reserve the term "particle" for objects that have just one location at a time and take a single path in going from one location to another, these propositions cannot both be true. Nor can they both be false, because a particle cannot reach the detector without passing through the slits. Prequantal common sense says that either *A* or *B* must be true and the other false. But as we have just seen, that hypothesis entails the absence of interference, in direct conflict with the experimental result. Hence, all possible joint allocations of truth values are blocked; we simply cannot assign them to these propositions as they stand.

Three possible routes of escape from this apparent impasse have been suggested, two of which I shall pass over with but scant mention in favor of the third, Heisenberg's objectification of probability. First, we might accept Niels Bohr's advice to avoid formulating propositions about the objects as they exist apart from ourselves and to speak instead only about the outcomes of actual experiments. If we followed such a rule when describing the double-slit experiment, we would not say that any electron passes through a slit, for in this apparatus no instrument detects its passage; thus, we would avoid the perplexing question of whether to affirm or deny *A* and *B*. Yet any proposition assigning a position on the terminal surface would prove to be unequivocally true in some trials of the experiment and false in others. This ability unambiguously to assign truth values to propositions would have been purchased, however, by giving up the right to think of objects as if they exist objectively in themselves, apart from our contact with them. Let us set aside Bohr's proposal as insufficiently realistic.

I shall also pass over attempts to produce an empirical logic specially tailored to quantum phenomena, because its applicability seems limited to experiments in atomic physics. Its advocates do not recommend it for ordinary discourse, not even for reasoning about the quantum theory or proving theorems within it. (See, e.g., Putnam 1968, Gardner 1971, Bub 1979, and Hellman 1981.) A "quantum logician" must adopt an equivocal use of the logical operators, altering their functions according to the meaning of the propositions to which they are applied. It seems fair to complain that, although quantum logic provides a coherent conceptual organization of the phenomena, it does not clear up the problem of how to think about them realistically.

However, by employing a modal logic of physical possibility, modeled on the standard one of logical possibility, we shall find it possible to speak coherently about quantum phenomena without the shortcomings of the two proposed solutions mentioned above. To qualify as an attractive alternative, this ploy must pass two tests: It must provide a *formal* solution to the problem of describing quantum phenomena coherently; and it must increase our understanding of the theory by supporting an *interpretation* that refers to objective properties of material things. In the following paragraphs I present some examples to show how a modal logic of potentiality and actuality permits a formally coherent description of quantum phenomena. Following that, I recommend an interpretation in terms of physical possibility.

Let us construct some descriptions of the double-slit experiment that use the modal qualifiers "potentially" and "actually." This expedient treats potentiality as an aspect of the objective world, like temporality. No assertion about the temporal world can be either true or false unless it carries at least implicitly a temporal qualifier; similarly, in forming a modal logic appropriate to quantum mechanics, we adopt the rule that validly formed assertions about the world must carry one of the modal qualifiers, "actually" or "potentially." Only then may they be assigned truth values.

We can find the rules for this manner of speaking by analogy to the standard modal treatment of logical possibility and necessity. Just as "possibly *A*" does not contradict "possibly not-*A*," so the conjunction "potentially the electron passed through slit *A* and potentially it passed through *B*" also escapes self-contradiction. Further, "not potentially *A*" means the same as "actually not-*A*," and "not actually *A*" is equivalent to "potentially *A* and potentially not-*A*, or actually not-*A*." Other analogies also occur.

Interpreters of quantum mechanics often say that we cannot make a classical picture of what the atomic particles are doing. Heisenberg's treatment of potentiality in the double-slit experiment illustrates the truth of this adage—if properly understood. It does not mean that we must refrain altogether from drawing pictures in the classical style; rather, we must fly to the opposite extreme and draw as many as possible. The result is anything but Newtonian. In the place formerly occupied by a single picture we must hang many, overlaid one on another within the frame of potentiality. For example, the electron beam spreads as it emerges from a slit not because some particles go one way and some another or because none goes anywhere but because each individual takes on the whole range of positions at the fluorescent screen. Indeed, an electron reaches each crystal there in two ways, arriving from slit *A* and from slit *B*. How can a single particle occupy more than one position, and how can it reach each of them by more than one route? It performs these feats not "actually" but "potentially." Let us see how these strange locutions flow from the theory.

Like any of the theories of physics, quantum mechanics consists of a formal calculus interpreted according to specified rules. With a single exception, the symbols on which it operates represent the standard mechanical properties, such as position, momentum, and energy. But the quantum theory also operates with another symbol, a complex number[2] called the probability amplitude. The theory specifies the state of a system by associating each possible value of the ordinary physical variables with a value of this new quantity. Its squared magnitude is related to ordinary probability by rules to be discussed below.

Although only the squared magnitude of a probability amplitude receives a direct interpretation, the complex numbers themselves also play an important role in the theory. On occasion, a straightforward application will produce two or more instances of a state of affairs, such as an electron having reached a fluorescent crystal by way of slit *A* and by way of *B*. Both possibilities are qualified as potential, but they are quantified with distinct complex numbers. In cases of this sort the theory merges the sepa-

2 / (For the benefit of readers unfamiliar with complex numbers.) The concept of a complex number is a generalization of the concept of a signed, real number. Signed numbers may be represented by the points on a line (say, the $x$-axis), those to the right of zero being positive and those to the left being negative. Complex numbers may be represented by the points in a plane; hence, they include as special cases the real numbers on the $x$-axis and the pure imaginaries, defined as those that lie on the $y$-axis. Just as two real signed numbers that lie on opposite sides of the zero point tend to cancel when added together, so two complex numbers lying in opposite quadrants of the plane tend to cancel when added. The *magnitude* of a complex number is the distance between its representative point and the origin, and its *phase* is the angle between the positive $x$-axis and the line joining the representative point to the origin. A pair of complex numbers of equal magnitude and opposite phase (the angles differ by $180°$) sum up to zero.

rate assertions of the same proposition into a single one bearing a probability amplitude that is the sum of those belonging to the combined assertions. Because the amplitudes may have opposite phases, the sum may be less than either of the separate values and as small as zero. On occasion, therefore, the individual assertions of a proposition, all of which contribute to the complete state-description, may nullify each other. In fact, this happens for certain positions in the detecting screen of the double-slit experiment, where the effect is called interference.

From these hints we see how a modal logic of quantum mechanics can work, paralleling the kind of reasoning we perform with logical necessity and possibility. More pressing than the details of the formal modal calculus, however, is the question of interpretation. How can we understand potentiality as an objective mode of being?

## INTERPRETING POTENTIALITY

I shall not take up here the deeper question of how to fit potentiality into a broad, realistic view of the world. That task must await the further exposition of some principles of the quantum theory. Let it suffice here to demonstrate that an interpretation parallel to that of logical possibility may also be constructed for quantum-mechanical potentiality. The central concept here is physical possibility, and the quantum theory's peculiar brand of it carries us along paths not charted by the two commonsense varieties. Let us note the differences.

COUNTERFACTUAL POSSIBILITY. Even though Newton's theory tells a rigidly deterministic story, its applicability to diverse objects gives it the flexibility to spin alternative tales. We can construct variations on the history of a system of Newtonian particles by imagining other positions and velocities than actually obtain, or by imagining systems composed of fewer or more particles of the same or other types. Within the constraints of any deterministic theory that lays down general laws but does not legislate specific circumstances, we construct physically possible worlds as alternatives to the actual one by inserting into the theory conditions contrary to fact. The same method serves for constructing possible worlds also within indeterministic theories, including quantum mechanics. The possibility that we envision in this way I shall denote by the term "counterfactual possibility," or simply "*C*-possibility." This kind amounts to nothing more than imaginability within the rules of a physical theory but contrary to the facts of the world as it is.

REAL POSSIBILITY. Alternative worlds constructed in this way are possible only in a weak sense, for Newtonian mechanics allows no laxity: Tweak one thread in the causal fabric it weaves, and the entire structure trembles. But, conceivably, Newtonian determinism does not hold a rigid grip on the world, so that there is some free play in nature's machinery. Charles Sanders Peirce (1892) urges such a hypothesis, pointing out that inescapable limits on the precision of measurement bar us from ever proving that complete determinism is a fact. No experiment could do more than set an upper limit on the slippage allowed among the parts of the great machine. Suppose, then, that a human being or an atom is really free, under the external and internal conditions prevailing objectively at a certain time, both to perform and not to perform a certain action. In that case, even an omniscient being would be obliged to hedge its predictions about future events, just because the things themselves have real powers to "choose" among alternatives. Yet when the predicted time has passed, the omniscient being would write a single, definite history. If an agent has the real ability to do an action at a certain time as well as to do some alternative, then, when the moment arrives, it is necessarily the case that either the action or its alternative gets done. The agent has no choice but to choose. All of this is perfectly commonsensical and coincides, I suppose, with what everyone not committed to Newtonian/Laplacean determinism believes. According to commonsense indeterminism the future is to some extent really open. The objects themselves have real abilities; there are objectively possible alternatives to the course of events. I shall call this kind of causal looseness "*R*-possibility." This sort of possibility applies, of course, only to the future. Though it may be multiple and indefinite, the past is always singular and definite. No agent ever avoids making its "choice" when the opportunity arrives.

Where can *R*-possible events be found? A complete answer to that question would carry us unnecessarily into moot issues of interpretation. A partial answer suffices here: All quantum theorists agree that *observation events* occur *R*-possibly. Interpretations differ, however, as to what kind of processes these are. Some say that any physical system that irreversibly changes its state when acted on by an atomic-sized object performs an *R*-possible observation event. Others say that only minds perform them. These and other proposals will occupy us in chapter 10.

HYPOTHETICAL REALISM. Observation events, being causal consequences of the microphysical processes they reveal, are distinct from them. We cannot tell a coherent story about the course of particle-diffraction experiments operationally, talking exclusively about the observations instead of the particles. Consider, for example, the arrival of a particle in a detector just behind one of the slits in the obstructed version of the double-slit experiment.

At the entry plane of the detector a microscopic activity starts a causal sequence that terminates in an observation event. The detector may be a Geiger counter, a photocell, a photographic emulsion, a scintillator, and so on. The list of currently used detectors is lengthy, and the list of all possible ones, if not infinite, is certainly open-ended. What common feature binds these devices into a single class? No usable criterion of membership can be found in the features of the apparatus itself. But the sequence that leads up to the lighting of a lamp in the front panel of a Geiger counter begins at the slit with a particle having a position there and a sufficient momentum in the forward direction. The position measurers are united into a class by the fact that the causal accounts of how they work all begin with the measured particle's having that position and momentum. (I shall adopt "passing through the slit" as a convenient equivalent to the more careful expression.) We cannot *define* the atomic activity in a slit operationally in terms of its effects, indefinitely various as they are; but, realistically and hypothetically, we can *conceive* of it as the particle's passing through the slit into the detector.

This interpretation implies that what happens in the slits is the same process in all experiments of this family, whether the slits are blocked by Geiger/Mueller tubes, fluorescent crystals, photomultipliers, or, indeed, whether they are left open. Consequently, instructive comparisons can be drawn between the standard double-slit experiment and the blocked version.

In the modified apparatus with particle detectors at the downstream side of each slit, we find that some particles possess the ability to cause observation events that reveal their presence in slit *A*, and a roughly equal number turn up at slit *B*. As we look back on the completed experiment we know that, for each particle, either it caused the *A*-observation or it caused an alternative, such as the *B*-observation. Are these results produced by exercising real possibilities? To find evidence for indeterminacy we must compare the two versions. The comparison reveals more than just the indeterminism of the experimental results; it also points out the limits of the concept of *R*-possibility and the need for a new, peculiarly quantal concept of indeterminacy.

We explain the interference pattern in the standard experiment by mentioning both the passing through slit *A* and the passing through *B* as we recount the history of each individual particle. The activity at slit *A* that in the modified apparatus grounds the possibility of an *A*-observation and the activity at *B* that grounds the possibility of a *B*-observation are both going on in the standard interference apparatus. Of course, the observation of a particle's passage through *A* is incompatible with the revelation of its passage through *B* (at the same time). This incompatibility holds just as surely for experiences of atomic particles as it does for those of commonsense things—as surely as seeing a baseball flying through one window never occurs with the vision of the same ball breaking through a neighboring one. Nevertheless, from the interference experiment we learn that the atomic activities that ground at least some incompatible observations are not themselves incompatible. (Can the same be said of the atomic goings-on that underlie the baseball experiences? I shall return to that question in chapter 10.)

Two conclusions follow immediately from the comparison of the two experiments. First, in the apparatus with detectors at the slits each particle that caused a passing-through-*A*-observation also was doing at slit *B* what might have caused a passing-through-*B*-observation instead. Therefore, the *A* and *B* observations were achieved by the exercise of an *R*-possibility; the observational outcome of the modified apparatus is objectively not determined. Second, because the activities at both slits contribute to the interference pattern in the standard apparatus, we must recognize an unprecedented kind of multiplicity, one that involves real alternatives for the course of events but in which the "choice" among them need not be made. *R* powers alone cannot accommodate the microphysical events that produce the interference phenomenon. The activity in the region of the slits, revealed in the blocked version by either the *A*-observation or the *B*-observation, goes on simultaneously in both slits, not alternatively. The particle does not "choose" between those activities as the interference experiment progresses. Because they both help to generate the future state, they have both "happened" (in a peculiar sense), as a matter of objective history. Hence, they do not occur as manifestations of *R*-possibilities. In addition to *C* and *R* possibilities, we must recognize a multiplicity in the activities of the particles themselves, one that does not become single as the indefinite future slides into history. I shall call it "quantal possibility," or simply "*Q* possibility." Consider two examples of the usefulness of this concept.

QUANTAL POSSIBILITY. A version of the Davisson/Germer experiment can be done with neutrons diffracting from a crystal. To explain the resulting interference pattern, we tell how each individual neutron interacts by means of the short-range nuclear interaction with every nucleus of the crystal. Each particle that contributes to the interference pattern has been deflected from its original course by a collision with nucleus number 1, an encounter with nucleus number 2, and so on. These interactions with the nuclei of the crystal lattice cannot be understood merely as *R*-abilities to generate observation records of the particle's presence at those microscopic locations. No measuring instrument could locate a neutron so precisely. Nor is it the case that, when the experiment is complete, one possible deflection by a nucleus has definitely happened, and the others definitely not. These collisions are not *R*-possible activities. Yet events of some kind they certainly are, because individually they cause a neutron to deflect from its original course, and collectively they determine that each neutron avoids certain regions of the pattern.

In the second example, the standard quantum-mechanical picture of the motion of atoms and molecules assigns characteristic shapes to the electrons' orbitals, the functions that describe the particles' potential positions relative to the nuclei. These functions have regions of greater and lesser probability amplitude as well as peculiarly shaped nodal surfaces where the amplitude drops to zero. These potential positions cannot be understood as causes of *R*-possible position measurements, again because no instrument could locate a particle that precisely. Yet observations related to such matters as the stabilities of atoms and molecules and their proclivities for linking themselves into larger structures are governed by the details of these potential positions. None of the positions becomes the exclusive one at any moment as history sweeps on; the molecule would not be stable if one did. They, too, are not *R*-possibilities; yet they form a part of reality. We must conceive of them in terms of another kind of multiplicity, namely, of options that need not be picked up. They are *Q*-possibilities.

A single, simply statable *Q*-possibility canot be defined in terms of a single *R*-possible event, or even in terms of a finite set of alternative *R*-possibilities, no matter how large the set may be. The *Q*-possibility may indeed be associated with an open-ended, and therefore essentially undefined, "set" of *R*-possible events. But such an association does not qualify as a reduction of the concept of *Q*-possibility because the members of this open-ended set cannot be picked out except by reference to the single *Q*-possible event. A complete explication of quantum-mechanical potentiality must relate it to the manifesting of *Q*-possible states of affairs. It must connect *Q*-possibilities both to direct measurements of them and to measurements of events to which the *Q*-possibilities make indirect causal contributions. Let us construct a formal interpretation of potentiality.

## CRITERION OF POTENTIALITY

I shall follow the lead of Einstein, Podolsky, and Rosen (EPR), who propose the following "criterion of reality":

> If, without in any way disturbing a system, we can predict with certainty (i.e., with probability equal to unity) the value of a physical quantity, then there exists an element of physical reality corresponding to this physical quantity. [1935, p. 777]

The reference to certainty in this criterion aligns it with Heisenberg's concept of actuality. Let us extend it to include potentiality.

In proposing a criterion of potentiality I shall use the term "system" to refer to a single particle or a collection of them; and the term "variable property" to refer to any of the "observables" of quantum mechanics—position, momentum, energy, angular momentum, and so on, belonging to particles singly or in groups. And by "measuring instrument" I shall refer to a thermodynamically irreversible device that is causally connectable both to an atomic particle and to a human brain (that is, observable by human senses) in such a way that some distinct states of the particle can generate distinct states of the device, which in turn causes distinct perceptual states of the brain. Finally, the term "observer" is left deliberately indefinite, in order not to anticipate the arguments of the next chapter: An observer is some system capable of being connected to the measured object in such a way that distinct states of the object cause corresponding states in the observer. For the present let us leave it an open question whether an observer is a physical or a mental entity, animal or mineral, simple or complex, whether it is the measuring instrument itself or something causally connected to it.

In the EPR criterion, "predicting with certainty" means deducing correctly from known facts and with the aid of a theory that a measurement will yield a single definite result. To varying degrees, measurements of physical quantities are always indirect. Measurement is a theory-laden art: The measured value is inferred from the result of the measurement, not given transparently. When we infer the approximate position of a particle from the behavior of a fluorescent crystal, the measurement is only modestly indirect; when we deduce the momentum of the particles in a beam from the size of the interference pattern they produce, the inferential chain is somewhat longer. When we explain the interference pattern in the double-slit apparatus by mentioning an individual particle's passage through a slit, we also infer a position, by means of theory, from the results of measurement; in this case, however, the inference points to more than one of the quantity's possible values. In the same spirit, we infer the shaped continuum of positions of the hydrogen atom's electron from many sorts of measurements, including spectroscopic data and facts about chemical reactions. By means of quantum mechanics we infer (correctly, as far as we can tell) not a single definite result for the value of a typical physical quantity but many values—not because the theory hesitates or hedges its bets but because all these values are "elements of physical reality."

Let us pull these considerations together into the following formal criterion: A variable property of a system has one of its possible values *potentially* at a certain time if we can predict correctly the subsequent observed behavior of the system on the assumption that the property has that value. The value obtains only potentially, that is, not actually, if at least one other value also contributes to the theoretically predicted behavior. A variable property has one of its possible values *actually* at a certain time if that value and no other contributes to the theoretical explanation of the system's subsequent behavior.

Two features of this criterion of potentiality and actuality need emphasis. "Subsequent behavior" includes but is not limited to direct measurements of the property; it also includes measurements of other properties that are causally linked to the property in question. Note, also, that according to this criterion actuality is merely a restricted form of potentiality. Both are elements of physical reality. I shall have something more positive to say about actuality below. But first let us draw out some of the meaning of this version of the criterion.

## APPLICATIONS OF THE CRITERION

TRAJECTORIES. Would any explanatory insight be gained if we thought of a particle as traveling simultaneously along several potential paths? A typical particle has at each instant several potential positions. Because all of them contribute to the story that explains the measurable properties of the system, they all participate in physical reality, and we are free to associate them in any way we wish. We could, for example, collect a temporal progression of positions in such a way as to mimic a standard Newtonian trajectory. Typically, many such collections are possible. But a grouping of potential positions would be merely an arbitrary imposition unless either experiment or theory justified assigning to it a common probability amplitude. Experiment does not, because the system is incapable of manifesting such a collection as a unit in a sequence of position measurements. The first interaction of the particle with a detector would introduce new probability amplitudes for the positions that lie farther downstream. At most, one of the potential positions can be revealed with the probability amplitude that the freely moving particle has. Nor does theoretical analysis naturally group coordinated positions together in such a way as to permit the extraction of a common probability amplitude from a coordinated set of positions and times. The reason for this difficulty lies in the technical fact that the phase velocity of the quantum wave differs from the velocity of the particle (which equals the group velocity of the wave). If the association is simply imposed on what the theory delivers, instead of being suggested by some hint from the dynamics itself, a mere conjunction of potential positions represents a trajectory rather weakly. I conclude that the criterion does not support an interesting concept of potential trajectories.

PAST INDEFINITE. Can we discover the actual existence of a trajectory after the fact? Suppose, for example, that a certain detector registers the particle in an arrival event that belongs to a particular trajectory. May we conclude from this fact that the particle has actually traveled straight from source to detector and not even potentially moved along any other line? According to the quantum theory such a conclusion would be false: It would amount to asserting, among other things, that if in this trial a detector had (*C*-possibly) been placed just at the nozzle of the source, it could not *Q*-possibly have registered the particle's emerging there at any time but the one belonging to this trajectory. The conclusion is false because emergings at other times remained as *Q*-possibilities until their opportunities had passed. Replications of the experiment, in other words, sometimes yield one of these results and sometimes the other. All of the potentialities possessed by a system contribute to its objective state until some of them are canceled as the wave function collapses during a measurement. Actualization does not operate retroactively. We cannot draw even so apparently innocent a conclusion as that the particle had an actual position right in front of the detector just before the moment of registration.

An object's possessing a certain potential value of a property amounts to this: The object has a propensity to manifest that value through its effects, either relatively directly in a measurement of the property itself or relatively indirectly in a measurement on another property causally dependent on the first. The criterion does not specify what it is for the object in itself to possess a potential value of any property, because it says nothing about the tendency except in relation to its effects in other things. From the viewpoint of realism, then, this criterion is desirable yet curiously unsatisfying. In explicating potentiality as a kind of propensity we imply, indeed, that it is an intrinsic property, lurking in the object even when we do not let it reveal itself; but, because we see only its effects, the propensity itself stays hidden. I shall return to this perhaps distasteful obscurity below, arguing that it is an inescapable feature of our epistemological situation vis-à-vis the world of objects.

The indefiniteness revealed by the quantum theory goes far beyond mere indeterminism. Not only is the future to some extent open, but even the past refuses to be pinned down. The history of the world contains alternative potential strands, all objectively there. In commonsense usage, potentiality points only toward the future, to what may yet come to pass, and multiple possibilities are either realized or rejected when their time comes; but in the quantum-mechanical sense potentiality remains multiple for all time. The past is just as indefinite as the future; reality itself is multiple. This multiplicity of present and past strongly offends our common sense. An objectively indefinite future might be acceptable, but how can we come to terms with an objectively indefinite past?

One mitigating consideration should be noted, however. One is strongly tempted to speak of quantum-mechanical indefiniteness in negative terms, as if the world pictured by the theory is somehow less substantial than the world of Newton, lacking something that Newton's possesses. But that manner of speaking undervalues quantum theory. The world of quantum mechanics is not less robust than the classical; far from wanting color, life, or activity, it teems with a superabundance. It is sometimes said that an electron "lacks a definite value of energy," as if the particle were less real than we thought it was in prequantal days. But in fact the electron is richer in its properties than classical physics allows for; it has the ability to reveal many different values of energy when put to the question by a measurement. The quantal picture of the world is not pale and shadowy, like a Monet cathedral in mist, but bewilderingly elaborate, like a Brueghel crowd scene.

SCHROEDINGER'S CAT. When precisely does the transition to actuality occur, and what sort of causal interaction is responsible for it? These questions are forced upon us by a thought experiment invented by Erwin Schroedinger (1935, p. 812) and now part of the standard lore of quantum mechanics. In Schroedinger's story, a cat is confined to an opaque box, which also contains a lethal device that either kills the cat or remains in ominous quiescence, depending on an atomic event that has two potential outcomes. Potentially, therefore, the device does its fell deed, and potentially it does not. And the cat, which for the purpose of this story is considered to be a mere machine, lacking a consciousness of its own, waits in a state of potential health and potential morbidity until the observer, raising the lid of the container and peering in, lifts one of those two possibilities into the realm of the actual. In his later views Schroedinger (1956) departed from the implicit dualism of this parable, choosing instead a version of idealism with a single, universal consciousness. Nevertheless, I shall refer to his earlier conjecture—that actualizations happen in the world of matter and that they begin at the portal connecting matter to mind—as Schroedinger's conjecture, or Schroedinger's model of the process of actualization. Heisenberg rejects this picture. He insists, instead, that "the transition from the 'possible' to the 'actual' takes place during . . . the physical, not the psychical act of observation," that is, as soon as the atomic object encounters the measuring device (1958, p. 54). In effect, Heisenberg adopts the additional postulate that macroscopic objects, of which measuring instruments are the outstanding example, do not share the indeterminacy of atomic particles; the modality of potentiality applies only to the microscopic objects of our study, not to the macroscopic instruments by means of which we study them.

Suppose that an observer examines the recording device in the double-slit apparatus long after the experiment has ended, finding that it records the previous arrival of a pulse from one of an array of detectors. In Heisenberg's view, the observer then finds out that the detector has changed at the earlier time from a state of actually being quiescent to a state of actually registering the arrival of a particle. The discovery is a transition merely in the observer's state of mind, but the discovered event is a prior transition undergone by the particle itself from potentially having many Q-possible positions to actually having just one. And all the other detectors, the observer also discovers, have been actually not activated all the time. Each potential history but one has now been contradicted (not just in our knowledge but also objectively) at the point where its assertion of multiplicity ran afoul of the uncompromising singleness of a measuring device. The plot thins during the course of the experiment, as the predictions of the various potential histories came due, one after another. In this paradigmatic situation, transitions from potentiality to actuality occur continually until, with a final rush at the moment of the actualization, all the surviving potential histories but one or a few participate in a general collapse. Or so says Heisenberg. In Schroedinger's model, all potential states, even of the macroscopic instruments, remain in force until the experiment registers in consciousness. Only then does the transition occur, everywhere and all at once.

In Heisenberg's view the observer's reading of the recording device reveals preexisting states of actuality. If our experience shows a particle detector to have received the particle at a certain time, then all the other detectors have been in states of actual nonactivation throughout, from the beginning of the experiment. Schroedinger's conjecture, on the other hand, retains potential positions everywhere until the moment that the experimental result registers in consciousness. Up to that very moment the particle might, with a definite probability, have revealed its presence elsewhere.

At this point in my exposition of the general features of the quantum theory I merely note these opposing conjectures about the transition from potentiality to actuality. Later, when I turn to the task of assessing antireductionist arguments based on quantum mechanics, it will be necessary for me to take a stand on the issue; then I shall argue for Schroedinger's interpretation. Before turning to those antireductionistic arguments, however, I must complete this survey of the quantum theory. Thus far I have illustrated its nature with paradigms that involve a single particle interacting with a measuring apparatus. In order to show the full force of the theory's insult to common sense, I must now turn to two additional stock examples of quantum systems, both of which involve pairs of particles. The first of these serves to lay to rest an attractive misinterpretation of the so-called wave-particle duality. The second introduces the perplexing problem of non-locality.

DUALITY. If we concentrate on single particles, we may be inclined to think that the wave that occupies one pole of the wave-particle duality vibrates in real, that is, physical, space—the same space in which the particle and its observer move. But that is not so. Consider the quantum-mechanical analysis of a particle confined to a cubical box. The wave for such a particle is a complex-number function of position between the walls of the box. The function itself receives no direct physical interpretation in the standard theory. Its squared absolute value, however, is a real-number function of position and does receive an interpretation as representing probability. Because the squared wave can be superimposed on the wanderings of the particle, it is easy to suppose that the wave and the particle coexist, or exist alternately, or in some other way share the physical space claimed by the particle. But that would be a mistake, as we can see when we turn to a system consisting of two particles confined to a single box. The wave function for such a system simply will not be settled into the particles' territory. The peaks and valleys of the wave spread out over a six-dimensional "space." Each point in the field over which the wave undulates represents a simultaneous pair of positions of the two particles; the $x_1$ component, for example, specifies the position of the first particle along the $x$-axis of the box, and the $x_2$ component does the same for the second. The domain of the function represents the set of all possible configurations of the two-particle system, not the set of spatial points in the box. The crests and troughs of a quantum-mechanical wave occupy a "space" never traveled by the particles. The wave cannot play Mr. Hyde to the particles' Dr. Jekyll, though that is what the notion of wave-particle duality seems to suggest.

In fact, the "space" that forms the domain of the wave function is a space of possibilities. Each possible configuration of the system has its representative in one of the points of this possibility-space. Regarding the box as a microcosm, we may see in one glance the multitude of all physically possible configurations of this small world. The squared absolute value of the wave function, by taking a value at each point in this space, assigns a probability to each possible configuration of the world.

THE EPR "PARADOX." Multiplicity may be the feature of quantum mechanics most repellent to common sense, but nonlocality runs a close second for that distinction. Both of these features are set forth in all their strangeness by a thought experiment devised by Albert Einstein, Boris Podolsky, and Nathan Rosen (1935), commonly known as the EPR paradox. The thought experiment, only apparently paradoxical, has been realized in several laboratories (Clauser and Shimony 1978; Aspect, Grangier, and Roger 1982; Aspect, Dalibard, and Roger 1982). The experiment exploits the fact that a composite system may have a single, definite value for some additive and conserved property such as angular momentum or energy, even though the particles that compose it equivocate. Typically, two particles initially closely associated in a single system and possessing a total value of zero for some additive, conserved property subsequently fly apart. Because the common property is a conserved quantity, the sum must retain its initial value of zero. Therefore, each particle must have the negative of the other's value. For the sake of illustration, let us suppose that the property in question is a component of angular momentum along some direction. Each particle possesses two potential values of the property, so that measurements can reveal either the positive or the negative value for particle number 1 and either positive or negative for particle number 2. Yet there are not four possible outcomes for a joint determination, but only two: In one scenario the first particle has the positive value and the second the negative, and in the other the assignments are reversed. It is not *Q*-possible for both to have the same value; that is why the total turns out to be zero in all *C*-possible worlds in which it is measured. In still other *C*-possible circumstances we measure the total angular momentum along other directions. Classical common sense tells us that the spin of one particle can be oriented definitely along just one direction in space. But quantum mechanics says that the particle possesses the same potential values along every imaginable direction. *C*-possible measurements can reveal some value along a certain axis, *R*-possibly the positive and *R*-possibly the negative; likewise along still another axis, and so on.

Accepting this pronouncement of the theory for the sake of argument, Einstein, Podolsky, and Rosen bring the following objection: Suppose that, while the particles are still in flight toward their respective measuring instruments, we decide to measure the *y* component of number 1's spin, getting, of course, a definite result, positive or negative. Whichever result turns up, we will then know with certainty that number 2, which we will not yet have touched or otherwise influenced in any way, has the opposite value, just as definitely. Therefore, because we will not yet have interfered with the second particle, it will already have possessed its value even before the contemplated measurement; therefore, it must possess it right now as we plan the next phase of the experiment. It must possess that as yet unrevealed value already, even though we may change our mind and decide to measure the first particle's spin along another axis instead. If we should do so, we know, the other measurement would reveal some definite value along that direction, and once this result has been recorded for the first particle we will know definitely that the second, still untouched, possesses the opposite value. Then, by another application of the argument we conclude that the particle already possesses some definite value along this other axis, as well. And likewise for every imaginable spatial direction: Because we could place ourselves in a position to know definitely about the second particle's component along any direction whatever, all without exerting any physical influence upon it, it must already, in and by itself, possess all of the information necessary to determine the results of any measurement we might *C*-possibly inflict upon it. How can this be? Because the theory performs altogether too well to sustain an accusation of incoherence, one might conclude that it is merely incomplete as to the story it tells of what the particle is doing. Perhaps a deeper structure of "hidden variables" underlies the property we know as angular momentum, and the other familiar properties as well, in such a way as to determine for each particle what shall be the outcome of any *C*-possible measurement.

This hypothesis of hidden variables does not command a large following nowadays, for various reasons. In the first place, in order to account for the perfect correlation between measurements made on widely separated particles, we would have to suppose that each carries with it a complete script to determine what values it will reveal when it meets an ideal measuring instrument. And that places a far too heavy burden on the information-carrying capacities of the infrastructure of the supposedly unitary particle. Second, according to a theorem of John S. Bell (1965), no hidden-variable theory that precludes instantaneous communication between the particles could account quantitatively for all of the correlations predicted by the quantum theory. This disagreement between quantum mechanics and the class of "local" hidden-variable theories sets up an oppportunity for an experimental confrontation. Experiments of this type have been carried out in several laboratories, with results that almost conclusively vindicate the quantum theory over its rivals. (See the review in Clauser and Shimony 1978, and the more recent work of Aspect, Grangier, and Roger 1982; Aspect, Dalibard, and Roger 1982).

The key assumption in the EPR argument is that properly conducted measurements always do nothing but reveal a state of prior definiteness. Therefore, when a definite value comes to light in a measurement we are entitled to conclude that, moments before, the object was already disposed to register that result and no other. But for this central premise Einstein, Podolsky, and Rosen offer no justification at all. Nor, obviously, do they feel the need of any: According to classical common sense that is exactly what a measurement should do. But just this classical truism is denied by quantum mechanics. In the transition to actuality one of a set of coexistent prior potentialities shoulders all the rest aside. The value is definite enough after the measurement has been recorded, but earlier than that matters stood quite differently. All the *Q*-possibilities were in effect then. So there will be no need to speculate about an elaborate level of hidden variables if we are willing to relinquish the commonsense and nearly sacred postulates of definiteness and determinism.

But there is more. If we grant that each particle possesses multiple potentialities before the measurement, carrying them around with it, as it were, and grant that the shedding of some of them in the transition to actuality is an objective event, how are we to understand the perfect correlation between the shedding that goes on in two widely separated, noncommunicating particles? Here on the right the first particle approaches a measuring instrument oriented along the *y*-axis. There on the left, possibly light years away, the second particle nears its detector, also oriented along the *y*-axis. The second measurement may happen so little later than the first that no material influence traveling at light speed or less could connect the two events. Hence, they are truly causally independent. Now, the first particle possesses two potentialities with respect to how it behaves in its measuring apparatus: On entering, it might *Q*-possibly bend in a direction that indicates a positive spin component, and equally objectively it might swerve in the opposite direction, indicating the negative value. According to quantum mechanics both possibilities are really there, and the eventual outcome, the actual registration of just one, is not determined by anything whatever. Yonder, light years away, the second particle faces a similar decision. It might reveal the positive value, and it might—really might—reveal the negative. The conservation law would be contravened unless the two values are coordinated properly, but how is this correlation to be achieved? In the absence of physical communication, how does each "know" which potentialities to erase so as to maintain the correlation? I shall return to this puzzling question in chapter 10.

TEN

# Mental Events in an Indefinite World

IN CHAPTER 8 I ARGUED THAT THE REDUCTION PROgram of atomistic materialism runs afoul of what everyone knows to be true of his or her own subjective mental episodes. I advocated a Cartesian dualism of mind and matter to resolve the discrepancy, claiming that only a mind not composed of particles could be performing the activities we know as sensory episodes. In this chapter and the following I reach the same position by an independent route. I argue that a straightforward acceptance of materialism leads to a gap in the causal story, revealing an activity for which no material agent will take responsibility. Again, a long-debated conjecture provides the solution: Only a nonmaterial mind could trigger the collapse of the quantum-mechanical wave function.

In the arguments of these chapters, I assume that our experiences put us in touch with an objective and at least partly nonmental world and that the present state of fundamental physics provides our most reliable knowledge as to the nature of matter. From particle theory, a branch of physics in constant flux these days, we get a fluid list of the fundamental particles and of their modes of interaction. From quantum mechanics we get a conceptual scheme for understanding change in general—both motion and transmutation—and how particles can interact to form durable structures.

Quantum mechanics, though a fundamental theory, may be fundamentally wrong. Overarching mechanical principles have been overthrown before. For that reason, any philosophical flour we might grind from the theory may have only a limited shelf life. We have, however, only two options: waiting for a completely trustworthy theory to come along (i.e., forever) or trying to interpret what we have, odd and fallible though it be. The quantum theory has survived a battery of increasingly sophisticated attempts to refute its central and most counterintuitive precepts. It has earned the right to be taken seriously. Still, if a radically different view of matter eventually supplants the quantum theory, then the task of interpretation must begin afresh. It cannot be helped. Only a limited amount can be established from first principles. I choose to take the risk of tentatively trusting the quantum theory in order to say something interesting and possibly not false about the world, rather than silently to wait for final truth. Quantum theory offers such a rich lode of philosophical ore that it would be a pity not to mine it.

Therefore, in these chapters I simply assume the truth of quantum mechanics as outlined in chapter 9 and search the theory for sources of light on how parts are related to wholes. The arguments that can be built upon quantum-mechanical principles divide into two groups. Some find in the theory's novel treatment of the interaction of particles a new sort of compositional holism. Others find in the theory's peculiar brand of indeterminism—especially as it comes into play in the process of measurement—hints of a new sort of unitary causal action by a nonmaterial mind.

## HOLISTIC FEATURES OF THE THEORY

Two closely related features of the quantum theory require us to treat conglomerates of particles in ways not required by earlier theories. These features may be called *nonadditivity* and *nonseparability*. Let us examine these examples to see whether they can support a new, quantum-mechanical holism.

NONADDITIVITY. This feature may be illustrated by a host of examples, including the EPR experiment discussed in chapter 9. The same point can be made more simply, however, by considering the angular momenta of the two electrons in a helium atom. Angular momentum in Newtonian physics is an additive quantity; that is, the value of the angular momentum of a collection of parts is given by the sum of the values belonging individually to the members. In its own way, quantum mechanics also treats the angular momentum of a composite system as a sum, because the operator that represents the angular momentum of the group is written as the sum of the operators for the individual parts. However, the quantum theory gives a strange new twist to the phenomenon: It shows that the whole system may have a definite value of the property while both parts remain indefinite. A helium atom may have a total angular momentum equal to zero, and have that value exactly, even though the two electrons whose motions generate the angular momentum have indefinite values of this property.

In such a state, and states like this are plentiful, the whole system is more definite—one might say it is more actual—than either of its parts. One might even want to add that the whole is more real than its parts, hence that its existence is not merely the outcome of their individual actions. But the case for such a statement is not a strong one, because quantum mechanics permits us to formulate, in a peculiarly quantum-mechanical way, an atomistic account of this definiteness of composite systems whose parts are indefinite.

The account draws upon our analysis of actuality in terms of physically possible worlds. In the case of the helium atom, the total angular momentum along a direction in space must be exactly zero in a two-component system when, in each potential state contributing to a superposition, the angular momenta of the parts have equal and opposite values. This example illustrates a general feature of the definiteness of composite systems, even those systems that are the subjects of the EPR experiment. The total value of any additive property becomes exact when the potential values possessed by the parts add up to the same total in each of the Q-possible states that contribute to the overall state of the system. Thus, even when the whole is definite with respect to some property while the parts equivocate, the definite value displayed by the whole is produced by the correlated potentialities of the parts. In every *Q*-possible world the property of the whole is the simple outcome of what the parts are doing.

NONSEPARABILITY. In experiments of the EPR type, when two parts of a system possess correlated potential states, any measurement that causes one part to actualize just one of its potential states also causes the other part to actualize its corresponding state. Both theory and experiment show that these correlated actualizations may occur even when the two parts are separated by a large distance. As we have seen, when a composite system whose total angular momentum is definitely zero separates spontaneously into two parts moving in opposite directions, each part carries two potential values, positive and negative, for this property, and these values may be realized along an infinite number of potential axes perpendicular to the line of flight. For each direction, the positive potential value for one part correlates with the negative potential value for the other. Now, suppose that the first part interacts with a measuring device and somewhat later, on the opposite side of the apparatus, the second part encounters another measuring instrument. The theory allows both devices to enter indeterminate states, composed of the correlated potential outcomes produced by the potential states of the two measured particles. But we know in fact that the two measuring instruments enter states with definite values—at least every device ever examined by a conscious observer has done so—and hence that the actualizations occur. According to an objective interpretation of quantum mechanics, each actualization is an event occurring in the observed system, not merely in the mind of the observer; Heisenberg's and Schroedinger's opposing conjectures about the transition to actuality agree at least on that point. Whether the first event results from the particle's encounter with the first measuring instrument or from the observer's inspection of it, the antecedent conditions do not suffice to determine the value recorded by the instrument. We must therefore consider the result to be partially uncaused. The "choice" of a positive or negative value seems to be freely made by the measured electron. Genuine novelty breaks into the causal web.

However, the value recorded in the second instrument is completely determined, yet not entirely by local influences. If the first measurement yields the positive value in a certain direction, and if the second instrument points along the same direction, then it is certain to register the negative, even if the second measurement happens only infinitesimally later than the first. These are puzzling facts, for two reasons. In the first place, the first measurement helps to determine the outcome of the second, even when no emissary, moving not faster than the speed of light, could pass between them. In addition, if two events occur nearly simultaneously in one inertial reference frame, they occur in reverse order in others; thus, we cannot point unequivocally to the agent of the supposed action. In attempting to reduce this compound measurement to a pair of causally connected single measurements, we find ourselves speaking of putative causal influences that propagate mysteriously from place to place without delay and with no need of physical intermediaries.

It is not self-evident, however, that the correlation of these two measurements results from an ordinary causal action of one instrument on the other. I suggest that the failure of this attempted reduction reveals not a flaw in the atomist program but our failure to reckon with the peculiar nature of the transition to actuality.

Traditionally, atomism has room for only two kinds of events: the shuffling of particles from place to place, as they assemble themselves into patterned clusters only to separate again; and the transforming of particles of one kind into particles of another. Even this second sort of event is admitted only provisionally, with the expectation that what appears to be a transformation will be revealed, following the example of chemistry, as the regrouping of other and more fundamental particles. And the causal action of standard atomism consists in nothing other than the influencing of some of these motions and transformations by others. Quantum mechanics makes no exception to this rule; indeed, within each Q-possible world it describes, the theory tells nothing but the standard sort of story; the ordinary canons of causality hold sway. The transition to actuality does not happen *in* any of them; instead, it simply prunes the luxuriating branches of potentiality. The pruning hook does not swing along a branch, as causal influences flow, but swings across it. Nor does the theory itself command the trimming; that task falls to the person who wields the theory, who *knows* that a measurement has delivered one of its *R*-possible results and not the others. At the time of the actualization the theorizer simplifies the story he or she is telling with the aid of quantum mechanics; presumably, therefore, the object correspondingly relinquishes some of its real possibilities.

Certainly, a kind of holism is displayed in the transition to actuality. But the unit to which this quantum-mechanical event points is not in general a composite, macroscopic *thing* in the usual sense of that term—in general not, for example, a biological organism or a piece of machinery. Rather, the unit seems to be an entire *Q*-possible scenario for the course of events. It involves pieces of many scattered commonsense things. Many such units participate in an actualization; all but one or a few participate by being cut off, thus ceasing to contribute to the total picture from the moment of the actualization onward, and the rest participate merely by escaping the general destruction, thus continuing to contribute.

Yet some active entity must be doing this metaphysical viticulture. If it could be identified it would qualify as the agent of a new kind of causal influence, operating from outside the manifold of space-time. As we have seen, Heisenberg and Schroedinger nominate rival candidates. But their dispute leads us away from the present theme of holism in the quantum theory; let us then defer that issue until we have considered how quantum mechanics treats interactions among composite things. The kind of holism that we seek would support our intuition that humans, and possibly other composite things as well, participate in causal interactions as units, not just as sums of the activities of their parts. To see what the quantum theory has to say on this subject, we must look at its prescription for how to describe the causal encounter of one structured collection of particles with another.

Like any other mechanical theory, quantum mechanics permits us to name conglomerates as units and describe them in terms of average or summed properties for convenience or by way of approximation, to simplify our description. That permission signifies nothing about the antireductive resources of the theory. Rather, the question is this: Does the theory *require* us sometimes to designate entire composite things as units, in order properly to describe their interaction? To what sort of unitary entities does the theory commit us?

## THE ONTOLOGICAL COMMITMENT OF THE THEORY

Like Newtonian mechanics with its three laws of motion, quantum mechanics builds on a basic law, in this case the Schroedinger equation or its equivalent, which predicts the behavior of a system only if its composition is specified in the boundary conditions. Both classical and quantum mechanics dictate the form of the specification. The objects are specified by means of the force function in the case of elementary Newtonian mechanics, the Hamiltonian function in the Hamiltonian reformulation of classical mechanics, and the Hamiltonian operator in quantum mechanics. When applying Newtonian mechanics to any specific system, one treats Newton's laws or their equivalents as a prescription for how to write the basic equation of motion of the system. Newton's laws contain a blank space, the filling of which turns a mere form for a differential equation into a specific equation for the system under consideration. Similarly in quantum mechanics, the Schroedinger equation prescribes how to construct specific differential equations for specific objects; the prescription form is filled in by writing the Hamiltonian operator appropriate to the system. This operator *defines* the object to which each quantum-mechanical description applies.

The Hamiltonian operator, representing the energy of the system, consists of two major parts, one for the kinetic energy and one for the potential energy. The kinetic energy expression is written as the sum of the kinetic energies of the parts, and the potential energy (like the force function in classical mechanics) represents the interactions among them. If a scientific theory reveals its ontological commitments by the entities it quantifies over, then the Hamiltonian operator in quantum mechanics, like its equivalents in classical mechanics, defines a physical system as a set of interacting parts. The events that transpire within a composite system are represented by the quantum theory as the combined motions and interactions of the parts. Although it departs from classical atomism in many respects, on this fundamental issue quantum mechanics stands squarely on tradition. We find, therefore, no reason to modify the classical dictum that a whole simply is what its parts do—that a living organism, for example, is simply one of the immensely complex patterned motions that atoms generate.

But what does the theory tell us about interactions *between* a pair of composite objects? If quantum mechanics is to restore the objects of everyday experience—ourselves included—to a solid ontological footing, it should justify our commonsense treatment of them as unitary causal agents in their interactions with other macroscopic things; and the justification should proceed by appealing to the way things are, not to approximations made for the sake of convenience, or by reason of the limitations of our ability to calculate upon large masses of data.

Queried in this way, however, quantum mechanics provides no reason to regard composite things as unitary agents. What we might hope to find—and what would certainly resolve the riddle of causal agency in a manner favorable to ourselves—would be a Hamiltonian that quantifies over composite systems (some of them, anyway) as units, representing interactions as occurring at least on occasion *between systems*, not always and only among their parts. Instead, we find that the quantum-mechanical analysis of a pair of interacting systems employs a single Hamiltonian, which quantifies over the same basic parts as did the individual Hamiltonians of the separate systems before they began interacting. For example, each individual hydrogen atom of an originally noninteracting pair is pictured as a proton and an electron. When the two atoms interact to form a hydrogen molecule, the plot may thicken but the playbill still lists entities of the same type; the interaction is pictured now as an event involving two protons and two electrons, that is, four entities, which reside on the original descriptive level. Causal agency continues to be described as the influence of particle upon particle, and the actions of one composite thing in touch with another are shown to be the actions of the parts.

A higher level of description that designates a composite system as an agent is simply not warranted by the quantum-mechanical treatment of interactions among composites. The exact analysis of an interaction does not transfer causal agency to either of the interacting subsystems as units. So we see that the atomist reduction program can be implemented also by the newer theory, at least in this respect.

Nevertheless, quantum mechanics seems to depart decisively from the Newtonian line by reserving a chair for consciousness. Operating within the older theory, one could isolate questions of mentality from discussions of basic physical processes and thus plausibly defer the mind–body problem until the final, mopping-up stages of the reductionist program. That deferral no longer looks plausible. Let us take a close look at the allegedly subjective features of quantum mechanics; perhaps we can use them to put up a radically new style of defense against the mechanistic reduction of human causal agency.

## THE ALLEGED ACTION OF CONSCIOUSNESS

Quantum mechanics suggests two possible lines of argument that could lead to a mentalistic retort to reductionism. One of them imputes subjectivity to the theory because of the central place it accords to probability, a prima facie subjective concept. The other alleges that the theory requires some causal agent to take on an assignment that no atom or group of atoms could perform, one that appears uniquely suited to consciousness. Let us consider, first, two possible intrusions of subjectivity.

IS QUANTAL PROBABILITY OBJECTIVE? Wigner (1961) builds an antireductionistic argument upon the probabilistic nature of quantum mechanics, claiming that a fundamental mechanical theory that gives an essential place in the workings of nature to probability places human subjective experiences at the center of the world rather than at its periphery, where atomistic materialism must have it. As we noted above, Heisenberg attempts to parry this sort of argument by producing an objective interpretation of probability as that concept functions in the quantum theory. So we must ask: Does Heisenberg's potentialism steer clear of subjectivity?

Heisenberg (1958) intends it to do so. "The probability function . . . contains statements about possibilities or better tendencies ('potentia' in Aristotelian philosophy), and these statements are completely objective, they do not depend on any observer"

(p. 53). Heisenberg's objective interpretation of probability finds an ally in the more extensively developed propensity theory of Karl R. Popper (1959; 1974). Popper defines propensities as "real dispositions; dispositions that determine relative frequencies . . . of any occurrences you may consider" (1974, p. 1130). Popper's way of objectifying probability will work for a physical system that does not obey strictly deterministic laws. Its behavior in the future is not merely an unfolding of its present state. At some or perhaps all moments in its history, it faces several real options regarding what to do next, independently of what we happen to know about it. At each moment the object has inherent tendencies to follow one or the other of its possible paths. If its behavior follows statistical laws, we can assign quantitative measures of probability that serve as predictions of the relative frequencies with which the various possibilities will be realized in a sequence of repetitions of the present conditions. Now, the quantum theory, unlike Newtonian mechanics, paints a radically indeterministic picture of the physical world. If the theory is correct and complete, then we are justified in locating tendencies toward mutually exclusive alternatives in single external objects themselves, independently of the contents of our store of knowledge. Heisenberg's and Popper's interpretations successfully counter antireductionistic arguments that attempt to build on the quantum-mechanical use of the concept of probability. In an irreducibly indeterministic theory, probability need not entail subjectivism.

DOES THE TRANSITION OCCUR OBJECTIVELY? A more difficult challenge remains. Heisenberg cannot avoid introducing a new kind of event into his objective picture of the quantum world, namely, the transition from potential to actual values of the measured properties of a system. The challenge, called the *measurement problem*, arises because the quantum theory assigns a probability amplitude to every possible configuration of a system and goes on doing so forever. Nowhere does the theory hint that some of the accumulating layers of potentiality are scrubbed away in these novel events, nor does it tell us when they might occur. But happen they must, for the conscious observer never enters a state in which experiencing something shares the stage with experiencing its contrary. When does possibility become actuality, and what object or agent bears responsibility for the transformation?

Schroedinger's (1935) parable of the cat proposes the hypothesis that actuality breaks in at the interface between consciousness and the world of atoms. Because conscious experience by its nature will accept none of the multiplicity that otherwise fills up the world of material objects, part of the clutter is cleared out whenever material things make contact with mind. Heisenberg attempts to parry this mentalistic thrust by insisting that the transition to actuality occurs at the point where the atomic object meets the measuring device, hence that it is "not connected with the act of registration of the result by the mind of the observer" (1958, p. 55).

If minds cause the transition to definiteness, then quantum mechanics has an answer to the question of whether human beings transcend and unify the causal actions of their atomic parts. Minds, in this view, take a hand in the conduct of the world's affairs—not by spinning within the atomic machinery but by exerting a new kind of influence from without. However, if the transition to actuality goes on independently of minds, this feature of quantum mechanics sheds no new light on questions about unitary causal agency. Consequently, an antireductionistic argument based on this feature must proceed by demonstrating the greater virtue of Schroedinger's version of the transition to actuality.

## POPPERIAN INDETERMINISM

Before taking up that task, however, I must first show that Heisenberg and Schroedinger differ over a substantive issue, not a mere pseudoquestion. Popper (1967) argues that questions about where the transition to actuality occurs are spawned by a mistaken interpretation of probability, from failing to recognize that probabilities are assigned in quantum mechanics relative to specified conditions such as the arrangement of the experimental apparatus and the initial motions of its parts. Probabilities, in Popper's explication, refer to objective dispositions or propensities in the apparatus itself; nevertheless, the sudden change in the values we assign to the possible outcomes of an experiment does not reflect an objective occurrence. Instead, what happens is a shift in our descriptive focus, from conditional probabilities that refer to the initial stages of the experiment to probabilities that refer to later conditions. Before turning to the debate over the agents of actualization, I must first show that Popper's argument does not dissolve the question at issue between Heisenberg and Schroedinger.

Popper constructs his explication of probability as propensity around three principles: (1) Propensities are inherent tendencies in things, not mere features of our knowledge or lack of it. (2) Propensities are properties of singular events, not just of classes or sequences of them. (3) Propensities are asserted hypothetically of physical systems, the hypothesis being testable by repeated trials of the experiments to which they are assigned (Popper 1959). These three features also characterize (albeit implicitly) Heisenberg's concept of potentiality as tendency, but there the analogy ends. Whereas Heisenberg views the simultaneous tendencies of a thing to do an action and all of its alternatives as a peculiar feature of quantum mechanics and as evidence that such things have a different mode of existence (the potential) than the objects described by ordinary common sense, Popper claims that the concept of propensity applies to Newtonian particles as well as to quantum-mechanical ones and that, therefore, no new mode of existence is introduced by quantum mechanics and no transition between modes need perplex us. Because the subsequent discussion will turn on the nature of quantum-mechanical transitions from the possible to the actual, we cannot ignore Popper's claim that such events occur also in a Newtonian context. Let us test the claim.

Can an individual trial of an experiment on Newtonian particles have an objective tendency or propensity toward two or more mutually exclusive outcomes? Surely not. In Newtonian determinism the future of an individual running of an experiment is already fixed when the objective initial and boundary conditions have been set up. Given its present state, whatever it may be, an individual Newtonian system is already committed to just one of the courses of action we in our ignorance reckon possible. Consequently, in any individual trial one and only one outcome is certain to follow—which one we usually cannot tell, because we do not know all the truth about the initial stages. Only our lack of knowledge about a Newtonian system justifies our speaking of probabilities; hence, these probabilities are not objective dispositions in the singular case. When applied to a Newtonian system, the second of Popper's three principles conflicts with the first.

It also conflicts with the third. Propensities in Popper's analysis are conditioned by the experimental arrangement to which they adhere, that is, by the initial and boundary conditions of classical or quantum mechanics. And a hypothesis about propensities must be tested by repeated trials of the experiment. Much depends, then, on what counts as a repetition; and that in turn depends on how closely we specify the conditions in our description of the experiment. If we characterize the experiment somewhat loosely, by not specifying the conditions down to the most minute detail, then states of affairs that differ objectively in properties that affect the outcome of the experiment will fit a single description, and we will count them as replicas of the experiment. Repeated trials, thus defined, will yield different results; consequently, propensities toward mutually incompatible outcomes may be attached objectively to the sort of entity that this description singles out. However, it picks out not an individual experimental apparatus but a class of them, a *kind* of experiment.

I submit that objective propensities pertain only to classes of Newtonian objects; singular cases admit only of subjective probabilities. We cannot find a model for Popper's concept of propensity in Newtonian determinism, because a rigidly deterministic world cannot have objective propensities that belong to singular events.

## PEIRCEAN INDETERMINISM

However, Popperian propensities do operate in an indeterministic world whose future is not contained in its present state. Now that quantum mechanics is well established, we can choose between two major and very different kinds of such worlds. An example of the first, prequantal sort is proposed by Charles Sanders Peirce (1892). He suggests that material objects may obey laws of Newtonian determinism only approximately, deviating randomly but circumspectly from them at any moment, as if by whim. In Peirce's speculation, whatever a material object may do it does definitely, with none of the equivocation we find in quantum mechanics. That Popper has in mind an indeterminism of this sort can be inferred from the way he uses retrodiction in a particle diffraction experiment (1967, pp. 26, 27): A particle moves through a single slit toward a planar array of detectors, where it localizes eventually at one of them. The quantum theory assigns probability amplitudes at the detectors for each moment in the particle's history. According to Popper, these amplitudes represent time-independent probabilities that are related only to the conditions obtaining at the start of the experiment. Later, when the particle adopts an actual location at some definite point, we use that datum to establish what the particle's actual path and velocity have been in its journey from the slit to the detecting surface. Relative to the initial conditions, the particle was disposed to move in many different directions; but relative to the conditions obtaining during its flight (conditions that were then unknown), it was disposed only to move along a single definite path and to strike just one point in the final plane. We discover which path has been the actual one when the particle strikes the detector. The earlier conditions were unknown to us at the time, but the measurement reveals them after the fact. Although it was not determined to pursue its chosen path at the moment it emerged from the source, it had made its choice by the time it had passed through the slit.

A Peircean indeterminism also aptly models Popper's thought experiment of a ball dropping through a pinboard—the sort in which the balls in repeated trials fall into various bins at the bottom, with frequencies corresponding roughly to the coefficients of the binomial theorem. Let us follow an individual trial of this indeterministic pinboard experiment. A ball, on striking the first pin, might—really might—bounce in several different directions, for the collision conserves momentum only approximately; consequently, both the ball's angle of approach to the next pin and its trajectory after striking it are even less well determined by the initial conditions. In a single trial of the experiment the ball settles into a bin in the bottom row by following an erratic but definite path as it bounces from pin to pin. In a second single trial, which starts out as an exact replica of the first—exact to the most minute detail—the ball exercises a different option, striking other pins and arriving at another receptacle. At the beginning of each individual trial the ball possesses objective dispositions or propensities to reach each one of the available bins, simply because its future is to a limited degree still open. Therefore, the event of the ball's arriving finally at a certain bin has a numerical probability relative to the conditions obtaining at the start of the experiment. Now, this assignment of conditional probabilities does not change; it may be tested by repeatedly restoring the same initial conditions and recording the relative frequency with which the ball arrives in that bin. Because each repetition of the experiment duplicates exactly the objective conditions of all the others, the propensity belongs objectively to the ball in that situation. The function that represents the probabilities of arriving in various bins is the analog in this experiment of the state vector in quantum-mechanical experiments. Nothing like a collapse of the wave packet happens here, because the conditional probabilities do not depend on time.

We can, however, construct something resembling the reduction of the quantum-mechanical wave packet. Let us define a time-dependent probability of the ball's arriving in the bin, relative to the changing conditions that obtain at each moment as the experiment develops. At the start this number is the same as the probability already referred to. But as the experiment progresses the conditions change, objectively. As the ball collides with the first pin it possesses objective dispositions both to move to the right and to move to the left, but it chooses just one of these options. And it goes on making such choices at each stage of its journey. Just as the ball strikes a pin in the bottom row, it must choose between the two receptacles immediately to its right and to its left—it can no longer reach the others. A different probability function applies to the final conditions than does to those at the beginning. At the end all the probabilities are zero except those for the two bins just below the pin now being struck, and for each of these the probability is now one-half. The experiment concludes with the ball firmly nestled in, say, the third bin. When we compute the probability of finding the particles in any bin relative to the final conditions, we find that the function has "collapsed" to the value unity for the third bin and zero for all others. In assigning a unit probability to just one of the possible outcomes and zero to the others, relative to the final conditions, we do no more than assert that if we look again we will still see the same result. No impenetrable mystery plagues us here; of the similar case of the flipping of a coin Popper enunciates the "trivial principle . . . that if we look at our penny a second time, it will still lie as before" (1967, p. 37).

This, then, is Popper's reconstruction of Heisenberg's transition to actuality: The objective possibilities in an indeterministic system become more and more restricted as the experimental situation develops. The discontinuous transition, he claims, consists of our shifting our attention abruptly from one set of conditional probabilities, which refer to the original stage of the experiment, to another set, which refer to the terminal stage. And the "state vector"—that is, the set of time-dependent conditional probabilities—changes nearly continuously, because choices are made continually as the experiment progresses.

Popper's analysis is certainly correct when applied to the sort of indeterminacy proposed by Peirce, which can be understood in terms of *R*-possibility alone. And the continual reduction of objective options does seem analogous to the reduction of possibilities in quantum mechanics. But in fact the indeterminate world of quantum mechanics differs radically from the world envisioned by Peirce, so radically that the analogy fails. *R*-possibility is not enough; we need *Q*-possibility, too.

## QUANTUM INDETERMINISM

To see how far Popper's analogy can be driven, and where it breaks down, let us alter Schroedinger's cat story by substituting for the cat an automatic mechanism. We place a radioactive nucleus, an emitter of electrons, near a crystal and a Geiger tube arranged so that an electron shoots out from the nucleus, scatters from the array of atoms in the crystal, and either hits or misses the tube. If the tube receives the electron it sends an electrical signal to a mechanism concealed within a box. This mechanism causes a small hammer to strike a silver watch, which was set running at the beginning of the experiment. The watch stops with its hands pointing to the time of the event. If, after an hour has passed, no signal has been received from the Geiger tube, this same mechanism actuates another hammer, which stops a gold watch. After two hours have passed, a human observer lifts the lid of the box, looks inside, lowers the lid, then lifts it and looks again. This contrivance matches Popper's thought experiment with a pinboard in four essential features. It includes the two measurements that occur in successive inspections by the observer. The apparatus includes something like the pinboard, namely, a lattice of atoms in the crystal. Third, the quantum-mechanical probabilities pertaining to the possible outcomes of the experiment (for example, the Geiger tube's being discharged or not) are assigned relative to the conditions obtaining at the beginning of the experiment; hence, as defined, they do not vary as the trial progresses. These conditions can be repeated exactly in successive trials, with the same state vector applying in every case. Finally, the physically possible outcomes picked out by the theory show the measuring instruments (the Geiger tube, the hammer, the watches, and the central nervous system of the observer) only in correlated states: In one such possibility, the Geiger tube lodges the particle, the gold watch ticks on, the silver watch is stopped at a position indicating the lapse of fifteen minutes since the beginning of the experiment, and the observer's brain encodes both a living image of the watches (from the second inspection) and a memory of the same scene (from the first). Another *Q*-possible picture painted by the theory duplicates the one just mentioned except that the hands of the silver watch indicate a different time; still another shows the Geiger tube untouched, the silver watch still running, the gold watch stopped at exactly one hour, and the observer's brain recording both the memory and the current image of the watches in this condition. In none of these distinct, *Q*-possible worlds does the brain of the observer encode a living image incompatible with the memory it retains, nor do these brain states fail to agree with the state of the watches. Thus, we may conclude that, in any physically possible world in which the atomic particle activates the Geiger tube, the first measurement records that fact and the second measurement corroborates the first.

It is hard to resist carrying this interpretation one step further by assuming that a measurement reveals the prior actuality of the *Q*-possible world to which the recorded result belongs. That would be appropriate in Peirce's indeterminism, which, although it cracks the rigid causality of the Newtonian world, retains its definiteness. The several threads of narrative to which we assign probabilities in a definite universe are realized in some trials of an experiment and contribute not at all to others—the ball finds its way to a bin by means of one zigzag path in one trial and a different path in another. Pursuing the analogy, we may suppose that in a given trial of this experiment the electron reaches the Geiger tube by colliding one by one with the members of one subset of the atoms in the crystal lattice, and in another trial it fails to hit the tube because it takes another path through the lattice. Like the ball in a single trial of the pinboard experiment, the electron continually makes choices, the discarded options making no further contribution to its progress in that particular trial until finally one and only one result wins the day.

Now many experiments with quantum processes do not reveal the error of such a view of probability. But experiments in interference, of which this atomic "pinboard" experiment provides an example, reveal that the world according to quantum mechanics is neither determinate nor definite. C. J. Davisson and L. H. Germer (1927), for example, in their study of the diffraction of electrons by a nickel crystal, found an interference pattern in the scattered beam: The electrons avoid regions of the detecting surface that they could easily reach if they collided with single atoms or sequences of single atoms of the crystal. The threads of the quantum narrative contribute—all of them—to each singular trial of the experiment. Normally, the strands separate permanently, and we do not experience difficulty with our mistaken assumption that just one of them (we do not know which) obtains in any singular case. But when particles diffract through slits, or collide with the atoms in a crystal, a dense new fabric is woven from the only temporarily separated threads; and we find the proof of their reassembly—and therefore of their continued contribution throughout the progress of the experiment—in the nonarrival of the particle, in all trials, at points on which it would sometimes land if it followed just one path in each trial.

The startling feature of the quantum-mechanical picture of reality is neither its indeterminism nor its use of conditional probabilities. Indeterminism is fairly easy to believe, and Popper argues persuasively that both classical and quantum-mechanical probabilities refer to the circumstances in which the dispositions come to be realized. Rather, the radical break between the quantum world and the world of classical common sense occurs over the issue of multiplicity versus definiteness. In prequantal indeterminism, free dispositions to do or not to do something point entirely toward the future, referring to causal sequences that an agent may initiate at a given time under the conditions then in force. An agent with that sort of freedom has not only counterfactual but also real possibility. I have called it *R*-possibility, to distinguish it from the *C*-possibility of Newtonian determinism and from Heisenberg's radically new concept, *Q*-possibility. If an agent can *R*-possibly perform an action at a certain time, and of course *R*-possibly not perform it, too, then when the time has passed it must be the case that the action either actually was performed or, though it might have been, actually was not performed. Real power abides in the agent, but the "choice" to exercise it or not must be made at the time and, once made, is recorded indelibly. Now we know from the Davisson/Germer experiment that it would be false to say, looking back on the completed process, that the particle actually collided with a given atom in the crystal (for that would entail that it actually did not bounce off from any other atom) and equally false to state that it actually did not collide with that atom. The scattering from atom number 1 figures causally in the story we tell to explain why every deflected particle avoided certain regions of the photographic plate, and so does the scattering from atom number 2, and so on. These *Q*-possibilities are not simply the real powers of common sense, not mere options that the freely acting particle exercises or refrains from exercising when the opportunity comes. Commonsense options crystallize as the fleeting present overtakes them; the commonsense past stands firm and singular. But in quantum mechanics the multiplicity is retained in what the moving finger writes. Even the past equivocates.

Hence, the probability amplitudes we calculate with reference to the initial conditions of a quantum-mechanical experiment do not admit of a continual updating as the experiment wears on. If quantum mechanics is correct, there are no hidden variables that could change objectively but under cover as the system evolves. New conditional probabilities are not called for toward the conclusion of an experiment—not because we happen not to know, or for inescapable reasons cannot calculate the altered conditions, but because the objective conditions themselves have not changed. Even relative to what the system is doing now (whatever that may be), long after the start of the trial, the probability at some future time of a given one among several Q-possible results remains equal to its value relative to earlier circumstances.

Popper's attempt to understand quantum-mechanical propensities as conditional probabilities of the familiar sort does not do justice to the radical many-sidedness of atomic objects. A thing's multiple propensities belong to it intrinsically and moment by moment, not merely in relation to its earlier circumstances. At each stage of its history, and in this metaphysically novel mode of being, the object acts (Q-possibly) in several mutually incompatible ways.

## WHAT CAUSES THE TRANSITION?

If the transition occurs objectively, it must occur somewhere and at some time; presumably, too, something must trigger the process. Where could this event occur, and by what agent's action? Let us consider, first, Heisenberg's account.

Heisenberg admits that the quantal world picture is less objective than the classical. The objectivity of prequantal physics entails the belief that we can "describe the world or at least parts of the world without any reference to ourselves." Now, although quantum theory "does not introduce the mind of the physicist as a part of the atomic event," nevertheless the new picture is "not completely objective" (1958, pp. 55, 56). Why does he make this admission?

In some passages Heisenberg suggests that a certain peculiarity of human language is responsible for "the paradox of quantum theory, namely the necessity of using the classical concepts" (1958, p. 56). Although he generally speaks in this context of concepts in the plural, he refers not to the ordinary physical concepts but to the metaphysical concept of potentiality. According to the quantum theory, it is the appropriate concept to apply to the particles, even to large systems of them, even to the collections of atoms that constitute the objects of ordinary life. Yet human beings cannot speak about macroscopic objects except univocally, that is, in terms of actuality. If the category of actuality were simply imposed on our scientific discourse by convention or by the limitations of the human brain, then the charge of implicating human peculiarities in the story about nonhuman matter would be well founded. But Heisenberg cannot intend us to take his claim in that sense. We do not lack the ability to speak of ordinary objects in terms of potentiality, and linguistic conventions can be transcended. The question is not whether we have the ability to utter them but whether claims of multiplicity are true of macroscopic things. Linguistic practice flows not from mere custom but from the facts of human experience. Our experiences of things are single; quantum mechanics pictures the things themselves as multiple: There is the "paradox." To the extent that we modify the atomic story by introducing elements of human experience, the quantal picture is not completely independent of "reference to ourselves." For example, information as to which particular potential event gets actualized must always be inserted into the story by appealing to human experience. However, we may reply that this appeal is required merely by the essential indeterminism of the world. We need to find out which possible outcome has won the lottery, but the drawing may nonetheless have been conducted, and its result recorded, entirely apart from human participation. In that case the involvement of human concerns in the scientific description would be minimal, and commonsense objectivity would survive. Heisenberg clearly intends us to adopt this view of the noninterventive role of human experience: "The observer has, rather, only the function of registering decisions, i.e., processes in space and time, and it does not matter whether the observer is an apparatus or a human being" (p. 137). So Heisenberg proposes the hypothesis that definiteness enters the world somewhere in the *physical* process in which the atomic particles interact with macroscopic instruments, before human observers engage themselves in the process. In this sense, too, subjectivity is kept at bay. Still, a problem remains.

Heisenberg points out that although we may freely enlarge the system beyond the atomic objects of measurement by including detectors, auxiliary measuring apparatus, secondary measurers of the first measurers, human sensory equipment, even brains, the quantum theory shows us nothing but multiplicity throughout the entire "closed system," no matter how far we extend its boundaries. However, we do find a way to put definiteness into the story. This is done "in the Copenhagen interpretation by the introduction of the observer" (1958, p. 137). This "observer" may be a mere machine; hence, no metaphysical novelties are implied. Even so, if we treat it as an ordinary collection of particles to which the laws of quantum mechanics apply in the usual way, we fail to get the definiteness we seek. Instead, this observing instrument must be introduced *ex machina*. We must insist that the multiplicity does in fact not obtain beyond this point in the measuring process. We exempt a portion of the system, the "observer," from the laws that govern ordinary objects (p. 137).

But how can we license the exemption? It requires a principled justification, a rule that extends the quantum theory by specifying the objective conditions under which the multiplicities predicted by the unmodified theory in fact do not happen. To accommodate the program of materialism, the new rule must not imply that anything but atomic particles, singly or in groups, participates in the transition to actuality—in particular, there must be no hint of a nonmaterial agent.

But the materialist program may fail. Perhaps definiteness does result from the interaction of the measuring instrument with a conscious mind. In what follows I shall argue for the dualistic alternative by means of a peculiarly vulnerable strategy. I shall not build a proof. Rather, having established in chapter 9 that the mind hypothesis is plausible, however distasteful it may be, I shall proceed negatively by attacking every hypothesis of the materialistic sort that seems remotely plausible. I do not know how to demonstrate that every conceivable materialist hypothesis must fail; but I hope to argue convincingly that the likelihood of success along that line is weak indeed. Finally, because one ought not to abandon a hypothesis, no matter how unpromising it has come to seem, without having a more promising alternative, I shall urge that we can adapt to the dualist conjecture's initially repulsive flavor—by dispelling part of it and by learning to like the rest.

## ALTERNATIVES TO THE MIND HYPOTHESIS

A measuring instrument is composed of particles just like those whose multiplicity it reveals to us. How, then, can we account for its steadfast rejection of potentiality? I shall consider seven strictly materialistic hypotheses about the process of actualization which, I submit, exhaust the range of even remote plausibility. I cast these hypotheses in the form of rules for actualizations. Were we to adopt one of them, it would function as an addition to the quantum theory, namely as a law governing the reduction of the wave packet.

RULE 1. Every macroscopic object that we notice, including the objects we employ as measuring instruments, exists only in the mode of actuality just because it is seen, because of its present or future connection to our senses. The atomic particles that we cannot perceive except by means of instruments may seethe with multiple possibilities, but the array of laboratory equipment that we attend to lies quietly definite; a watched potentiometer never boils.

Clearly, Heisenberg's program cannot accommodate this rule; for, by making current or projected perception part of the conditions determining whether an object can be actual or not, it inserts human sensory organs and perceptual dispositions into the measuring process—the very result his account of the process of actualization is designed to avoid. What goes on in the interaction between a particle and a measuring instrument ought to depend only on what it is doing then and there, not on relations that the device sustains with sentient beings: Neither its origin in an instrument shop nor its future inspection by a research assistant can add anything to the properties it carries to the scene. Rule 1 fails to conform to Heisenberg's program.

RULE 2. Every macroscopic object, and therefore also every instrument, exists only in the mode of actuality by virtue of its being a composite thing.

Against this hypothesis stand arguments proposed in chapter 1 for causal interactions in general and others proposed in the present chapter specifically for the interactions of quantum mechanics. These arguments show that causal interactions between composite objects, or between a particle and a composite thing, can be understood adequately only if we describe the interacting systems at the level of their parts. A detector, therefore, does not act as a whole when it swallows up a particle; that interaction, like all that occur among composite things, can be adequately represented only by a Hamiltonian that identifies the atomic parts as the actors. We cannot maintain the view that a particle interacting with a composite thing engages in an event different in kind from its interactions with a small group of particles of its own sort. Interacting with a composite thing just is interacting with such particles.

Besides, counterexamples to this rule are easy to find. We have seen, for example, that sometimes a pair of particles jointly possesses multiple potentialities. Even more conclusively, a variation of Davisson and Germer's experiment has been performed with helium atoms, each of which is composed of not less than six particles (Estermann, Frisch, and Stern 1931). The result is essentially the same as for electron diffraction: When a beam of helium atoms passes through a crystal of lithium fluoride, an interference pattern forms, showing that each atom scatters potentially from each of the atomic centers in the crystal. Clearly, composite objects sometimes exist in states of multiple potentiality, and rule 2 is contradicted by experiment.

RULE 3. Macroscopic objects are invariably actual just by virtue of their being macroscopic.

This principle can be stated more explicitly in three versions, with various degrees of strength, as follows: First, and most strongly, we might say that a macroscopic thing always has actual values of its *macroscopic* properties such as total mass, total linear or angular momentum, position of the center of mass, and the like. Second, we might say that a macroscopic thing is actual only in those properties currently under observation. Finally, we might allow a macroscopic object to have a range of potential values for its macroscopic properties but require that the range be so restricted as to be indistinguishable by macroscopic measuring instruments from a single, definite value.

The second version pushes the problem of definiteness back from the detecting instrument toward the conscious observer. Heisenberg's program, which aims to make the transition to actuality an issue to be settled among the material things themselves without the participation of mind, would not be furthered by this conjecture. It concedes too much to the line of interpretation that leads to Schroedinger's conjecture, and I shall not consider it further here.

Consider the first and boldest formulation: The macroscopic properties of a macroscopic thing are always actual. Despite the fact that the parts of a composite system always teem with potentiality, this suggestion cannot be dismissed out of hand. We have seen examples of definiteness constructed out of indefiniteness even in some very simple systems. The total angular momentum of the two electrons of a helium atom, for example, may have a value precisely zero, though each particle posseses both positive and negative values potentially. Along with this principle we shall also wish to maintain the conservation laws of mass-energy, linear and angular momentum, and the rest, as we do, for example, in analyzing the EPR experiment. Now let us see whether these two principles can be maintained within the laws of quantum mechanics as we have them.

Consider the Davisson/Germer experiment. The system consists of an incoming particle and a crystal lattice. The particle may be prepared initially in a state of definite linear momentum, as a plane wave of arbitrarily large extension across the wave front. Such a particle has precisely zero values of its linear momentum components in directions perpendicular to the propagation of the wave, and a precise nonzero value, related to the wavelength, in the direction of propagation. In these initial conditions, we describe the two-part system by assigning values of momentum and other properties to the incoming particle independently of assignments made to the lattice. Initially the particle has a definite momentum because of its manner of preparation, and the lattice has a definite momentum *ex hypothesi*, because it is a macroscopic thing. Therefore the entire system has a definite total momentum, the sum of the momenta of its macroscopic and microscopic parts.

Now let us apply the quantum theory to this example of scattering from multiple centers by adapting the analysis of the double-slit experiment. After some time has elapsed the description of the system can no longer be factored into independent parts. The story shows the particle arriving at any given detector in the terminal surface by scattering potentially from one lattice point with a potential momentum such as to carry it to the detector, from another lattice point with another potential momentum such as to carry it to the same detector, and so on. To each of these potential changes of the particle's momentum corresponds a change in the crystal's, so that the sum of the particle's and the crystal's momenta after the potential collision equals their sum before. We know from our analysis of the resulting interference pattern that the scattered particle exists in a superposition of several distinct momenta, because it converges from all lattice points to a single point on the detecting surface. Hence, the lattice possesses potential momenta that range just as widely as do the potential momenta of the scattered particle. We cannot understand the interference pattern without postulating the many converging potential momenta of the particle; and we cannot maintain the conservation law without postulating corresponding diverging potential momenta for the lattice.

Rule 3 stipulates that the crystal simply changes from its definite initial momentum to some definite final momentum. But the scattered particle's momentum is linked to the crystal's by a conservation law, as in the standard EPR experiment. Consequently, the particle must reduce its potential momenta to the subset that correlates with the crystal's definite, though unmeasured, value. But any such subset would be too meager to account for the observed interference pattern. Because the particle carries the same momentum into each potential interaction with a scattering center, and the crystal recoils (on this hypothesis) with just one definite momentum, the particle scatters with precisely the same potential momentum from each center. But equal momenta are parallel and do not converge to make an interference pattern. If we retain the conservation laws and the standard quantum-mechanical analysis of the diffraction experiment, we must allow that even the properties of macroscopic objects can exist in states of potentiality.

True, the potential momenta of the crystal in this example are all too small to be measured by the techniques of classical physics, such as measuring the velocity of the crystal; hence, there is no possibility of showing by such measurements that the crystal has any one of these momenta, much less several. But the practical unobservability of multiplicity in this example is not significant if our aim is to say what goes on among the material things whether or not we look at them.

In Schroedinger's thought experiment we can easily distinguish the potential states of the cat, but their alleged simultaneous contribution *in potentia* cannot be demonstrated by an interference pattern. In the Davisson/Germer experiment we can prove the existence of the crystal's potential macroscopic states, but a human observer cannot distinguish them. The two experiments complement each other. Taking them together, the conclusion seems inescapable: Neither individual particles nor macroscopic collections of them are immune to quantal multiplicity of any degree.

Nevertheless, that argument *proves* only a small degree of multiplicity. Perhaps something in the nature of things keeps the range of potential values so small as to escape detection by direct measurement; hence, measuring instruments would always look definite, even when they are not. This third possible explication has weaknesses of its own. First, it strains out a merely quantitative gnat while swallowing the camel of nonactuality. If an ordinary object has distinct potential values of position, momentum, and so on, no matter how nearly equal they may be, it has no actual value of these commonsense properties whatsoever. That is a radically different claim from the commonplace fact that we can never measure such a property with unlimited precision. This principle asserts that the property is not actually there. The commonsense realist about laboratory equipment should not accept that. Second, no more comfort can be extracted from this defense than the new parents got from observing that their unplanned baby was a very little one. Even if a macroscopic object started out with ranges of potential momenta and positions that satisfied the minimum allowed by the uncertainty principle, and if no further potential values were introduced by interactions with other things, the quantum theory shows that the eventual growth of the object's potential positions would be limited only by the amount of time available.

The principle might be rescued by adding that there is a law at work that cuts off the spreading potentialities as they verge on macroscopic distinguishability. But this attempt to patch up the rule looks suspiciously ad hoc. These macroscopic properties and their ranges are built up of sums of the corresponding properties and ranges of the parts. The elaboration, then, amounts to an imposed limitation on the potential values of the parts. But we know that the individual parts can have potential values that spread over macroscopic ranges. With respect to position, for example, each conduction electron in a piece of metal has a wave function that extends from end to end of the wire. So the limiting process must apply not to just any macroscopically distinguishable range but only to those coordinated potential values of the parts that would, if not suppressed, cooperate to make portions of the whole object's range discriminable by a macroscopic detector. Notice that there is no agent responsible for this pruning of potentialities. The particles must exercise self-restraint, with an eye, as it were, on the audience. I judge that this proposal of a merely apparent actuality in macroscopic things has passed over the line that separates the barely plausible from the excessively ad hoc. But others may judge differently; certainly sneering at an idea is not as effective as refuting it, and I have not refuted this one.

COULD it be that any interaction between a particle and any other material thing triggers the transition to actuality? Such a proposal could be formulated thus:

RULE 4. Whenever circumstances present a particle with a "choice" among alternative potential interactions with other objects, it will actualize just one of them.

This conjecture appeals strongly to commonsense intuitions about potentiality. In fact, it scarcely amounts to an addition to the contingent laws of quantum mechanics, being a simple unpacking of the commonsense meaning of potentiality. The possibilities of ordinary indeterminism, what I have called *R*-possibilities, look toward an open future; but when the opportunity presents itself, the free agent must make its choice. The result is then engraved in the history books. Despite its appeal, we may dismiss this candidate immediately, for the experiment of Davisson and Germer contradicts it, too. An electron or an atom of helium, facing potential interactions with a myriad of scattering centers in a crystal, interacts actually with no single lattice point but scatters potentially (in the sense of *Q*-possibility) from each.

Yet interacting with a detector differs in one suggestive respect from scattering by a crystal. A collision with the loosely bound conduction electrons in a photosensitive surface occurs inelastically and irreversibly. The incoming particle transfers an appreciable amount of energy to an electron residing originally in the target, and the repeated trials of this event do not belong to the same *C*-possible world. Instead, they make up a statistical ensemble of the sort treated in thermodynamics. As Leon N. Cooper and Deborah Van Vechten (1969) point out, only in statistically irreversible processes does the object impress on the measuring device a permanent record of its presence; consequently, thermodynamic irreversibility must characterize any instrument that might be used for measuring. This point is significant because, as these authors also point out, the scattering interference experiments occur reversibly, and these experiments generate our chief evidence that contrary possibilities coexist in the objects themselves. Let us take a closer look at this type of experiment.

The common element in the design of interference experiments is this: The experimental apparatus must possess two or more distinct Q-possible histories which are made to converge on a single outcome. And the evidence is negative: It consists of the nonoccurrence of a common result which would happen if the histories were traced out singly. In order to overcome the normal inconclusiveness of negative evidence, the experimenter must construct a multitude of replicas of the experiment and show that the result is missing from the entire set. For example, a large number of particles, each with the same well-defined energy, are sent through the double-slit apparatus one after the other; and their number is made so large that the frequency with which each Q-possible result turns up may be taken as a reliable indication of its probability. Hence, the absence of recorded electrons at a certain place in the completed interference pattern, formed by millions that do arrive at other places, tests the quantum-mechanical prediction that alternative C-possible paths converge and cancel at that point.

The evidential value of an interference experiment derives from its replicability. Repeated trials contribute to a single, sufficiently well-defined interference pattern just because they reproduce the same C-possible world and therefore the same set of Q-possibilities. Because of the essential design of interference experiments, such direct evidence of indefiniteness can be obtained only with respect to those portions of an object's Q-possible histories whose separation can be undone in the same way in each replica of the experiment. Consequently, we know that we will never be confronted by direct evidence of indefiniteness in any process complicated enough to involve a multiplicity of C-possible states, as always happens in thermodynamic irreversibility. In such conditions, no distinguishable interference pattern will be found, whether or not a transition to actuality takes place in the process. The absence of a pattern in irreversible processes cannot be counted for or against either of the rival conjectures. Insured against direct contradiction, then, let us propose another rule.

RULE 5. The participants in an interaction actualize their relevant properties just in case the interaction proceeds irreversibly.

This rule offers two advantages: It cannot be proved wrong in an interference experiment, and it focuses on just the feature of macroscopic objects that makes them employable as measuring instruments. The unfalsifiability of rule 5 assures that we can safely adopt Heisenberg's conjecture as a conventional prescription for choosing the point at which we insert fresh information about the result of a measurement. But if Heisenberg's conjecture is to serve his purpose, any rule we may offer in support of it must function as more than a heuristic device; we must be able to treat it as a hypothesis about the world of objects. But how can we evaluate an experimentally unfalsifiable hypothesis? Because a test lies beyond our reach, we must rely on other considerations, of which logical consistency is the most important. Let us inquire whether rule 5 fits logically into the rest of our attempt to interpret quantum mechanics objectively. We shall find that it does not.

The difficulty stems from the rule's reference to irreversibility. Statistical thermodynamics says that an irreversible process takes a system from a state of lower to one of higher probability. The relative probability of the initial and final states may be viewed from two perspectives: from the outside, with regard to the experimental conditions required to set the process in motion or to reverse it; and from the inside, with regard to the inner workings of the system's parts. From an external vantage point we characterize an irreversible process by contrasting the relative simplicity of the apparatus by which the parts are set in motion with the complexity—indeed, the practical unattainability—of the apparatus required to reverse their motions when they have attained the final state. Referring to the simplicity or complexity of the apparatus by which we manipulate the experiment focuses attention away from the atomic objects and toward the experimenter's limited knowledge of and control over atomic events.

Internally described, the probability of a state is a measure of the number of distinct patterns of motion of the microscopic parts (the number of distinct microstates) that we group together under a single macroscopic, and therefore partial, description. The internal perspective is equally subjective, because it connects the probability of a state to the degree of detail we build into our description of it. From either perspective, then, the concept of probability is used subjectively in thermodynamics, in precisely the sense from which Heisenberg's potentialism is designed to protect the quantum theory.

Heisenberg (1958) comments on a certain lack of objectivity in this proposed rule.

> At this point quantum theory is intrinsically connected with thermodynamics in so far as every act of observation is by its very nature an irreversible process. . . . The irreversibility is . . . a consequence of the observer's incomplete knowledge of the system and in so far not completely "objective."
> [Pp. 137, 138]

The thermodynamic distinction betweeen reversible and irreversible processes makes essential use of the notion of statistical assemblies. "If [one] tries to call a system's belonging to an assembly 'completely objective' [one] uses the word 'objective' in a different sense from that of classical physics" (p. 138).

Because Heisenberg explicitly disavows an interpretation of "observer" that would limit the term to conscious beings, we must interpret "incomplete knowledge" as an inability to discriminate between microscopically distinct states of the measured system, that is, as a tendency for the "observer" to respond in a single way to a group of distinct microstates of the object system. And yet Heisenberg says that even this metaphysically parsimonious account of the transition to actuality is not completely "objective." Why does he make this admission? He does so because, in saying that groups ("statistical assemblies") of distinct potential processes lead to the same result, we focus on a selected portion of the causal consequences of the interaction, namely, the glowing of a lamp or the swinging of a galvanometer needle, ignoring various microscopic distinctions that still obtain in the objects themselves. In effect, we say that nothing *significant* distinguishes the resulting states of the system-plus-apparatus, nothing noticeable to a further observer of that system. Thus, an implicit reference to "knowledge" remains in the story. That is the sense—an important one, I submit—in which Heisenberg says that the story is not completely objective.

The criticism may be put crudely thus: On one occasion an electron interacts potentially with a group of atoms arranged to form an array of photomultipliers, initiating in those devices potential processes of which large groups result in the same outcome, such as the lighting of a certain lamp, and other large groups result in the lighting of another lamp, and so on. On another occasion the electron interacts with a group of atoms arranged in a crystal lattice, initiating potential processes in the lattice that cannot be sorted into groups according to distinct macroscopic outcomes. The interactions in these two cases are distinguished by their outcomes in the large, many-atom system with which the electron interacts. But the question of whether the electron does or does not reduce its range of potentialities in an interaction ought to be settled by what is going on there and then, not by what will happen on some future occasion. Why should the natures of the two outcomes matter to the electron so strongly as to induce it to actualize just one of its potential interactions when it faces several photomultipliers, and to retain them all when it faces the prospect of being scattered by the atoms in a crystal? The conjecture that the nature of the potential outcome of an interaction induces the transition to actuality looks strangely like crediting prescience to the particle.

A rule of a different sort has been proposed by Richard Schlegel (1980, pp. 212, 213). He casts his principle in the form of a limitation on the sort of superpositions that may occur in nature. Schlegel introduces the notion of the "modified general Lorentz group" of transformations, defined as "the standard velocity transformation, spatial translation and rotation, space but not time inversion, and charge conjugation." The operations of this group represent the symmetries inherent in the basic interactions of physics. Schlegel notes, as a "generalization from experience," that the various Q-possible states of a particle, its superposed states, are related by members of this group. Thus the various potential positions of a particle can be transformed one into another by spatial translation; and a particle's various potential momenta are interchangeable by velocity transformations. The multiplicity of a particle's states is achieved, Schlegel suggests, by means of the transformations of the modified general Lorentz group. The "restricted superposition hypothesis," then, can be formulated thus:

RULE 6. "The only states which can enter into a superposition are those which can be reached, one from the other, by the operations [of the modified general Lorentz group]" (p. 212).

Consider two successes of this hypothesis. First, it does not forbid macroscopic things to exist in states of superimposed potentiality. For example, it accommodates the superposition of momentum states that we must assign to the recoiling crystal in the Davisson/Germer experiment; these states can be transformed one to another just as the superposed momenta of a single particle can. Second, if the principal is applied to composite systems as wholes, it forbids superpositions of macroscopically distinguishable states. A blackened grain at one point in a photographic plate cannot be converted into a blackened grain elsewhere by displacing the plate, or rotating it, or by any combination of operations applied to the plate as a unit. The conversion can be made but only "in a highly derivative manner"; that is, only by applying the transformations separately to the individual particles that compose the system (Schlegel 1980, p. 213).

Despite these successes, the hypothesis fails to accommodate superpositions that we know to be present in many-particle systems, for example, in EPR experiments. Consider a system that separates into two equal parts while conserving energy and linear momentum. Let it be a sodium dimer, say, initially having zero total momentum in some inertial reference frame and an indefinite position. Let it start out in an antibonding state whose energy is not sharply defined, in accordance with a lifetime *T*. Later, at a time less than *T*, the system's *Q*-possible states include (1) the still intact dimer, (2) a pair of sodium atoms moving with equal and opposite momenta of a certain magnitude, (3) the same pair moving with equal and opposite momenta of a different magnitude. These three are typical of the members of the superposition. No transformation of the modified general Lorentz group nor any combination of them, applied to the whole system, can transform one of these states into another. However, although a single transformation to a moving reference frame can connect the undissociated dimer at rest to the rest frame of *one* of the separated atoms, a different transformation is needed to reach the frame of the other. Yet another connects the rest frame of one of the separated atoms in state 2 to the rest frame of the same atom in 3; but a different transformation is required to connect the superposed states of the other atom, because it is moving in the opposite direction. If it is to work in this experiment, the restricted superposition hypothesis must be applied only particle by particle. But that reading of the hypothesis will not solve the measurement conundrum. Such an interpretation would not forbid the photographic plate in the double-slit experiment to exist in superposed states. And, because each particle's potential state in the dead cat is related to its state in the living one by a combination of members of the modified general Lorentz group—a different combination for each particle—Schroedinger's cat is allowed to retain its several degrees of health.

Finally, suppose that the quantum system adopts a narrower range of potentialities under a variety of circumstances but that no specifiable common factor in them determines that it must do so. That is the conjecture proposed by Nancy Cartwright (1983). It is questionable whether this proposal should be called a rule, but I shall do so anyway and formulate it in Cartwright's own words:

RULE 7. "There need be no general characteristic true of situations in which the evolution is deterministic [i.e., no loss of potentialities] and false when the evolution is indeterministic [the wave packet is reduced]" (Cartwright 1983, p. 201).

In support of this proposal Cartwright asserts that we have many examples of experimental situations, in addition to measurements, where the wave packet is reduced. Thus,

> Von Neuman claimed that reduction of the wave packet occurs when a measurement is made. But it also occurs when a quantum system is prepared in an eigenstate, when one particle scatters from another, when a radioactive nucleus disintegrates, and in a large number of other transition processes as well. . . . There is nothing

> peculiar about measurement, and then there is no special role for consciousness in quantum mechanics.
> [1983, p. 195]

The plausibility of Cartwright's proposal depends on whether this assertion is correct. Let us test it. Do we have reason to believe that potentialities are erased in apparatuses that prepare beams of particles in eigenstates? Consider one that prepares atoms in eigenstates of angular momentum, such as the Stern/Gerlach experiment. (Preparations of this sort have been discussed in Wigner 1963, p. 159, and in Feynman, Leighton, and Sands 1965, pp. 5–9.) A typical apparatus separates excited, metastable helium atoms, which have three potential orientations of total *z* component of spin, plus, zero, and minus. These atoms pass through a region of nonuniform magnetic field, emerging on the far side in three beams, one for each of the three eigenvalues of total spin component. Cartwright seems to claim that each atom, originally owning all three potential values, has chosen just one of them by the time it reaches the far side of the magnet. Unlike the double-slit experiment, in which each individual particle passes through the apparatus potentially in every possible path, in an experiment that emits beams of distinct eigenstates, each particle passes definitely along just one of the three possible paths.

As Wigner's and Feynman's discussions show, orthodox quantum theory does not condone this story. In principle, an experiment could show which account is correct. The preparation experiment can be modified by sending into it a beam of particles all of which are in an eigenstate for a different orientation of magnetic field, and hence in a well-defined superposition of the three eigenstates for the orientation of this magnet. The magnet then produces three distinct beams. Beyond it another device brings the separated beams back together. Finally, a second Stern/Gerlach separator, oriented along the direction of the original, incoming eigenstate, tests the condition of the particles. If the atoms undergo a transition to a definite eigenstate in the first separator, then they will constitute a mixture of eigenstates in the recombined beam; that is, some will be in one eigenstate of orientation to the separating magnet's field and some in another. None will have the definite orientation it had as it entered the apparatus. With respect to that axis of orientation each will now be in a superposition.

However, according to the orthodox theory the reconstituted beam is restored to its original eigenstate. This result means that each individual particle passes potentially through each beam, interfering with itself in the region of reunion, where the interference reconstitutes its original eigenstate. An apparatus that prepares beams of distinct eigenstates does not send one particle definitely into one beam and another definitely into another; each particle goes potentially into every beam. Or so says the orthodox theory. Intuitions differ as to whether it can be trusted to this extent. What would happen if the experiment were performed? Wigner says, "There is little doubt that in this case the orthodox theory is correct" (1963, p. 161). Cartwright, on the other hand, entertains a large doubt.

What can we learn about Cartwright's conjecture from actual experiments? Part of her claim concerns an apparatus that produces nonoverlapping beams of particles in distinct eigenstates. One well-known optical device provides the evidence we seek. (Experiments with photons, though perhaps less satisfying than those done on non-zero-mass particles, are often easier to perform.) The polarization beam splitter, a variant of the Nichol prism, accepts photons in an input beam and sorts them into two mutually perpendicular output beams in such a way that the photons in one have a horizontal linear polarization and those in the other are polarized vertically. This device does for photons what the Stern/Gerlach magnet does for spin-one-half particles. The output beams could be sent separately into other experiments, in the interpretation of which one would normally treat each beam as delivering particles in a well-defined state, not merely components of a superposition. But do the particles really enter definite states as they pass through the beam splitter? We can find out by pursuing an analogy to the experiment discussed by Wigner and Feynman.

Let the input photons be prepared in an eigenstate of linear polarization along a line oriented at forty-five degrees to the vertical. Each photon in this beam has an equal chance of emerging in the horizontally or the vertically polarized output beams, having made a transition from its original state. Mirrors placed in the paths of the emerging photon beams make them converge at some distant point. When we test the reunited beam with a polarization analyzer, we find not a mixture of two kinds of particles, half in one eigenstate of the separator and half in the other, but just one kind: All the photons have the eigenvalue that they carried into the beam splitter.

Wigner's confidence is vindicated, at least for photons. Each particle samples both beams. Therefore, contrary to Cartwright's conjecture, the individual photons do not adopt exclusively one or the other of the two eigenstates offered to them. Here is an apparatus that prepares particles in distinct eigenstates, yet fails to reduce the wave function.

Cartwright also rejects the orthodox interpretation of scattering:

> A particle with a fixed direction and a fixed energy bombards a target and is scattered. . . . We may circle the target with a ring of detectors. [But] even without the detectors, the particle must be travelling one way or another far from the target.
> [1983, p. 194]

Well, that supposition appeals very strongly to our classical intuition, but the Davisson/Germer experiment refutes it. An individual particle retains its manifold potential positions and momenta after scattering potentially from each atom in an array of targets in a crystal. Only a spontaneous reduction after the particle scatters, while it is in flight toward the detectors, could save Cartwright's assertion that the particle has a definite trajectory "far from the target." Perhaps particles spontaneously shed their potentialities while in solo flight between collisions—the more probably the longer the flight. This hypothesis, too, could be tested; it implies that the interference pattern would gradually be washed out as the distance between the detectors and the scattering crystal increases. Certain it is, however, that orthodox quantum theory does not accommodate this sort of spontaneous reduction; neither, so far, does experiment.

The conjecture that radioactive decay produces particles with definite trajectories would be harder to test. The particles emerging from the beta decay of a collection of nuclei could in principle be allowed to enter a double-slit apparatus. According to the orthodox theory, each beta particle passes potentially through each slit, interfering with itself in the plane of the detectors beyond. An interference *pattern*, however, will not be built up by these particles because the individual nuclei do not emit their electrons in phase; hence, the maximums and minimums of one particle's probability distribution do not coincide with those of another.

Cartwright proposes that the orthodox theory must be modified to accommodate these alleged cases of spontaneous reduction of the wave packet. If such reductions indeed occur, then we do not need the hypothesis that consciousness plays a special part in quantum phenomena. But we have no evidence to support Cartwright's conjecture and much that weighs against it.

None of these seven attempts to make sense of the transition to actuality accomplishes what we demand of it. I submit that, if we insist on speaking only about material particles, any attempt to interpret quantum mechanics realistically will fail. However, we could continue to speak of the events in the laboratory next door as if they run on without help from ourselves, provided that we add to our inventory of its contents another causal agent that is not a particle or a group of them, namely, the mind of the investigator who labors there.

Persons who are unwilling to abandon the physicalist theory of mind will find such a proposal unacceptable. But those who already suspect the physicalist program could find a place for minds, for in doing so they would merely be granting employment to an acknowledged applicant. As an inducement to the former group, I have offered in chapter 8 an argument for dualism that flows naturally from the central theme of these essays, namely, the tension between unity and plurality that strains even a Newtonian world view. But the Newtonian and quantum-mechanical arguments stand or fall independently. Both support a metaphysical conclusion so widely doubted as almost to require parallel and independent buttressing. Let us examine more closely the implications of the proposal that minds effect the transition to actuality. Indeed, short of abandoning realism, we seem to have no alternative.

## THE MIND HYPOTHESIS

Why are actualizations associated with potential interactions in a photomultiplier and not with those in a crystal lattice?

Nothing that appears at all relevant to our concerns distinguishes the events as to their objective, intrinsic properties, but there is one obvious difference in their causal consequences: Because of the way the apparatus is arranged, potential collisions in distinct particle detectors lead to experientially distinct potential brain states in the graduate student who is conducting the experiment, whereas potential collisions with distinct atoms of the crystal are not so coupled to an observer's central nervous system. Should we then conclude that cortical neurons possess in themselves the power to compel transitions from the possible to the actual? No, we have shaken off essentially the same error in connection with rules 2, 3, and 4. Neurons contain the same atomic particles as are found in crystal lattices and photomultipliers, and their causal connections with other pieces of matter proceed by means of the same types of interaction.

Quantum mechanics, relentlessly applied, indicates that interactions among material objects spread potentiality more and more widely. Now potentiality has been interpreted only partially and indirectly, merely as a tendency to generate experiences, usually incompatible ones. It is, of course, much more than this, for the multiple activity that underlies it goes on whether minds are connected to it or not. Nevertheless, it is proper to inquire as to when these tendencies get realized. Toward what definite result does an indefinite system tend?

The answer proposed conjecturally by John von Neuman and by Wigner is this: A brain, sharing the multiplicity of a larger system to which it is coupled by means of sensory organs and measuring instruments, tends to produce a definite state in a metaphysically distinct kind of entity by means of another kind of interaction, one that joins the material and the mental orders. Taking Schroedinger's conjecture seriously, we conclude that quantum mechanics speaks the truth in all of its assignments of potentiality to material objects, up to and including the neurons in a brain, being curtailed only at the point where it induces a mind to undergo an actual experience. This is actuality in its primary sense. And the mind reacts upon the particles. In that transaction between ontological categories, and only there, do some of the correlated potentialities of cerebral cortex, retina, photomultiplier, and scattered electron vanish from the objective world, leaving a much reduced set.

This condition is often called actuality among the particles. The definiteness achieved here is, of course, limited to the set of properties involved in the chain of causes that connects the traveling electron to the cerebral cortex. In the plane of the detectors the particle acquires a more nearly definite position but not a definite momentum, because those instruments have been connected to the observer's sense organs in such a way that distinct positions, but not distinct momenta, lead to distinct subjective experiences.

Admittedly, Schroedinger's conjecture seems impossibly fanciful. Instinctive, naive realism leads us almost irresistibly to treat our experiences of the world as utterly transparent, as placing us in direct contact with the perceived thing. We pay attention to the block of stone, not to the eyes and fingertips through which we experience it. Only by philosophical effort are we able to distinguish the experience from its object.

Experience never superimposes incompatibles. Just so, no material thing big enough to be seen or felt or heard has ever been experienced in incompatible states. As with our bodies, so with our tools; we project our experiences out to the very tip of the measuring instrument that mediates them. No cell viewed through a microscope, no particle located by a detector, is ever "seen" in incompatible states. Only with difficulty, keeping in mind the uncompromising results of interference experiments as well as the more subtle indications of quantum mechanics, can we avoid the erroneous generalization that those objects are inherently as definite as the experiences. And, provided we restrict the generalization to thermodynamically complex systems, we can keep up the pretense. Just as the artist leaves his brushes in the studio when the painting goes to the gallery, so we exclude the experimenter's retina and photomultipliers from the scientific picture of the objective world. Indeed, we gain a considerable convenience in exposition if we yield to our innate proclivity to think of the act of observing as merely revealing to our receptive minds the results of previously completed transitions to actuality. No practical harm results, either, provided only that we do not attribute actuality more lavishly than the subjective experience warrants us to do.

Because we can never control the microscopic parameters of a measuring instrument so minutely that repeated trials of an experiment could generate an interference pattern for the instrument itself, Heisenberg's conjecture that measuring devices prick the bubble of potentiality cannot even in principle lead us to err in predicting observations. The disagreement between his and Schroedinger's conjecture, therefore, carries no meaning whatever in the context of an instrumentalist view of science. If experiences are all we can ever know or care about, then the precise locus of the transition to actuality matters not a whit. But Heisenberg is concerned to maintain the realist doctrine that a knowing subject makes contact with objects that are other than self and that our best physical theories reveal something of what goes on in the objective world. Consequently, the practical indistinguishability of his and Schroedinger's divergent conjectures does not diminish their philosophical importance. We want to know what entities comprise the furnishings of the world; and one criterion of what to place on our inventory is the consistency of the story we can tell about the machinery of nature. We have seen that, although Heisenberg's conjecture sets minds off from the world of material objects, it commits us to a distastefully arbitrary treatment of measuring instruments, whereas Schroedinger's allows us to place all material things and their interactions under the dynamical laws of quantum mechanics. On the latter view, all of the parts of a system share in its possibilities, and all participate in the transition to actuality. Only Schroedinger's speculation applies quantum mechanics consistently to all material things without implying the presence of hidden variables and without introducing arbitrary distinctions among macroscopic objects. To the extent, then, that we are guided by the current state of scientific theory, we are impelled, or at least nudged, toward a metaphysical dualism of matter and mind.

Although dualism fits not at all comfortably into the atomist program of Democritus and Lucretius, physics has reached it by following the program faithfully step by step, yielding only to the facts that have turned up along the way. Quantum mechanics makes room, as Newtonian did not, for a new kind of causal action, in addition to mechanical causation. By admitting minds as the agents of actualization we can regard as more than merely illusory our intuitions about ourselves as unitary causal agents who sometimes introduce novelty into the flow of events.

Indeed, quantum mechanics seems to deliver what Charles

Sanders Peirce and William James call for in their attacks on determinism. Writing before the advent of quantum mechanics and trying to find room for the exercise of human will in the course of events, Peirce wants to admit "pure spontaneity . . . as a character of the universe" (1892, p. 333). He advocates a doctrine of absolute chance not for its own sake but because chance loosens "the bond of necessity," thus making "room for another kind of causation, such as seems to be operative in the mind" (p. 334). Peirce is content to postulate a severely limited indeterminism, one that lurks within the gaps left in the scientific world picture by the inescapable imperfections of scientific instruments (p. 329). Daring more than Peirce, James (1897) anticipates almost exactly the flavor of the potentialist interpretation of quantum mechanics as he attempts to support "our ordinary unsophisticated view of things." "To that view," he says, "actualities seem to float in a wider sea of possibilities from out of which they are chosen; and *somewhere* . . . such possibilities exist and form a part of truth" (p. 150). Like Peirce, James takes an interest in chance because of the space it clears for volition. Human choosings, he says, seem to have "the strange and intense function of granting consent to one possibility and withholding it from another, to transform an equivocal and double future into an inalterable and simple past" (p. 158).

Quantum mechanics sets a limit to the program of atomistic reduction and provides an important supplement to its model of causal agency. It does so by forbidding the reduction of consciousness and by assigning a peculiar task to minds. In one interaction, material objects induce a mind to undergo a state of consciousness and the mind reacts upon the material system, causing transitions to actuality. In this new type of causal process lies the possibility of a new reply to mechanistic reductionism, one that is forbidden by Newtonian determinism and is unimaginable in the context even of Peirce's indeterminism. Quantum mechanics does not dictate the details of this reply, but a little cautious speculation may permit us to guess its general trend.

As a cautionary transition to the next chapter, let me emphasize that the success of quantum mechanics permits us—indeed, some feel that it encourages us—to adopt an instrumentalist view of scientific theorizing, grounded on an idealist metaphysics. Schroedinger has demonstrated this in one of his later essays

(1956). If that is our choice, however, then quantum mechanics functions merely as a calculating device for relating one set of experiences to another, and there our investigation must end; we can ask no further questions about the nature of things. But if we persist in applying the categories of actuality and potentiality to the world of objects, then we can ask and answer further questions. Such activity is preferable to silence, even though the answers we breathe out may seem to have been inhaled from a pipe. Reading quantum mechanics realistically, as the correct and fundamental story about the way things are, we find it possible to make some progress toward a picture of the general scheme of things. Inevitably, the picture will have regions of obscurity, even blank spaces, but we can also hope for areas of clarity, fantastic though they may seem. Let us make the attempt.

ELEVEN

# Notes for a Quantal World Picture

## INTRODUCTION

LET ME NOT RAISE FALSE EXPECTATIONS: I SHALL NOT quell the major objection to matter–mind dualism. My aim in this concluding chapter is more modest. While acknowledging the problems of dualism and the misgivings it arouses, I want to recommend the philosophical challenges it lays before us. The objection is serious, but I submit that none of our alternatives is problem-free; hence, we can only choose to replace one complex of puzzles and embarrassments by another. We can, however, try to choose wisely. If the arguments of the three preceding chapters carry the load I have placed on them, an atomistic materialism is untenable. And I have set its nonrealist alternatives outside the range of these essays, for two reasons. First, idealisms and phenomenalisms cannot do justice to our strong sense of being acted upon by external, independently existing agents. Second, they fail to provide the impetus for further inquiry that we get from an attitude that grants real causal agency to molecular, atomic, and subatomic particles. Only microphysical realism, or something practically indistinguishable from it, namely, a willingness to act *as if* the invisible particles are really doing things out there, could have produced molecular biology, structural chemistry, and particle physics. Merely looking for mathematical or verbal formulas to correlate experiences, I submit, would not sustain or even make sense of the advance of modern natural science. As guides for inquiry, idealisms and phenomenalisms are stultifying.

Nevertheless, to many thoughtful persons the dualism I have endorsed will seem intolerable. What remains, then? Just this: to find a way to tolerate it. As an initial effort toward that end, I shall try to peer a short way ahead into the terrain opened to us by a Western, realistic interpretation of the quantum theory. I want to show that the dualist's position is more than tolerable—it is even interesting. To support that claim, I shall pose some questions of the sort that could not arise without at least a crypto-realist interpretation of atomic theory but that make sense as puzzles within a realistic dualism. Further, I shall try to show that something interesting comes from this speculation; that is, that it leads to some more or less plausible conjectures.

Dualism's main objectionable feature is highlighted by these questions: How could metaphysically distinct things—an individual mind and the shifting coalition of atomic particles that constitutes an individual brain—achieve the intimacy that dualism assigns to them? How can we understand the ability of a mind to be acted upon by one brain rather than another, and to react upon an even larger collection of particles as it induces the transition to actuality? The opacity of this puzzle is widely felt. Hilary Putnam (1979), quoting Shimony, asks, "By virtue of what *properties* that it possesses is 'consciousness' able to affect Nature in this peculiar way [reducing the wave function]?" and replies, "No answer is forthcoming to [this question]" (p. 165).

Two sorts of response may be adopted here. Let us see whether either can help us.

First, we can call for patience and further study. This plea, however, must be supported by some indication that the patience will be rewarded, that study might produce some plausible and enlightening stories. Of course, further study might refute indeterminism. It is conceivable that potentialism may yet be rooted out of the quantum theory if experimental attempts to show the presence of hidden variables finally succeed. But that outcome does not appear likely. A general ontological program such as dualism will probably not be established or overthrown by further work in the laboratory. Rather, it must recommend itself by bearing other intellectual fruit. One of the hallmarks of a promising paradigm is its ability to generate specific puzzles—interesting, limited questions to which plausible answers can be proposed. If dualism leads us only into an embarrassed silence, we would do well to give it up. But if it inspires a line of investigation, even merely of interesting speculation, then it will have earned our serious attention.

The second kind of response has good credentials but must be used extremely sparingly lest it lose its force. Under certain circumstances we may legitimately point out that, in a contingent universe, not every fact gets explained. The basic facts about the nature of things are simply there. Were we to adopt this attitude toward matter–mind interaction, we would simply admit the mystery. We have admitted several others, equally opaque but now familiar and therefore almost comfortable, into the world picture of modern atomistic science. The basic laws of mechanics might have been other than what we now hold them to be. Aristotle might have been right; so might Newton; Einstein might be wrong. Why does the universe realize these mechanical laws rather than others? Why does the electro-weak interaction display the features it does and not others? Why does the fine structure constant have just that value and not some other? Why do fundamental particles come in just these categories rather than others? Mysteries such as these will not be dissipated when theorists succeed in deriving some or all of them from deeper principles; the aura will simply float over to those principles. Despite its inner coherence and austere, abstract beauty, the universe, like a work of art, is ultimately a contingent fact, which is to say it is unexpected and unexpectable.

By virtue of what property does a mind interact with a set of particles? Well, one might also ask for the properties that enable two electrons to exchange virtual photons. The answer, electrical charge, is not an explanation but merely a name for the propensity. Now it may turn out that the collapsing of wave packets is not a fundamental fact of mind–matter interactions, in which case Shimony's and Putnam's question will have an interesting answer in terms of whatever turns out to be fundamental. However, this collapse is the only indication we get from quantum mechanics that consciousness can take a hand in the affairs of ordinary matter; hence, it looks very much like the fundamental fact about their interaction. And truly basic propensities do not receive explanations. So we will not violate the rules of natural philosophizing if we simply build into our account of the transactions between minds and particles the propensity of a mind to trigger the "transition to actuality." Just how far can we carry this response? How much can legitimately be consigned to the category of basic, unexplained, contingent fact? This question must remain open. Its answer must await the results of attempts to solve the specific puzzles posed by a dualistic, quantal ontology.

Certainly, we must not assemble a roster of ultimate facts too freely. Inevitably, we will begin to regret the number of items on the list and to demand an explanation in terms of physical—or possibly even mental—mechanisms. The ad hoc is as undesirable here as in explanations of particle interactions; hence, we must view with suspicion each item in our tentative catalog of fundamental facts, asking whether some may be understandable in terms of others. But we cannot do without the list. The universe is contingent. I shall, therefore, propose a partial list of facts of common experience that may have value as evidence.

Building on these shreds of sometimes dubious evidence, I shall propose a picture, plausible though inevitably sketchy, of one possible combination of ontology and epistemology that is not inconsistent with the interpretation of quantum mechanics urged above and may even cast some light upon it. Let me emphasize that I do not claim that the fragmentary philosophical position to be outlined here is dictated by quantum mechanics, although I think it has informed the thinking of some quantum mechanicians from the beginning. Other views, radically different, may also be consistent with the theory—for example, a thoroughgoing idealism. Quantum mechanics permits much. But I shall not soar on newly unfettered wings over the speculative vistas opened by the theory. Rather, I shall attempt to preserve as much as possible of a prequantal, realistic epistemology, one that respects the deep moat that modern physics seems to dig between appearance and reality.

As evidence that this partial world picture deserves attention, I shall conclude by drawing from it some questions about specific aspects of the interaction between matter and mind and some puzzles about the place of mind in the larger scheme of things.

## BACKGROUND FOR SPECULATION

KNOWN AND KNOWING THINGS. Interpreting quantum mechanics realistically has led to an ontology in which the causal agents belong to two distinct orders of being: the material, whose units are the particles of physics, and the mental, consisting of individual minds. A mind is induced to perform the activities that count as experiences of the material world as it interacts with the particles whose existence we postulate in theoretical physics. Though they interact, these objects exist independently of ourselves and of one another. In this assumption we extend conjecturally to material things the same independence we know by intimate acquaintance in our own activity as interacting but individual persons. We know the objects not directly but only through their effects on consciousness. That is the case even for commonsense objects. What the keyboard of my word processor is in itself I cannot say; but I do know that something is going on out there now that is like what has gone on often before and that is capable of generating what I have learned to call keyboard experiences. And the something that abides, not the experiences that come and go, is the keyboard to which I refer.

But the quantal concept of potentiality gives a deeper significance to the distinction between the way things are in themselves and the way they appear to us. The theory shows that our epistemic connection to the object must, of physical necessity, be limited to only some of its aspects. The object is singular and definite in any aspect it presents to consciousness, whereas it teems with multiple alternatives in most of the features not available for scrutiny. We cannot, therefore, directly experience the quantum multiplicity of external things and can, indeed, conceive of it only indirectly, as an ability to affect ourselves in several diverse ways. In what, then, does a material system's ability to generate two or more logically incompatible sense experiences consist? We cannot say much in answer to that question. At best we can multiply the kind of statement we make about ordinary, definite objects: "Something is going on out there (the particles are doing it) of the sort that has been partly responsible for the experiences I have learned to interpret as live-cat experiences, *and* the particles are also doing something of the sort that has been partly responsible for what I have learned to interpret as dead-cat experiences."

OBJECTIVITY. The granting of independent ontological standing to the objects that underlie our experiences is, I submit, the core of the scientific attitude toward nature. Objectivity is the foothold we must not lose as we resist the antirealist tug of the quantum theory.

The objective attitude can be seen more clearly in contrast to what many practitioners of the humanities find to be a satisfactory working relationship with nature. Aldous Huxley (1963) typifies this other stance in an essay that makes a powerful case for quite another sort of reply to reductionism. Huxley's remedy for the cold mechanism of the atomist philosophy is a metaphysics that places Mind at the center of things. Huxley attractively presents the literary side of the culture gap: Literature interprets human experience of all sorts, from the nearly ineffable to the completely public (William Blake, say, to Alexander Pope), by "purifying the words of the tribe" to get precise yet multiple meanings. Literature subordinates *things* to *experiences*; it looks at things always and only in relation to the human mind, only as contributors to human meaning. Certainly, Huxley would make one exception to this rule. Other persons would not be thus subordinated to the artist's experiences: Persons, and they alone, would be accorded a transcendent status as beings-in-themselves. Respect for persons requires that one not view them merely in relation to one's own inner life. Indeed, Huxley does briefly adopt an even broader objectivity when he asks,

> How did the illimitable inane get on without the perceiving, feeling and thinking inhabitants of this and all the other dark little worlds of woe, bliss, love and frustration—not to mention poetry and science? And how will it get on when we are all gone?
> [P. 63]

But otherwise he focuses exclusively on experiences—how to sort them out, how to express and enhance them. Indeed, with regard to inanimate things Huxley seems to believe that scientists, too, do nothing other than organize human perceiving and thinking (leaving feeling for others to explore); that they interpret experiences of the most public sort by means of words stripped down to single meanings and of concepts whose sole justification is that they serve "operationally" to tie one set of inner events to another in a logical network.

That, however, is not at all what most scientists think they do. Most of them are realists. I submit that the essential spirit of science, the attitude that alone makes possible such an unprecedented relation between humankind and nature is this: consciously and deliberately to approach inanimate things with the same humility, the same delicate hesitation to impose one's own interpretative scheme upon the other, that we accord (in our better moments) to other persons. In science the word for this attitude is "objectivity"; when we adopt it toward other people we call it respect. Dealing objectively, respectfully, with nature, scientists attempt to focus not *on* their own experiences but *through* them to the things themselves. Unable to approach nature without some presumptive system of concepts, they nevertheless try to employ that system so tentatively and with such humility as to give nature every chance of refuting it. That is the experimental method: to make nature itself an active party in the debate over the nature of things. This, of course, is not to say that the artist's attitude toward the world, which is equally respectful in its own way, is less worthy than the scientist's objectivity; the artist has noble but different aims. Still, nature does not thrust its self-revelations upon us. The sculptor, who focuses centrally on the emerging figure and only peripherally on the stone, hears only part of what the marble whispers to a mineralogist.

How can we reach out to the reality beyond experience? Beginning with the Greek atomists, natural philosophy has offered one way, the path of hypothetical reasoning, paved with the concepts of theoretical science. But Huxley does not believe that concepts of any sort can help us break out of the closed circle of our ordinary perceptions—hence his operationism with regard to theories. How, then, can we reach out? He recommends another path, the way of mystical experience.

Huxley seems to employ a restricted sense of the term "know," according to which the only real knowledge is *self*-knowledge; hence, the only way to know another thing is to become one with it; hence the importance of the mystical emptying of self. But, without denigrating this sense of the term, I submit that we would blind ourselves to an important aspect of our connection to the world unless we used "know" also in other senses. Let us stipulate that one can also have knowledge *about* another person or thing—knowledge mediated by sensory experience and conceptual interpretation, fallible, usually only approximate, often mixed with error, but knowledge nonetheless. Let us assume the possibility of objective knowledge.

I mean by this term more than merely knowing how to cope with external objects. That is yet a third type of knowledge, the practical. But we can also have conceptual, theoretical knowledge of other things. In what does such knowledge consist? It is a more distant relation than union with the object yet more intimate than merely using it for one's own purposes or responding to it in survival-promoting ways. It consists, rather, in putting one's self into a kind of limited, partial resonance with the object, in adopting an internal state that reproduces some features of its formal structure. The structure is then known in the intimate sense of being actively and consciously embodied, and the object is known indirectly by this sharing of structure. There is nothing mystical about this kind of knowledge. The laws of mechanics, for example, reproduce, as mathematical entities, something of the formal structure of the activities of the material objects, and as those laws become encoded in our brains we acquire theoretical knowledge of the things whose activities are thus mimicked.[1]

The conjecture that knower and known belong to metaphysically distinct categories may seem to place too large a distance between them, as if the mind were locked away inside the cranium, compelled to view phantasmic figures projected by the cerebral cortex. I suspect that much opposition to the theory

1 / Robert Greenler, for example, in the preface to a book on atmospheric phenomena, expresses a sense of resonating thus with the object of knowledge: "The beginning of my interest lies in my childhood awe of the beauty of the rainbow. My response to something that I like is to try to personalize it by my own participation. Trying to understand [these phenomena] is one of my forms of personal participation" (1980, p. ix).

stems from this interpretation; certainly, it was the source of my own reluctance. But, in fact, dualism preaches no such isolation. Even ordinary perceiving involves participation in the object of knowledge. The familiar occupants of our perceptual world—the creamy cloud twisting across an aquamarine sky, the purple iris stretching up from the margin of a shallow pool, the fragrant, gritty strawberry—are all of them produced by intimate collaboration between the mind and the several sets of particles that undergird the sky, flower, and berry experiences. In sensory perception the collaboration gains more from the contribution of the mind than from the formal character of the material object, though both help to shape the activity; in scientific, rational understanding the balance shifts toward the object's structuring. But the knower and the thing known contribute cooperatively to the experience in both types of knowing. There occurs a kind of union between knower and external object, a merging in a common creative exercise. This is not in itself that "oneness with the universe" of which mystics speak; but I surmise that the direct apprehension of this mutuality contributes to the mystical experience.

All this cooperation notwithstanding, in maintaining objectivity we systematically eliminate ourselves, the knowing subjects, from the story we tell about the way things are. How far can this practice be carried? A. Peres and W. H. Zurek (1982) claim that the scientific story must eventually refer to the storyteller because quantum mechanics is essentially self-referential. They suggest that this feature of the theory explains why we must draw that strangely elastic line between the object, to which quantum mechanics applies, and the observer, to which it does not. Quantum mechanics, they say, is *universal*, because anything whatever may be placed on the object side of the boundary, but it is not *closed*, because not everything can be placed there. Therefore, the boundary does not mark the place where mind acts upon matter; rather, we draw it, somewhat arbitrarily, because of "a logical necessity of any theory which is self-referential, as it attempts to describe its own means of verification" (p. 810).

Such is not the case, however; the goal of objectivity is not lost. To see this, consider the example of Schroedinger's cat. In that experiment we can avoid the problems of self-reference if we step outside the laboratory and determine the animal's condition by questioning the person who is performing the experiment. In doing so, of course, we assume that when we receive an answer the editing of potentialities has already happened, in virtue of the registering of the surviving scenario in the consciousness of the other person. This assumption allows the storyteller to deal with the interface between object and observer without having to refer to himself. Not only does the assumption save the theory from possible problems with self-reference, but it is one we should wish to make in any case—indeed, we have already made it. It amounts simply to choosing against solipsism. In this example we reap two additional benefits: We gain a reason for drawing the line between object and subject where we do; namely, that quantum mechanics details the activities of material particles but not of minds. And we can continue to stand outside the story we tell about the world out there. The storyteller's own mentality, special concerns, and values still are kept from complicating the tale. Mentality per se has not been excluded, because the story mentions the other person's mind; but the program of objectivity survives.

CAUSATION. Because objects come in two general types, we can imagine three broad categories of causal activity: interactions among material things, between matter and mind, and among mental entities. The first category, including the gravitational, electrical, and other interactions, has formed part of the traditional subject matter of the sciences since Newton. Interactions of the second, which cause minds to undergo conscious experiences and particles to make the transition to actuality, have been addressed by physical science for the first time in the quantum theory. I shall raise some questions about both in the following paragraphs. But concerning the third imaginable kind of interaction, the direct action of mind upon mind, I shall have nothing to say. The quantum theory does not speak about it, and what few data we have on the issue are anecdotal or, if systematic, still moot. I do not deny the possibility of extrasensory knowledge, but I shall base my discussion on the supposition that communication always occurs through the employment of sound waves, signal flags, the postal service, or some other material bearer of messages.

Some distinctions will be helpful. I shall call the sort of interaction that goes on among the objects themselves *primary causation*, to distinguish it from and grant it priority over the correlations we discover in ordinary experience and through scientific study, which I shall call *phenomenal causation*. In order to make sense of the experienced correlations we must conceive of primary causation, but we do not know it experientially, because it operates behind the experiential scenes.

However, primary causation does not lie entirely beyond our grasp. In perception, and perhaps in volition as well, the mind interacts by primary causation with the material objects of knowledge, through the mediation of the brain. Here is a single example of primary causal interaction of which we have something that goes beyond hypothetical, conceptual knowledge—in fact, a kind of direct intuition. When an object acts upon the subject, not only is the mind caused to undergo experiential episodes, but it also feels constrained by an independent reality. Here we encounter the causal interaction among things in themselves from within, as it were. Our feeling of passivity in receiving sense impressions and our sense of being causally active when choosing and deciding are examples of a kind of intuition distinguishable from the sensory mode of knowing, though not, of course, separable from it. Together they amount to a direct experience of the subject-object relation. This is an intuition of the interaction between a mental entity and the external material thing we conceive of, through interpreting the phenomena, as the cerebral cortex.

Living with this intuitive grasp of causal agency, we are bound to feel disappointed with the picture of causation that emerges from physics. Phenomenal causation is unsatisfyingly inert. Even potential energy, which at first glance seems like the active principle we seek, turns out to have an explication in terms of the same "constant conjunctions" that we codify in the equations of mechanics. As David Hume saw, we can tell that phenomenal correlation is merely the appearance of causal action without the substance thereof by its failure to display any hint of necessity. The necessity and initiative are both there in the objects, but, except for the compulsion we feel when receiving sense impressions and the initiative we think we exercise when choosing, the active power does not reach into our experience. Insofar as it resides in transactions among other things than ourselves, we do not and, it seems, cannot touch it. How, then, do we come to know about causal activities carried on by material objects? We know them only hypothetically, by speculating about the ordinary correlations of commonsense experience.

SPACE-TIME. Having made a radical distinction between objects and their appearances, we must view the space-time of physics as belonging to the phenomenal realm. It is not a container for the minds and particles that compose the objective world but the manifestation in experience of the formal structure of the interactions that take place among the material objects only. The subjective qualities of space and time—the vastness of space, for example—are generated by the mind; like any other sensory qualities, they are activities that minds do. But the structure of space-time, as we have learned from Einstein, is a subject for empirical research. We build our understanding of physical geometry upon measured relations among events. The "points" of space-time are physical events, and these come in just two kinds: First, there are the actually measured ones, in which a causal interaction transpires between an object and a measuring instrument, for instance, the registration of a moving particle at a certain location by its contact with a detector. Second, there are other events, not directly measured but inferred from measurements, for example, the passing of a photon through a region of empty space. This sort, though it may not involve actual causal interaction, nevertheless can be conceived of only in terms of physically possible interactions: If a detector had been waiting at the location of the moving particle, it would or Q-possibly might have registered its presence there. Space-time consists of a set of relations among actual and possible causal transactions, transactions that we do not directly experience but must conceive of in order to make sense of our experiences. The geometrical structure of space-time is the shadow cast on the screen of experience by the limitations that inhere in those interactions.

About the objects the quantum theory can say only a limited amount. Constructed to be a means of helping us make conceptual sense of our experience of the world, it cannot give us experiential knowledge of the objects that lie beyond experiences and help to shape them. Quantum mechanics, like any other physical theory, can aid us at most only in conceiving of them. More no doubt goes on "out there" than we can ever capture in words and concepts. Conceptual knowledge, hence all of science, must be incomplete in this sense. The incompleteness is not a peculiar fault of the modern theory, not a demerit in comparison with classical mechanics; rather, it is an essential limit on any conceptual knowledge of that which causes our experiences.

## PUZZLES AND CONJECTURES

With these broad outlines of an epistemological and ontological program to guide us, let us proceed to test the program and our interpretation of the quantum theory by posing some questions and proposing answers to them. The purpose of this exercise is not to establish any solid facts about the quantal world picture. Rather, I wish merely to substantiate what I claimed above, that the activity licensed by a realistic (or crypto-realistic) interpretation of the quantum theory is preferable to the silence that follows upon a merely instrumentalist interpretation.

DOES MIND ACT UPON MATTER? With regard to mind–matter transactions we have assumed that minds play a role not only in receiving the action of matter but also in reacting on it to catalyze actualizations, and perhaps more. The transition to actuality occurs in the objective world, as a correlated group of atomic particles is shorn of part of its accumulated wool of potentiality, thereby becoming more nearly definite with respect to those properties that connect it to a conscious experience. This action is performed by the group of correlated particles because of the mind's reaction upon them. They act in concert, as a peculiar sort of unit, so that the actual state bursts into the space–time manifold like a log bobbing up through the surface of a pond. One end may break the surface slightly later than the other, and if the log is very nearly horizontal the two events may be so nearly simultaneous that a physical signal cannot move from one to the other. Though they are connected, neither event causes the other. Analogously in the EPR experiment, the actualizations of particles that have interacted in the past are connected and correlated without being physical causes one of another. So this kind of action intrudes upon the fabric of space-time without disrupting its causal structure; its thrust runs not within the manifold of actuality but across it.

This uniquely quantum-mechanical activity offers a new perspective on mind–matter interaction. If this is the way mind traffics with matter, then one of the traditional perplexities of interactionism is neatly averted, namely, the question as to how a mind could deflect an atom from its appointed path. Minds, as agents of actualization, stand outside the atoms' scrimmage, neither pushing nor being pushed.

ARE MINDS MERELY PASSIVE? Let us see whether we can do without the assumption that mind reacts upon matter. We have rejected Heisenberg's conjecture that the transition to the actual occurs at the point of contact between the atomic object and the measuring instrument and have placed it instead on the doorsill between matter and consciousness. But we have accepted without criticism his suggestion that definiteness is to be found not only in our subjective experiences but also in the objective world. Suppose, however, that definiteness obtains nowhere in the material order but only on the mental side of the portal. Perhaps the mind achieves the definiteness of its experiences merely by filtering, by refusing to accept for home viewing all but one of a measured object's potential properties, while leaving them all to contribute to the thing's objective state.

This conjecture will show in a somewhat clearer light if we ask a related question: When two spectators view the same apparatus, do their minds experience the same actual state of the object? Here we face a perplexity that cannot be resolved by doing an experiment; the problem of intersubjective agreement troubles us just as deeply in quantum-mechanical as in classical dualism. The inability of the quantum theory to answer the question may be seen by applying the analysis of the EPR experiment to the case of two observers looking at the same apparatus. To make the illustration more lurid, let us suppose that the observed object is the cat (but a mindless one) of Schroedinger's parable. The two groups of photons carrying information from the body of the cat to the eyes of the viewers act like the correlated particles in the EPR experiment, because they originate in the same object. A straightforward application of the quantum theory produces descriptions of two principal potential states of the coupled material system that consists of the cat, the ambient light, and the bodies of the observers. In one potential state the Geiger tube receives the atomic particle, the cat lies inert on the floor of its box, images of its sorry state form upon the retinas of both spectators, their brains encode the retinal images, and sounds of dismay issue from their throats. In the other potential state the Geiger tube is untouched, the animal springs from its prison, the retinal images of this escape take shape, the two brains support the corresponding patterns of neuronal firings, and the vocal cords of both persons generate tones of gratification. Finally, the quantum theory produces no assertion of a potential state of this correlated system such that the retina and visual cortex of one observer record a dead cat and the other's a living one, nor is either's vision contradicted by what he hears the other say. Moreover, if any single observer looks twice at the cat, the potential states induced in that person's brain are self-consistent. In some potential scenarios the current image induced by the second inspection and the memory left by the first one both record a living cat, and in others they record a dead one; but in none do the present image and the memory disagree. (See, e.g., Everett 1957.)

Now let us suppose that the first viewer's mind passively receives just one of its brain's collections of correlated potential properties into its own merely subjective actuality while leaving all potentialities to contribute undiminished to the state of the material object. On that supposition we would expect the second person, on glancing at the cat, to be able to receive the alternative potential world into consciousness. Because each potential world contains only mutually consistent values of the correlated properties, even the properties of the other observer's body, neither mind could be aware that the other has actualized (that is, passively received) a different potential world. Consequently, the hypothesis of passive reception without a corresponding reduction of potentiality in the material world, including the brain, leads to serious doubt about agreement among minds.

Those doubts might be resolved, or rather prevented from arising, by following Schroedinger (1956; 1958) eastward, that is, by adopting a metaphysics in which there are not many individual minds but only one universal consciousness. Nevertheless, although by this postulate we could avoid the question of whether distinct minds agree, we cannot avoid a closely related problem, also generated by the supposition that the objects retain their tendencies. The problem concerns the agreement of a single mind with itself over stretches of time.

The mind, we know from introspection, never experiences the world in toto; rather, impressions of objects enter consciousness often in small pieces and haphazardly. Therefore, as an observer peers twice in succession into the cat's cage, two opportunities are presented to the material system to deliver one or another of its possible exports to consciousness. Let us suppose that in the first instance the lot falls on the experience of a defunct cat. If the material object retains its full range of dispositions, the brain still has two tendencies: to deliver a current experience and a memory of a dead cat, and to deliver an experience and memory of a living one. Consequently, when the experimenter looks again, the mind may receive in the second shipment a subjective state consistent within itself but inconsistent with the earlier experience. Would the person know that such a thing had happened? Not unless a mind keeps a store of memories apart from its brain. A discrepancy between successive experiential states of a single observer would remain undetected for the same reason that a similar discrepancy between distinct viewers also goes unnoticed: At each moment a person's experience is totally self-consistent, both with regard to his own memories and with regard to the physical characteristics of the other spectator.

We find that the hypothesis of passivity leads to a radical skepticism not only about the states of others' minds but also about the past states of one's own. Surely we stare here at a solipsism of the most advanced degree. How can we escape it? Only by adopting (as we are free to do) the most effective reply to solipsism, that is, by choosing not to believe it.

Passing on, then, to an alternative conjecture, let us assign a slightly more active role to the mind. Suppose that the registering of an experience in consciousness triggers a reduction in the range of possibilities objectively present in the observed system. This conjecture would give us a reason to believe that distinct minds agree as to the actual values of the variable properties of things. One observer looking at a system previously inspected by another, or the first observer looking again, would have an experience consistent with the first observation, because all tendencies to produce inconsistent experiences have been rooted out of the objective world. They are no longer there to be actualized. Thus, the threat of solipsism recedes.

Having readopted the interactionist conjecture, we must compile an inventory of new, fundamental, and therefore unexplainable facts about mentality. To the head of the list goes the ability of a brain to induce a mind to perform specific conscious episodes. The other end of this same interaction is the mind's ability to induce an actualization in the material system. This reaction of mind upon matter raises another question.

DOES A MIND DIRECT WHAT MATTER DOES? Does the mind merely trigger the actualization, letting the outcome fall as it may, or does it sometimes select? Most evidence indicates that the mind is very passive indeed. That certainly is the case in ordinary perception. The brain labors vigorously in interpreting the incoming stimuli by recognizing patterns and processing signals in various ways, but the mind itself simply receives the result of all this activity. It is just our felt passivity in this relationship to the external world that generates our sense of being acted upon by something "out there." In our emotional life, too, matter often acts upon mind; fear, joy, lust, awe "overcome" us; they are called passions with good reason. In addition, we have noted above how much that counts as intelligence—such activities as solving problems and inventing plots for novels—is carried out by the unconscious machinery of the brain. By and large, bright ideas, such as the solution to an anagram or the principal theme for the adagio movement, simply "occur to" us. In these cases matter, principally the brain, is the active party and mind the passive one. Indeed, there is only one area of human experience where almost everyone feels that the mind assumes an active role, namely, in making decisions. That, I say, is the nearly unanimous feeling; whether it can be supported by reasoning based on solid evidence remains to be seen. At this point I simply note the subjective fact: We seem to be connected with external reality quite differently when ordering lunch than when tasting it.

There seems, indeed, to be a certain lack of symmetry between the active and passive involvements of mind with brain, between willing and sensing. Of the multiplicity that quantum mechanics assigns to external things we get no intimation in any instance of sensing, but we do sometimes experience something rather like a superposition of several potential alternatives when engaged in choosing among options: Occasionally "yes" and "no" seem really to float together in some vestibule to the world of actuality.

If a moral can be drawn from this observation, it would be that the active connection of mind to matter differs in some respects from the passive, that when actively choosing we touch some potentialities before they are erased.

Although none of these anecdotes from common subjective experience carries enough weight to compel us toward one conclusion rather than another, they are the only clues we have. Let us see what can be done with them.

HOW DOES THE TRANSITION TO ACTUALITY OCCUR? Do particles pass on actuality from one to another? Does it progress like the fall of a line of dominoes, with the loss of potential values of some property by a single atom in the cortex triggering correlated losses in its immediate neighbors, and so on? No; as I have argued above, no principled account can be given of this triggering that does not attribute it to the interaction between mind and matter. Well, then, what mechanism mediates the interaction? This question, too, includes a mistaken assumption. We should not expect to get answers by borrowing from atomistic ways of thinking.

There are two reasons against forcing atomistic analogies upon mind, one evidential, the other prudential. As to evidence, we quite simply have none that points toward an atomic constitution of mind. The original impetus toward an atomic hypothesis for matter came from the observation that most substances admit of division into parts, which manage to exist on their own while retaining some of the properties of the parent lump. But in minds we find nothing analogous to the partitioning of a block of marble into solid, sharp-edged chips, or of a barrel of beer into independently drinkable pints. I consider this sort of divisibility to be a necessary condition for the plausibility of an atomic hypothesis; without it, other indications of multiplicity will settle more comfortably into other conceptual schemes. The prudential consideration is this: Extending atomism to the mental sphere would entail abandoning a promising program. The atomic hypothesis conflicts sharply with some entrenched intuitions about human beings as causal agents and about the unity of consciousness. Introducing minds as agents of an entirely new sort of causal action promises to bring ontology into line with intuition. Of course, agreement between intuitions and scientific hypotheses does not guarantee truth, for both are fallible, but a clash between them must be taken as a warning; hence, flags of peace are a welcome sight. An atomic hypothesis applied to mind would rescind the promise of harmony by reintroducing the problem of unity also in this other category of being.

We do find in mental events a multiplicity of sorts, but it seems to be a multiplicity of activity rather than of composition. I have urged as a principle of method that we conceive of mental episodes as activities of mind rather than as component parts. We say that a mind does several things, perhaps even simultaneously, but we refrain from saying that it consists of several pieces. If there were any prima facie evidence to make an atomic conjecture plausible, the next step would be prescribed by paradigms drawn from the atomic theory of matter: Having recognized multiple doings or undergoings we would postulate multiple substantial parts. In standard atomism no intrinsic change occurs; apparent examples of it are shown to be changes merely in the spatial alignments and interactions of the enduring atoms, not in their intrinsic properties. However, we have no evidence that anything like that goes on in mental episodes, nor have we any clue to what either the eternal, intrinsic properties or the extrinsic relations of mental atoms could be. We need an entirely new way to conceive of change with transtemporal self-identity. To understand mental activity, we need a conceptual scheme cut loose from the program of Democritus.

WHERE DO MIND AND MATTER TOUCH? Just where in the brain does the mind contact matter? Where is the point of entry from one world to the other, and if it is a portal rather than a mathematical point, how wide is it? The bizarre flavor of these questions surely reveals an underlying conceptual muddle. The questions assume that the interaction occurs in space, but we must not treat the relation between matter and mind on the model of that between particle and particle. However we may come eventually to think about this metaphysical transaction, we must not try to push it into the web of space-time. As I have argued above, space-time is the phenomenal manifestation of limitations in the interactions among the particles. We have no reason to expect spatiotemporal relations also to manifest limitations in the interaction between mind and matter.

Where is the point of contact between mind and matter? This question requires delicate handling. We may choose to read it literally, understanding by the point of contact between two things the region of space that they occupy jointly. On that reading the "connection" has no location. Because it does not exert or suffer physical forces, a mind does not live in the spatiotemporal world. If we interpret the term more loosely, stipulating that the point of contact is the place where the mind's effect is manifested, then the point turns out to be the gerrymandered region occupied by all the particles whose potentialities are pruned in the reduction of the wave function; and this sphere of influence may extend far beyond the confines of the body, and even of the galaxy. Both of these answers have their merits. But a more nearly commonsense reading of the question promises a fairly commonsense answer. Let us define the "contact point" as the set of material objects which, in the relevant experience, affect the mind directly, not through physical interactions with other things; in that case empirical research is likely to identify a fairly small region of the brain, a small but shifting set of cortical neurons, as the physical side of the door between matter and mind.

But what a strange door. Why is the passage between the two worlds positioned just there? In virtue of what property do the neurons take on their vestibular role? Or, if the neurons are not wholly responsible for this liaison, what property of minds disposes them to adopt brains, and not some other complicated assembly of atoms, as their means of contact with material objects? It seems obvious that no sort of answer to these questions can be looked for from the atomist program.

HOW CAN THERE BE ACTION AT A DISTANCE? Nowhere does quantum theory deviate more sharply from the traditional principles of natural science than in its assertion that a single measurement can induce widely separated particles to adopt definite, correlated values of certain properties. Quantum nonlocality does not contradict the principle that the causal action of one particle on another must occur by means of intermediaries that travel at finite speeds across the intervening space. In the transition to actuality no forces are exerted, no photons or gluons are exchanged. It happens not because of interplay among particles but because of an interaction between mind and matter.

Nevertheless, a very great affront is offered to our rooted notions about the absolute importance of spatial separation as a limiter of causal interaction. As I have interpreted it, the collapse of potentialities in widely separated particles seems to put a mind on intimate terms with (to say "in contact with" would introduce precisely the wrong metaphor) any number of particles anywhere in the universe.

The particles conduct their causal affairs according to their own regular and limited ways. The potentiality-limiting activity of a mind in no way abrogates the orderliness of those activities. But we must remorselessly deflate the claims of physical space-time to be the arbiter of all primary causation. The daunting vastness of the space between earth and the Andromeda galaxy is no more than the manifestation in consciousness of what little we can resonate with in the rules of interparticle behavior. One feels the strongest reluctance to suppose that a mind could induce a proton in another galaxy immediately to lose some potential positions; yet this feeling amounts to an illicit (though well nigh irresistible) application to one kind of interaction of rules that inform another and fundamentally different kind.

Though we cannot experientially know primary causation, yet we must conceive of it; what, then, can we say about it? Negatively, we can say this: Because it takes place among objects that lie behind and transcend our experience, primary causation almost certainly transcends its own phenomenal appearance; in particular, it includes a type of transaction not found anywhere in sensory experience, namely, the interaction between material objects and a mind. We should not assume that this type of primary-causal transaction would show much similarity to the sort that takes place among material objects, which we experience phenomenally as forces. The latter have their own characters and inherent limitations, which manifest themselves as spatiotemporal contiguity and separation. Consequently, although the maxim "no action at a distance" applies to the phenomenal manifestation of the primary-causal transactions among the particles, we have no ground for supposing that a suitable translation of it can be applied to a radically different kind of transaction, namely, that between material objects and consciousness. The reduction of the wave packet, the correlated deleting of quantum-mechanical potentialities, is not achieved by one particle exerting a force on another; hence, we have no reason to expect that the rules by which we express the possibilities and limitations of the transition to actuality could be stated in the language of space-time.

CAN MINDS INTERFERE? The potentiality-editing influence of a mind reaches not only to the particles directly under observation but beyond them to correlated particles widely separated in physical space. Opportunities should sometimes arise, therefore, for a single particle to be implicated in the transitions being induced simultaneously in separate laboratories, though the linking particle is not present in either. In that case, the definite result experienced by one consciousness will have been achieved not by interaction with its own measuring instrument but by the other mind, even though no communication of the usual sort has passed between them. This sounds uncomfortably like a license for mental telegraphy. Hence, we must ask: Is there any natural limitation on the ability of our minds to tamper with perceivable states of affairs far removed from ordinary spheres of causal influence?

Indeed there is such a limitation. It arises because most potential states of affairs at the level of particles do not correspond to distinct states of consciousness, and only those that do are eligible for erasure in the transition to actuality. Consider just one artificial but revealing example. Suppose that an experiment of the EPR sort produces a pair of electrons from an initial state of zero angular momentum. The separating particles then have correlated potential values for their spins along a continuous range of directions perpendicular to the line along which they separate. Let the left-hand particle encounter a magnetic field oriented vertically, so that the electron is obliged to adopt a definite spin value along the vertical line. Let us set two particle detectors beyond this analyzing magnet in such a way that a particle deflected upward enters one of them, triggering a train of electrical signals that terminates in the lighting of a red lamp; and a downward deflected particle lights a green lamp. In the left-hand beam we place a corresponding arrangement of analyzing magnet, detectors, and red and green lamps, but there the separation occurs along a horizontal axis. When the right-hand particle undergoes its transition to actuality—let us say to the upward orientation, lighting the red lamp—the left-hand particle adopts a definite downward orientation. However, both particles retain the complete range of potentialities for orientations along the horizontal axis. Consequently, the left-hand electron has lost none of its options with regard to a horizontal deflection and may Q-possibly trigger either the red or the green lamp at its end. The potential outcomes of measurement at one end of the experiment are quite independent of those at the other. Therefore, the transitions to actuality induced by an observer sitting at one detecting station would not limit the range of possible red or green experiences of someone at the other end.

Indeed, the experiment must be carefully contrived, as it was in the prototype invented by Einstein, Podolsky, and Rosen, in order to avoid this orthogonality, or a near orthogonality practically indistinguishable from it. In the standard experiments of the EPR type that have been carried out, analyzers are indeed set up at other than exactly orthogonal angles, but even in these cases only extended repetitions of the experiment, statistically analyzed, are able to manifest the quantum correlation. Individual trials, or haphazard sets of them, the sort of thing that casual observation of the world consists of almost exclusively, would fail to turn up anything noticeable. In the general case, the perceivable consequences of the collapse of Q-possibilities at one location correlating with a collapse elsewhere would be negligible.

I think it is obvious that we can easily generalize this result to cases where the orthogonality is not spatial but is quite as effective as in this example. Particles and the more complex systems that they encounter, left to themselves, cannot be expected to sort themselves into aligned measuring devices. The physical interactions that lead eventually to a perceptual experience in one observer's mind will normally not alter in any noticeable degree the possible experience-generating interactions in another's perceptual apparatus.

And if this lack of spontaneous alignment is the rule in external things like particle detectors, we may be sure that only a fantastic coincidence could produce a perceivable correlation in the Q-possibilities that burgeon within different brains as a result of the signal processing and logical manipulations that occur there. If persons make choices by selecting from among Q-possibilities that are generated in the brain and presented by it to consciousness, different volitional agents will act upon their own options with practically complete independence, despite the universe-wide correlation that quantum mechanics reveals.

Should we wonder which of two spectators really triggers the actualization of an extended system when the two experiences happen so close together in time and far apart in space that no physical signal could connect them? No, we have seen that questions about temporal priority in such cases erroneously imply that the triggering of a transition to actuality takes place within the space-time manifold. No causation in the usual sense—that is, no pushing of particle against particle—goes on in an actualization, and both observers passively receive its results; hence, the anomalous possibility of signaling faster than light does not arise.

CAN A MIND SELECT POTENTIAL STATES? Consider a further speculation, which grants a still more active role to minds and raises a difficult question about causal priority. Suppose that on occasion an individual mind can actively select which of an object's potential states shall become actual, "granting consent to one possibility and withholding it from another," as William James (1897) describes volition. Could we maintain such a conjecture consistently with what we have learned from quantum mechanics?

Here we raise the possibility of violating the principles of special relativity. To see this, consider an EPR experiment in which the two observers measure the polarization of a pair of correlated photons. Let one of them passively receive and the other actively select the state to be actualized, with the selection occurring in such a way that horizontal and vertical polarizations turn up with roughly equal frequency in the long run. Even with this restriction, the active mind could select a string of horizontal and vertical actualizations (corresponding to the zeros and ones of a binary code) that carry a message. Then, because the actualizations of the two separated parts of a correlated system happen simultaneously, the active person would be able to transmit a signal to the other one with less delay than would be experienced if an actual physical intermediary traveled from sender to receiver. But a superluminal transfer of information, according to special relativity, entails the possibility of sending signals from the present into the past, as well as other paradoxes of causation. That uncomfortable result might provide reason enough for discarding the hypothesis of active selection.

We could avoid the paradoxes by placing an attractive but ad hoc restriction on the hypothesis. Intuition suggests that choosing influences only the causal chains that proceed outward from our brains to the world of objects. We certainly feel passive enough when merely perceiving: Both scientific experiments and horse races frequently defy our expectations. Our active intervention in the world's affairs seems to be limited to the occasions when we assert ourselves in deeds or words.

Suppose, then, that a mind's direct powers of active selection can reach only those potential states of its brain that are no longer coupled, via EPR correlations, with other portions of the universe. That supposition is plausible because the required uncoupling of distant, correlated objects does occur just where it is needed—in the interactions that accompany observations. For example, if two distant particles have correlated values both of position and of momentum, as in the original thought experiment of Einstein, Podolsky, and Rosen (1935), and if an observer makes contact with one of the particles by means of an instrument that measures position, then the person's mind induces the measured atomic object to adopt a single, definite location. But the interaction between that particle and its position detector introduces by physical necessity a range of potential momenta in the particle, as the uncertainty principle states. These new potential momenta are not correlated with the potential properties introduced at the site where the other particle interacts with its measuring instrument. Similar interactions, hosts of them, occur in the causal chain connecting that instrument to another spectator's cerebral cortex. Still more occur within the cortex as it processes sensory data and assembles blocks of neuronal connections, which if called upon could direct alternative programs of bodily motion. Each of these introduces fresh potentialities that bear no correlation of the EPR sort with the propensities branching out in the other body.

Consequently, if each mind exerts a choice only over potential brain states whose properties have been disconnected from those of objects outside the brain, a nonmaterial volition could direct the transitions to actuality without engendering a conflict between distinct minds. Yet this influence could have macroscopically distinct effects on publicly observable events as distinct as the two states of Schroedinger's cat because, although the mind intrudes upon the space-time world only by means of the second kind of causation, its choices are amplified by the first kind, by the neuronal and muscular mechanisms that connect the brain to the limbs and larynx, manifesting choices and resolutions made internally.

But this speculative excursion, brief and hesitant though it has been, has passed well beyond the territory mapped out by the quantum theory. It can claim our attention mainly because it fails to contradict that specific theory, demonstrating by example the hospitality of quantum mechanics to the idea that human beings influence the course of events as units. Whereas a belief in human causal agency could be embraced in the nineteenth century only in spite of the atomistic mechanics of Newton, this speculation shows that one can fit the belief into our present intellectual framework without darting anxious or apologetic glances toward the physics laboratory.

## CONCLUSION

Speculations such as these could be multiplied indefinitely. But let us halt and take our bearings. What, if anything, has been accomplished toward answering the reductionist picture of living things? The objectionable feature of atomism, as I have formulated it, is this: It portrays every activity performed by a composite thing, even by a living organism, as nothing other than the compounded activities of the particles that compose it. An organism, in this picture, does not act as a causal unit; it is a spectacle performed by a multitude of actors. If we accept the atomist ontology, those statements follow almost immediately, for, according to atomism, there is nothing to perform activities over and above the particles; having enrolled them, we can find nothing to put alongside them. We can, indeed, designate conglomerates of atoms by single names and thus treat them as if they were unitary actors, but we have found no activity done by a group of atoms that cannot be understood, and more thoroughly at that, as the sum of the activities of the parts.

To this understanding of the world dualism offers a radical alternative, because it provides a richer cast of characters. In addition to the multitude of activities continually being carried on by the atoms that compose the nerves and muscles of a living organism, there are also the activities of its mind—at least in human beings and possibly in other sentient animals as well. The bodily activities are indeed pluralistic; they are done by a throng. We have, however, no reason for trying to understand the various things a mind can do as being built up from changing combinations of simpler, endlessly repeated activities of "mental particles." There is no evidence for that view and nothing to be gained from it. According to the speculative sketch we have drawn, the activities of a mind are performed by a unitary actor, one not merely designated as such by others for their own convenience but unitary in itself.

We do have examples of unitary agents in the material realm: They are the particles identified (provisionally) by physics. What a fundamental particle does is not done for it by component parts—it has none. Yet, despite their essential simplicity, these units can perform a repertoire of activities. A quark, for example, can interact with other charged particles by sending and receiving virtual photons; it can also exert forces on other quarks by emitting and receiving virtual gluons. This example differs in important respects from the unitary activities of minds. The causal action of the brain on consciousness is not to be conceived in terms of the exchange of material emissaries between the participants. Nevertheless, the creating and the annihilating of field particles by electrons and quarks do exemplify self-contained activities performed by structureless units. So, also, do the activities we call mental events. A mental event or process is performed by a single thing, a mind; it is not the work of a committee. A swirling crowd of particles stimulates the mental activity and partly colors it. But what a mind does—the mental portion of what a person does in sensing, imagining, willing, and evaluating—is done by that unitary actor itself, not by a host of parts on whose existence it might depend.

This speculation may be criticized on the grounds that it rows against the tide of scientific and philosophical thinking that began to flow in the days of Copernicus. We no longer think that humankind dwells at the center of the solar system, or is at the center of the universe. We now believe that our age, midway through the lifetime of the sun, is a fairly representative slice across the long journey of the universe from big bang to heat death. We now understand our species to occupy an unremarkable place on the evolutionary tree: Though we can claim to be the product of aeons of evolutionary change, the same can be said of every extant kind. Each species is the best in the world at what it does, and none does it perfectly. How, then, can we justify distinguishing ourselves as a metaphysical union of material and nonmaterial actors? A self-description so flattering must be viewed with caution.

But it should not be dismissed merely on that account. It may be right, for all that. Arguments are not lacking to support the description. They deserve to be studied—with caution, indeed, because they appeal to our self-esteem, but also with careful attention because they carry important implications.

This view of human nature would lend theoretical support to our belief that benefits and harms done to human beings have direct ethical relevance, whereas the effects of our actions on inanimate objects have only derivative relevance: Our estimation of ethics would be secured. This description would make room for the sense one gets of being in touch with a reality not oneself and not merely particles, either, when one communes with other persons: Our estimation of social life would be ratified. This view would tolerate the conjecture that the experiences of mystics of all traditions reveal some reality beyond the individual mystic's central nervous system and his or her personal history: Our estimation of religious traditions would be elevated. These implications are grounds for taking the speculation seriously, though none provides reasons for accepting it. Just as it must not be embraced merely because it favors us, so it ought not be scorned just because it raises the threat of irrationalism. It is good to see the subtle attractions of the position in order not to succumb to them; but the arguments must stand or fall on their own merits.

Throughout this book, I have sought to reconcile the intuitions of ordinary experience concerning causal action and individual existence with the informed intuitions we get from scientific study of the nature of things. From personal experience we form the notions of causal agency and individuality. From natural philosophy we hear that these ideas apply properly and primarily to the fundamental particles. Impressed by the success of reductionism, we suspect that they do not, after all, apply to ourselves. There is dissonance, indeed. But we can restore a measure of harmony by enlarging our ontology. The arguments I have collected here make room for the distillations of ordinary human experience and the carefully crafted ideas of rational science to collaborate in peace.

# BIBLIOGRAPHY

Achinstein, Peter. 1977. "Function Statements." *Philosophy of Science* 44:341–67.

Ashby, William Ross. 1960. *Design for a Brain*. 2d rev. ed. New York: Wiley.

Aspect, Alain; Dalibard, Jean; and Roger, Gerard. 1982. "Experimental Test of Bell's Inequalities Using Time-varying Analyzers," *Physical Review Letters* 49:1804–7.

Aspect, Alain; Grangier, Philippe; and Roger, Gerard. 1982. "Experimental Realization of Einstein-Podolsky-Rosen-Bohm *Gedankenexperiment*: A New Violation of Bell's Inequalities," *Physical Review Letters* 49:91–94.

Ayala, Francisco. 1970. "Teleological Explanations in Biology," *Philosophy of Science* 37:1–15.

Beckner, Morton. 1959. *The Biological Way of Thought*. New York: Columbia University Press.

———. 1968. "Teleology." In R. P. Edwards, ed., *The Encyclopedia of Philosophy*. New York: Macmillan.

———. 1969. "Function and Teleology." *Journal of the History of Biology* 2:151–61.

Bell, John S. 1965. "On the Einstein Podolsky Rosen Paradox." *Physics* 1:195–200.

Blanshard, Brand. 1958. "The Case for Determinism." In Sidney Hook, ed., *Determinism and Freedom in the Age of Modern Science*, pp. 3–15. New York: New York University Press.

Boorse, Christopher. 1976. "Wright on Functions." *Philosophical Review* 85:70–86.

Bub, Jeffrey. 1979. "Some Reflections on Quantum Logic and Schrödinger's Cat." *British Journal for the Philosophy of Science* 30: 27–39.

Campbell, Donald T. 1960. "Blind Variation and Selective Retention in Creative Thought as in Other Knowledge Processes." *Psychological Review* 67:380–400.

———. 1974*a*. "Unjustified Variation and Selective Retention in Scientific Discovery." In Francisco J. Ayala and Theodosius Dobzhansky, eds., *Studies in the Philosophy of Biology*, pp. 139–61. Berkeley: University of California Press.

———. 1974*b*. "'Downward Causation' in Hierarchically Organized Biological Systems." In Francisco J. Ayala and Theodosius Dobzhansky, eds., *Studies in the Philosophy of Biology*, pp. 179–86. Berkeley: University of California Press.

Campbell, Keith. 1976. *Metaphysics*. Encino, Calif.: Dickenson.

Cartwright, Nancy. 1983. *How the Laws of Physics Lie*. Oxford University Press (Clarendon Press), and New York: Oxford University Press.

Casteneda, Carlos. 1974. *Tales of Power*. New York: Simon and Schuster.

Causey, Robert. 1969. "Polanyi on Structure and Reduction." *Synthese* 20:230–37.

Clauser, John F.; Horne, Michael A.; Shimony, Abner; and Holt, Richard A. 1969. "Proposed Experiment to Test Local Hidden-Variable Theories." *Physical Review Letters* 23:880–84.

Clauser, John F., and Shimony, Abner. 1978. "Bell's Theorem: Experimental Tests and Implications." *Reports on Progress in Physics* 41: 1881–927.

Cooper, Leon N., and Van Vechten, Deborah. 1969. "On the Interpretation of Measurement within the Quantum Theory." *American Journal of Physics* 37:1212–20.

Cummins, Robert. 1975. "Functional Analysis." *Journal of Philosophy* 72:741–65.

Darwin, Charles. 1859, 1872. *The Origin of Species by Means of Natural Selection*. 6th ed., rep. New York: Burt.

———. 1890. *The Variation of Animals and Plants under Domestication*. 2d ed., rev. London: Murray.

Davisson, C. J., and Germer, L. H. 1927. "Diffraction of Electrons by a Crystal of Nickel." *Physical Review* 30:705–40.

DeVries, Hugo. 1889, 1910. *Intracellular Pangenesis*, trans. C. Stuart Gager. Chicago: Open Court.

Dewey, John. 1910. *The Influence of Darwin on Philosophy, and Other Essays in Contemporary Thought*. New York: Holt.

Drell, Sidney D. 1978. "When Is a Particle?" *American Journal of Physics* 46:597–606.

Einstein, Albert; Podolsky, Boris; and Rosen, Nathan. 1935. "Can Quantum-Mechanical Description of Physical Reality Be Considered Complete?" *Physical Review* 47:777–80.

Enc, Berent. 1979. "Function Attributions and Functional Explanation." *Philosophy of Science* 46:343–65.

Esterman, I.; Frisch, R.; and Stern, O. 1931. "Monochromatization of de Broglie Waves of Molecular Rays." *Zeitschrift für Physik* 73: 348–65.

Everett, H., III. 1957. "The 'Relative State' Formulation of Quantum Mechanics." *Reviews of Modern Physics* 29:454–62.

Faber, Roger J. 1984. "Feedback, Selection, and Function: A Reductionistic Account of Goal-Orientation." In R. Cohen and M. Wartofsky, eds., *Methodology, Metaphysics, and the History of Science*, pp. 43–135. Dordrecht: Reidel.

Feyerabend, Paul K. 1963. "Materialism and the Mind–Body Problem." *Review of Metaphysics* 17:49–66.

———. 1970. "Consolations for the Specialist." In Imre Lakatos and Alan Musgrave, eds., *Criticism and the Growth of Knowledge*, pp. 197–230. Cambridge University Press.

Feynman, Richard P.; Leighton, Robert B.; and Sands, Matthew. 1965. *The Feynman Lectures on Physics*. Vol. 3. Reading, Mass.: Addison-Wesley.

Fodor, Jerry A. 1968. *Psychological Explanation*. Englewood Cliffs, N.J.: Prentice-Hall.

———. 1975. *The Language of Thought*. New York: Crowell.

Forester, Cecil Scott. 1964. *The Hornblower Companion*. Boston and Toronto: Little, Brown.

Gardner, Michael R. 1971. "Is Quantum Logic Really Logic?" *Philosophy of Science* 38:508–29.

Glansdorff, Peter, and Prigogine, Ilya. 1971. *Thermodynamic Theory of Structure, Stability, and Fluctuations*. New York: Wiley-Interscience.

Goosens, William K. 1978. "The Reduction of Molecular Genetics." *Philosophy of Science* 45:73–95.

Gould, Steven J., and Lewontin, Richard C. 1979. "The Spandrels of San Marco and the Panglossian Paradigm: A Critique of the Adaptationist Programme." *Proceedings of the Royal Society of London* B205: 581–98.

Green, Michael B. 1979. "The Grain Objection." *Philosophy of Science* 46:559–89.

Greenler, Robert. 1980. *Rainbows, Halos, and Glories*. Cambridge University Press.

Heisenberg, Werner. 1958. *Physics and Philosophy*. New York: Harper.
Hellman, Geoffrey. 1981. "Quantum Logic and Meaning." In Peter D. Asquith and Ronald N. Giere, eds., *PSA 1980*, vol. 2. East Lansing, Mich.: Philosophy of Science Association.
Hempel, Carl Gustav. 1965. *Aspects of Scientific Explanations*. New York: Free Press.
Hull, David. 1974. *Philosophy of Biological Science*. Englewood Cliffs, N.J.: Prentice-Hall.
Huxley, Aldous. 1963. *Literature and Science*. New York: Harper and Row; rep. 1982, New Haven: Leete's Island Books.
James, William. 1897, 1956. "The Dilemma of Determinism." In *The Will to Believe, and Other Essays in Popular Philosophy*. New York: Longmans, Green.
Lucretius Carus, Titus. 1968. *The Way Things Are: The "De Rerum Natura" of Titus Lucretius Carus*, trans. Rolf Humphries. Bloomington: Indiana University Press.
Mackie, John Leslie. 1974. *The Cement of the Universe; A Study of Causation*. Oxford University Press (Clarendon Press).
Manier, Edward. 1971. "Functionalism and the Negative Feedback Model in Biology." In R. C. Buck and R. S. Cohen, eds., *Boston Studies in the Philosophy of Science*, vol. 8. Dordrecht: Reidel.
McNulty, P. J.; Pease, V. P.; and Bond, V. P. 1978. "Visual Phenomena Induced by Relativistic Carbon Atoms with and without Cerenkov Radiation." *Science* 201:341–43.
Meehl, Paul E. 1966. "The Compleat Autocerebroscopist: A Thought-Experiment on Professor Feigl's Mind–Body Identity Thesis." In P. K. Feyerabend and G. Maxwell, eds., *Mind, Matter, and Method: Essays in Philosophy of Science in Honor of Herbert Feigl*, pp. 103–80. Minneapolis: University of Minnesota Press.
Mill, John Stuart. 1859, 1975. *On Liberty*, ed. David Spitz. New York: Norton.
Nagel, Ernest. 1961. *The Structure of Science*. New York: Harcourt Brace and World.
———. 1977. "Teleology Revisited." *Journal of Philosophy* 74:261–301.
Nissen, Lowell. 1981. "Nagel's Self-Regulation Analysis of Teleology." *Philosophical Forum* 12:128–38.
Peirce, Charles Sanders. 1892. "The Doctrine of Necessity Examined." *Monist* 2:321–37.
Peres, A., and Zurek, W. H. 1982. "Is Quantum Theory Universally Valid?" *American Journal of Physics* 50:807–10.
Polanyi, Michael. 1968. "Life's Irreducible Structure." *Science* 160:1308–12.

Popper, Karl R. 1959. "The Propensity Interpretation of Probability." *British Journal for the Philosophy of Science* 10:25–42.

———. 1967. "Quantum Mechanics without 'the Observer.'" In Mario Bunge, ed., *Quantum Theory and Reality*. New York: Springer-Verlag.

———. 1972. "Of Clouds and Clocks." In *Objective Knowledge: An Evolutionary Approach*. Oxford University Press (Clarendon Press).

———. 1974. "Replies to My Critics." In Paul A. Schilpp, ed., *The Philosophy of Karl Popper*, pp. 961–1197. La Salle, Ill.: Open Court.

Popper, Karl R., and Eccles, John C. 1977. *The Self and Its Brain*. New York: Springer-Verlag.

Powers, William T. 1973. *Behavior: The Control of Perception*. Chicago: Aldine.

———. 1978. "Quantitative Analysis of Purposive Systems: Some Spadework at the Foundations of Scientific Psychology." *Psychological Review* 85:417–35.

Putnam, Hilary. 1968. "Is Logic Empirical?" In R. S. Cohen and M. Wartofsky, eds., *Boston Studies in the Philosophy of Science*, vol 5. Dordrecht: Reidel.

———. 1979. *Mathematics, Matter, and Method*. 2d ed. with additional chapter. Cambridge University Press.

Quine, Willard V. O. 1960. *Word and Object*. New York: Wiley.

Rosenblueth, Arturo, and Wiener, Norbert. 1950. "Purposeful and Non-purposeful Behavior." *Philosophy of Science* 17:318–26.

Rosenblueth, Arturo; Wiener, Norbert; and Bigelow, Julian. 1943. "Behavior, Purpose, and Teleology." *Philosophy of Science* 10:18–24.

Rousseau, Jean Jacques. 1791, 1947. *The Social Contract*, ed. Charles Frankel. New York: Macmillan (Hafner Press).

Ruse, Michael. 1973. *The Philosophy of Biology*. London: Hutchinson.

Ryle, Gilbert. 1949. *The Concept of Mind*. New York: Barnes and Noble.

———. 1954. *Dilemmas*. Cambridge University Press.

Schlegel, Richard. 1980. *Superposition and Interaction*. University of Chicago Press.

Schroedinger, Erwin. 1935. "Die gegenwartige Situation in der Quantenmechanik." *Die Naturwissenschaften* 23:807–12, 823–28, 844–49.

———. 1956. "On the Peculiarity of the Scientific World-View." In *What Is Life? and Other Scientific Essays*. Garden City, N.Y.: Doubleday.

———. 1958. *Mind and Matter*. Cambridge University Press.

Smart, J. J. C. 1962. "Sensations and Brain Processes." In V. C. Chappell, ed., *The Philosophy of Mind*, pp. 160–72. Englewood Cliffs, N.J.: Prentice-Hall.

———. 1963. *Philosophy and Scientific Realism*. London: Routledge and Kegan Paul.

Taylor, Richard. 1950*a*. "Comments on a Mechanistic Conception of Purposefulness." *Philosophy of Science* 17:310–17.

———. 1950*b*. "Purposeful and Non-purposeful Behavior: A Rejoinder." *Philosophy of Science* 17:325–32.

Whorf, Benjamin Lee. 1956. *Language, Thought, and Reality: Selected Writings of Benjamin Lee Whorf*, ed. J. B. Campbell. Cambridge, Mass.: MIT Press.

Wigner, Eugene. 1961. "Remarks on the Mind–Body Question." In I. J. Good, ed., *The Scientist Speculates*, pp. 284–302. London: Heinemann; and New York: Basic Books, 1962.

———. 1963. "The Problem of Measurement." *American Journal of Physics* 31:6–15.

Williams, George C. 1966. *Adaptation and Natural Selection*. Princeton, N. J.: Princeton University Press.

———. 1977. *Sex and Evolution*. Princeton, N. J.: Princeton University Press.

Williams, Mary B. 1970. "Deducing the Consequences of Evolution: A Mathematical Model." *Journal of Theoretical Biology* 28:343–85.

———. 1973. "The Logical Status of the Theory of Natural Selection and Other Evolutionary Controversies: Resolution by Axiomatization." In M. Bunge, ed., *The Methodological Unity of Science*, pp. 84–102. Dordrecht: Reidel.

Wimsatt, William C. 1971. "Some Problems with the Concept of 'Feedback.'" In R. C. Buck and R. S. Cohen, eds., *Boston Studies in the Philosophy of Science*, vol. 8. Dordrecht: Reidel.

———. 1972. "Teleology and the Logical Structure of Function Statements." *Studies in the History and Philosophy of Science* 3:1–80.

———. 1974. "Complexity and Organization." In K. Schaffner and R. S. Cohen, eds., *Boston Studies in the Philosophy of Science*, vol. 20. Dordrecht: Reidel.

———. 1976. "Reductionism, Levels of Organization, and the Mind–Body Problem." in G. Globus, G. Maxwell, and I. Savodnik, eds., *Brain and Consciousness*, pp. 199–267. New York: Plenum.

Wittgenstein, Ludwig. 1958. *Philosophical Investigations*. Oxford: Blackwell Publisher.

Woodfield, Andrew. 1976. *Teleology*. Cambridge University Press.

Wright, Larry. 1973. "Functions." *Philosophical Review* 82:139–68.

———. 1976. *Teleological Explanations: An Etiological Analysis of Goals and Functions*. Berkeley: University of California Press.

# INDEX